Magic Mush
Explorer

"Psilocybin is getting a lot of attention lately as its therapeutic potential is being rediscovered after decades of not simply neglect, but of active suppression and prohibition. Those who follow this blooming resurgence of psychedelic research will already be aware that this simple, nontoxic molecule may harbor the potential to treat addictions, depression, traumatic memories, and even blunt the sting of death itself by alleviating the existential anxiety and loneliness of terminally ill patients about to cross that final threshold. What is rarely acknowledged in the staid scientific literature of clinical studies and neuroscientific assessments of psilocybin is that these emerging therapeutic applications, as important and promising as they are, barely scratch the surface of what we can learn from the intersection between a suitably primed hominid nervous system and this ancient fungal teacher, far older and far wiser than our species.

What Simon G. Powell articulates clearly and argues compellingly in *Magic Mushroom Explorer* is that psilocybin not only opens the portals to visionary dimensions but also constitutes a tool for the exploration of reality, a tool every bit as important to scientific inquiry as the telescope or the microscope. While these instruments open sensory windows on realms of cosmic vastness or microscopic dimensions, psilocybin is another kind of 'lens,' a lens that enables us to interface with and engage in dialog with the inherent intelligence that permeates all of nature.

Simon's book discusses all these highly charged ideas in a charming, easily understood, humorous, and utterly engaging manner that will resonate with experienced psilocybin explorers and that may just open the eyes of those who are not (yet) experienced to the possibility that nature is richly blessed with unimagined realms of intelligence, mystery, and complexity. With this book, his third, Simon has knocked it right out of the park (or perhaps right into the park, since parks seem to be the frequent home of his little fungal friends)."

DENNIS MCKENNA, PH.D., ETHNOPHARMACOLOGIST, COFOUNDER OF THE HEFFTER RESEARCH INSTITUTE, AND AUTHOR OF *BROTHERHOOD OF THE SCREAMING ABYSS*

"Here is the thought-provoking description of the author's spiritual quest, his profound discoveries, and their implications for renewed research with psychedelic substances, reawakening us to the sacredness of nature and life itself. In and through the pitfalls and pinnacles of his journey is the transformation of a curious and courageous young man into a mature modern prophet and social critic. Fascinating read!"

WILLIAM A. RICHARDS, PH.D., JOHNS HOPKINS SCHOOL OF MEDICINE

"Simon G. Powell, a credible psychonaut, has written a book that should be welcomed as our overpopulated species attempts to transition to sane drug policies and respect for native wisdom, integration with nature, and, ultimately, planetary maturity and ecological stability."

DORION SAGAN, AMERICAN SCIENCE WRITER, ESSAYIST, AND THEORIST

"The author informs, muses, and amuses as he chronicles his psilocybin explorations and insights into natural intelligence. He writes in joyfully plain English, tells compelling stories, and gets excited by all of life. Definitely outside the box."

JEREMY NARBY, AUTHOR OF *THE COSMIC SERPENT*

"Simon G. Powell's most profound insight is that nature is intelligent, not in the way that we think of intelligence as confined to the human mind, but that intelligence is an intrinsic property of the whole of nature. He calls for a new science of 'psilocybinetics' that views life anew under the 'perceptual lens' afforded by the mushroom. It is an interesting and provocative read!"

DAVID E. NICHOLS, PH. D., PRESIDENT AND COFOUNDER OF THE HEFFTER RESEARCH INSTITUTE

Magic Mushroom Explorer

Psilocybin
and the
Awakening Earth

SIMON G. POWELL

Park Street Press
Rochester, Vermont • Toronto, Canada

Park Street Press
One Park Street
Rochester, Vermont 05767
www.ParkStPress.com

Text stock is SFI certified

Park Street Press is a division of Inner Traditions International

Note to the Reader: This book is intended for informational and educational purposes only. All recounted actions undertaken by the author were done so at his own risk and with the benefit of years of experience. None of the author's ventures should be blindly copied by others. Neither the author nor the publisher assumes any responsibility for physical, psychological, or social consequences resulting from the ingestion of psilocybin.

Library of Congress Cataloging-in-Publication Data
Powell, Simon G.
  Magic mushroom explorer : psilocybin and the awakening Earth / Simon G. Powell.
    pages cm
  Summary: "A visionary guide to safely using psilocybin mushrooms to tap in to the wisdom of Nature and reconnect humanity to the biosphere" — Provided by publisher.
  ISBN 978-1-62055-366-4 (pbk.) — ISBN 978-1-62055-367-1 (e-book)
  1. Psilocybin—Psychological aspects. 2. Mushrooms, Hallucinogenic—Psychological aspects. 3. Gaia hypothesis. I. Title.
  BF209.H36P689 2015
  299'.93—dc23

                                                    2014021681

Printed and bound in the United States by Lake Book Manufacturing, Inc. The text stock is SFI certified. The Sustainable Forestry Initiative® program promotes sustainable forest management.

10 9 8 7 6 5 4 3 2 1

Text design by Debbie Glogover and layout by Priscilla Baker
This book was typeset in Garamond Premier Pro with Sanvito, Andrich, and Helvetica Neue used as display typefaces

To send correspondence to the author of this book, mail a first-class letter to the author c/o Inner Traditions • Bear & Company, One Park Street, Rochester, VT 05767, and we will forward the communication, or contact the author directly at **www.simongpowell.com**.

Contents

༄༄༄

Foreword by Rick Doblin, President of MAPS   **vii**

Prologue: A Question of Substance   **xi**

1

Mushroom Fever   1

2

Avalonia Psychedelica   60

3

Natural Intelligence   107

4

The Powell Report   142

5

The Sacred Pattern   186

6

Idris Nemeton   234

About the Author   265

Foreword

❦

By Rick Doblin, President of MAPS

Simon G. Powell is a literary and cultural figure visioning a new reality. *Magic Mushroom Explorer: Psilocybin and the Awakening Earth* is devoted to the author's search for truth, using psilocybin as a guide. Simon's personal experiences and deep connection to nature and psilocybin balance his philosophic inquiry and political commentary. Innovative concepts such as *natural intelligence* (chapter 3) and the *sacred pattern* (chapter 5) are informed both by psychedelic journeying and evolutionary science. Firsthand experiences are recalled throughout the book. Psilocybin is at the crux of Simon's search for truth, and both the substance and the man come through in this writing.

For every advance in psychedelic science there are many setbacks. In 2005 Simon, who is British, presented the Powell Report (chapter 4) to the House of Commons in an attempt to keep fresh psilocybin mushrooms legal or at least to persuade the U.K. government to gather more safety evidence (unlike other countries, fresh unprocessed psilocybin mushrooms were legal to possess in the U.K. at that time). On July 18 of that year, the U.K. Home Office labeled the mushroom as Class A, illegal. Simon and I share a common goal of ending prohibition and making psychedelics legally available. This book is one effort to communicate the benefits of psychedelics and the harsh reality of their criminality.

The 1950s and early 1960s were a time of discovery. Psychedelic research flourished. A renewed focus on health and well-being emerged. People embarked on personal and spiritual exploration, both with and without the aid of psychedelics. In the mid-1960s and '70s, fear began driving drug policy, escalating the War on Drugs and rendering the use of psychedelics for research into therapeutic, religious, and neuroscience purposes taboo, as well as outlawing all nonmedical use. The Controlled Substances Act was passed in the United States in 1970. In 1973 the U.S. Drug Enforcement Administration (DEA) was established, merging the Bureau of Narcotic and Dangerous Drugs and other federal offices. Marijuana, LSD, and psilocybin were criminalized.

We are progressively recovering from the trauma caused by years of misinformation and reactionary politics. Since 1986, when I founded MAPS (Multidisciplinary Association for Psychedelic Studies), we have made several breakthroughs. None of the drug breakthroughs was a big surprise; psychedelic therapists and users knew the benefits. The most celebrated breakthroughs have been bureaucratic and political. The year 2014 brought forth exceptional success at MAPS: we published our study on LSD-assisted psychotherapy in subjects with anxiety from life-threatening illness, which was the first new study of the therapeutic use of LSD in more than forty years; after twenty-two years MAPS overcame the emphatic and antiscientific blocking by the National Institute on Drug Abuse (NIDA) and the DEA of our medical marijuana research and obtained approval for our marijuana/PTSD Phase 2 drug development study in veterans; our MDMA-assisted psychotherapy research expanded into an international series of Phase 2 MDMA/PTSD pilot studies; a new study was initiated into the use of MDMA in reducing social anxiety in adults with autism; and two new studies were planned for the use of MDMA in subjects with end-of-life anxiety related to life-threatening illnesses and tinnitus. Similarly, the Heffter Research Institute has supported studies of psilocybin for the treatment of anxiety associated with cancer, alcohol, and tobacco addiction, and for catalyzing spiritual experiences; and the Beckley Foundation has initiated LSD and psilocybin brain scan studies. There is now more psychedelic research taking place than at any time in the last forty years. The messages and understandings written in this book will further facilitate the expansion of psychedelic research and the mainstream use of psychedelics for beneficial purposes.

Simon writes about the world's environmental peril. His entire motivation is to bring up from the underground the potential of psilocybin and other psychedelics to profoundly contribute to a healing process that is desperately needed. His book makes a compelling argument for the need for Western society to move to a post-prohibition world. *Magic Mushroom Explorer* presents a glimpse of what lies beyond the War on Drugs and offers insights about how to get there and what to do once there. Read it and wake up!

RICK DOBLIN earned his Ph.D. in public policy from Harvard's Kennedy School of Government, where he specialized in the regulation of Schedule I drugs. He is the founder (in 1986) and president of the Multidisciplinary Association for Psychedelic Studies (MAPS, www.maps.org), a nonprofit research and educational organization that sponsors FDA-approved research into the risks and potential therapeutic benefits of Schedule I drugs such as MDMA, psilocybin, and marijuana.

A Note to the Reader

PROLOGUE

A Question of Substance

⟡

The modern age in which we live is marked by a number of great triumphs. The gradual eradication of diseases such as smallpox and polio, for example. Or the development of rockets able to leave the firm grip of the earth's gravity and boldly venture into outer space. Or the technological ability to communicate across the globe in the blink of an eye. But there is another triumph of the modern age that is rather more sinister and not as widely acknowledged—namely, the triumph of image over substance. Images are easy to manipulate. That we are so easily swayed by them means that we ourselves are easy to manipulate. Political propaganda relies heavily upon image manipulation, as does the consumer market. The aim is to control our attention and our values, to make us think in a certain way and to conform to the wishes of the image manipulators. Political parties, for instance, present the public with well-manicured images, beneath which may be nothing permanent or substantial. Their catchphrases, emblems, smiling faces, and sound bites might be appealing, yet they often lack real substance and guarantee nothing. Likewise, the world of commerce involves engineering brand images that may camouflage a lack of anything truly substantial underneath. The creation of a brand or a new political party is a game of imaginative fakery, the sort of activity traditionally practiced by illusionists. But rather than conjuring something out of thin air on a theater stage and making a local audience gasp in awe, political maneuvering and brand development take place on the cultural stage and garner the collective attention and financial support of millions of people. In one way or another, images lacking substance now dominate people's lives.

What modern culture lacks is something beyond consumerism and politics, something more fulfilling than mere words and slogans, something more rewarding than passing fads and fashions. What we rightly yearn for is some sort of *real substance,* a substance that delivers, a substance that can grant us real, lasting meaning and that can genuinely empower us. To really empower us would be to make us feel really alive, really inspired, and full of joy, hope, and even unconditional love. In other words, a real substance would provide us with *spiritual sustenance*—something we would know by the undeniable feeling of it. By *spiritual,* I do not mean anything wishy-washy or "New Agey"—I am referring to a positively charged, emotional connection to some larger pattern of meaning beyond the shallow promises of political parties and the corporate advertising industry. Spiritual sustenance implies feelings connected to the larger biospherical (and cosmic) whole within which we live and which sustains us and from which we have become inexorably alienated.

Not to be confused with religion, this notion of spirituality gels with popular science author Carl Sagan's take on spirituality. With sentiments echoing Einstein's pantheistic views, Sagan describes spirituality as follows in his book, *The Demon-Haunted World: Science as a Candle in the Dark* (1995):

> When we recognize our place in an immensity of light-years and in the passage of ages, when we grasp the intricacy, beauty, and subtlety of life, then that soaring feeling, that sense of elation and humility combined, is surely spiritual.

Whatever your metaphysical stance, it is evident that many of us suffer existential malaise and are very far from enjoying such transcendent feelings. New commercial brands might look bright and colorful, new political slogans might arouse enthusiastic cheers, but by buying wholeheartedly into these kinds of thing we are simply going around and around in the same circles. The props may change their name and shape, but the game we are asked to play remains the same. Real meaning is not forthcoming, and the prizes are illusory.

When you boil it all down, when you get to the heart of modern Western culture, the acquisition of more possessions, more dollars, and a higher social status are touted as the chief aims of existence, certainly over and above any spiritual interests we might have. To amass as much cash as possible and to surround ourselves with as much stuff as we can find room for are the overt agendas of our consumer culture. Yet huge houses, designer clothes, flashy cars, and fancy restaurants don't provide what the human spirit yearns for. They can certainly provide novelty and a sort of instant feel-good factor, but they generally lack lasting meaning and fail to deliver spiritual nourishment. In fact, if you really think about it, the race to acquire material stuff is just another case of chasing substances with no real substance.

Many of us are so famished inside that we will latch on to virtually anything that convinces us that it has substance. We grab meaning from a pompous job title, the size of a bank account, the breadth of an audience, the number of names dropped in an online career profile, the volume of social media friends we have, the amount of letters we have after our name, the logo emblazoned on a wristwatch, or the sight of a brand-new car parked in our driveway. We chase after mirages and idols, driven by the belief that if we obtain some social circumstance, or surround ourselves with prestigious items, or achieve some social status, then we will be happy and fulfilled. But when we get there, or we obtain the stuff we desired, we soon become accustomed to that new state of material affairs and find that those things do not really satisfy after all. So we strive for yet more stuff; we aim for even greater social heights. The game of "chase the image" takes over. It is like the world we are holding in place consists of things that cannot really be held, hugged, or cherished because they are no more substantial than projected images and empty promises.

In an age when image has triumphed over substance and in which we are obedient consumers buying an endless supply of objects that never really give us meaning, and where we vote for political parties that invariably end up doing what we in no way voted for, eventually the proverbial shit will hit the fan. More and more people will wonder how on earth they believed all the hype and worshipped so many insubstantial images. Why did we think some politician could really change anything? Why did we put our well-being and autonomy in their hands? Why did we buy into consumer materialism? Why do we continue to pillage the environment for profit? Why do nations continually exploit one another? Why have we played these banal, divisive, and ecologically damaging cultural games for so long? Note that I am not having a go at civilization or technology here—at least not in the pure sense of those terms. I am not suggesting we should abandon technological society and head back to the caves. Far from it. My point is simply that we worship material wealth and accept status-quo thinking at our peril. Everything in its rightful place is all well and good. And technology and goods *do* have their place, as do civil servants. Ultimately, their place is defined by how much we value them.

This implies that our value system is in dire need of an overhaul. We need to reappraise our core values. We need to reevaluate those substances, drives, and yearnings that we currently endorse and esteem. We also need to redefine what *wealth* really means—whether it is to be measured in terms of material substances or is more to do with inner well-being. Once our value system has changed along with our ideas about what constitutes real wealth, then culture will change. Until this change in values occurs (which is really a change in consciousness), we will continue to be robotic consumers obediently buying into an endless mass of insubstantial stuff that does not fill the existential void within. In consequence, both the biosphere and the collective human spirit will continue to suffer.

Needless to say, I am not alone in stating this. At the current time there are all manner of social movements and social ideologies that are challenging our value systems and our modern way of life. There are the various Green Movements, the Occupy Movement, the Zeitgeist Movement, the growing interest in permaculture and self-sufficiency, and all manner of sustainability movements. In one way or another, large groups of people, particularly the youth and the dispossessed, are challenging the status quo and looking for alternative cultural modes of being. All I am really offering to this fervent mix of transitional ideologies is knowledge of a substantial substance that can act as a useful catalyst, particularly with regard to helping us retune to a larger pattern of meaning.

So what is this substance that I have been carefully spiraling around? Let me cut straight to the chase. The substance in question is found inside an actual living organism—namely, a mushroom—seemingly no more than a humble fungus. I say "seemingly" for good reason, for the truth is that this mushroom is actually a catalyst for the aforementioned lofty spiritual feelings described by Sagan. I would go a bit further, however, and submit that at the very deepest core of spirituality there is a felt connection not just to the larger cosmos but to some kind of "higher-order purpose" within it and, moreover, that this mushroom can potentially connect one to it. That is its ultimate promise and payoff.

Endowed with that sort of power, this particular mushroom is assuredly a candidate for the legendary philosopher's stone of the ancient alchemists. Sought after for millennia, the hallowed philosopher's stone lay at the heart of alchemy. On a superficial level the philosopher's stone was deemed to be able to transform base metal into gold. Although gold was thought to be obtainable through convoluted alchemical dabblings with forge and furnace, at the end of the day gold is but a physical metal. Any true mystical seeker would well know that gold could not be the real pursuit of alchemy. There had to be more to alchemy than the quest for a cold and inert shiny metal. Indeed, the real meaning of the philosopher's stone was its ability to perfect and enlighten humankind and to confer immortality. This suggests, of course, that the philosopher's stone had to be some kind of substance with real substance.

Here is a description of the mythical philosopher's stone from *Through Alchemy to Chemistry* (John Read, 1957):

> They held that although the Stone was infinitely difficult to attain, yet it lay at hand, diffused throughout Nature and awaiting anybody having the clear alchemical vision enabling them to pick it up.

And here is a really fascinating description from the anonymous author of the 1526 alchemy book *Gloria Mundi:*

> It is familiar to all men, both young and old, is found in the country, in the village, in the town, in all things created by God; yet it is despised by all. Rich and poor handle it every day. It is cast into the street by servant maids. Children play with it. Yet no one prizes it, though, next to the human soul, it is the most beautiful and the most precious thing upon earth, and has power to pull down kings and princes. Nevertheless, it is esteemed the vilest and meanest of earthly things.

Although I have handpicked these descriptions for purposes of effect, they really could be veiled descriptions of a mushroom. Indeed, as evidence that most Europeans distrusted mushrooms during the heyday of alchemy and really did consider them to be the "vilest and meanest of earthly things," we need only consult the *Grete Herball,* by Peter Treveris, published in the same year as *Gloria Mundi* and which had this to say about them:

> There be two maners of them; one maner is deadly and sleeth them that eateth of them and be called tode stooles, and the other dooth not.

Even this latter it was claimed: "be peryllous and dredfull to eate."

Whatever the popular consensus is today regarding mushrooms, I specifically have in mind mushrooms that contain *psilocybin,* one specific "brand" of mushroom, if you will.* However, unlike manufactured brands that may be all glitz and packaging, the psilocybin brand of mushroom really delivers. Thus, the rest of this book concerns the astonishing realms of experience that psilocybin can potentially grant. I would hope that long after I have left this mortal coil, other informed and educated adults might follow the same trail and delight in the same perceptual wonders that I have been fortunate enough to have experienced. That is actually my main wish—that other bold voyagers educate themselves, ready themselves inwardly, and share the same majestic forms of consciousness that I have repeatedly enjoyed and can thence spread good word of this—for the benefit of both humanity and the biosphere.

All this might sound overly bold, pretentious even, yet such is the

---

*Psilocybin mushrooms are not to be confused with the bright red, white-spotted fly agaric mushroom whose psychoactivity is totally different but which is sometimes referred to in the press as being a "magic mushroom."

psychological power of psilocybin. Indeed, recent studies at the prestigious Johns Hopkins University in which psilocybin was administered to healthy volunteers found that most of them described the experience as being one of the five most spiritually significant experiences of their lives. Even more impressively, almost one-third of those volunteers described their psilocybin experience as *the* most spiritually meaningful experience of their lives. Strange how this kind of thing is not permanent front-page news.

Elsewhere, I have talked about the psilocybin mushroom as being an "antidote" against ecological destructiveness and ecological insensitivity (I state this in my *Manna* documentary film, which can be viewed on YouTube). But it is much more than an ecopsychological catalyst. The main virtue of psilocybin is the incontrovertible spiritual charge that it carries. This charge is so strong that one becomes immediately empowered. Through psilocybin, the "center of action" is not some trendy nightclub or some new mobile app. The "place to be" is no longer some other city or the fashionable part of town. Where "it's happening" is not some new art scene. The place to be is not somewhere else. *You become where it's at; you become the center of significant action.* Which is to say that psilocybin can initiate the most profound state of consciousness imaginable. It brings you into the full glory of the living moment. In terms of your own life story, the psilocybin experience can be of immense significance, similar in scope and kind to the moon landings or the fall of the Berlin Wall.

If you are really fortunate, the psilocybin mushroom may grant a full-blown mystical experience—as it seems to have done with some of the subjects in the Johns Hopkins studies. This is not to be sneered at. Such mystical peak experiences are likely the greatest psychological events that one can go through in this lifetime—although they are beyond words. One's being becomes fully connected to the whole. One feels the interconnectedness of everything along with the wisdom that somehow suffuses all life on earth. It can feel as though one is suddenly awakening from a long slumber into some larger transcendental reality. No wonder then that these mushrooms were considered sacred by historical native peoples in Mesoamerica. Psilocybin mushrooms are like living symbols that can literally be digested. It is as if human life is part of an epic, unfolding cosmic story, or cosmic game, and that within this game-cum-story are buried here and there clues and "power-ups," these being special "plot devices" to help us on our way. Moreover, I suspect that once psilocybin's potential is fully realized and harnessed by modern humans, then everything will change for the better, particularly in terms of our relationship with the biosphere and with one another. On that quixotic note, let us jump right in at the deep end.

Psilocybe semilanceata, *or Liberty Cap,*
the world's most prolific magic mushroom

1
Mushroom Fever

〜〜〜

All of us, at some time or another, ask deep questions about the meaning of life. Why are we here? Indeed, why is *anything* here? Why are there three spatial dimensions and a temporal dimension? Why are there specific laws of nature and specific forces of nature? What happens when we die? And so on. Some of us look to science for an explanation of how and why we are here. Some find answers in religion. Some find answers in New Age ideology. Others think that there are no answers to be had and that we should just get on with life. Still others, like tireless alchemists, spend their whole lives searching for an elusive "something"—some revelation, some encounter, some discovery—that might resolve these biggest of existential questions.

Whatever we conclude about the meaning of life, we can all agree that life is astonishing. I mean, really, it is truly incredible that there is a reality process replete with law and order on all scales and that we can consciously delight in it—maybe not all the time, but at least some of the time. To exist within a universe too big and too old to really grasp, whose complexity and ability to surprise appear infinite, cannot be brushed aside as if it was some minor incident. Even a single, solitary sunflower seed is remarkable when you think about it, when you consider what it can grow into and that its future young flower buds will track the movement of the sun and dine on its generous output. Who would imagine something so tiny could be in harmony with something as massive as a star? Further, the explosive birth, long life, and eventual death of energy-emitting stars also ties in with a bigger picture, as stars arise only because of cosmic laws and forces. The universe is not just vast but interconnected in more ways than we can ever imagine. Even the tiniest details link up to bigger and bigger webs of relationship. We thus find ourselves part and parcel of an especially interesting and especially profound reality process.

Curiously, some scientists go out of their way to contest such sentiments. Take popular physicist Lawrence Krauss, who in a talk titled "A Universe from Nothing," delivered to the 2009 Atheist Alliance International annual conference and available on YouTube, says this about the universe: "It's big, rare events happen all the time, including life, but that doesn't mean it's special." I see. We must have been hoodwinked. Then again, if a universe able to craft smart, multicellular, bipedal scientists such as Krauss from humble bacterial origins is not "special," then what sort of universe would make us raise an eyebrow in surprise? How high do we set the bar? What kind of creative potential does a universe have to be endowed with before we concede that we *do* exist in extraordinarily special circumstances?

To be sure about all this, the mystery of existence becomes even more profound when we consider consciousness. Given that our conscious experience is *the only thing we know to exist with absolute certainty,* this means that the universe we know is the universe as perceived and conceived by consciousness. This applies as much to aboriginal conceptions of the universe as it does to the latest scientific conceptions of the universe coming from physicists and cosmologists. In other words, consciousness is *fundamental* and certainly not a trivial, insignificant feature of reality. Consciousness actually matters more than so-called matter.

It is also the case that consciousness is not fixed. There are different kinds of consciousness. At any one moment we can be more, or less, conscious. The more conscious we are, the more awake we feel and the more real reality feels. In fact, the word *consciousness* means to "know together." By definition, an increase in consciousness therefore involves the knowing of more together, or more at once. This explains why the "expansion of consciousness" is often talked about in terms of an increase in perceptual clarity and conceptual clarity.

Following on from this, the suggestion arises that if we want to understand something as deep as the meaning of life, then it makes sense to do this with a very clear kind of consciousness. Answering a question like that, or formulating some sort of answer, should not be undertaken casually or sloppily. The mind needs to be keen. Consciousness needs to have clarity. Serious questions whose answers might well affect what we make of our lives and how we live our lives warrant a seriously sound kind of consciousness. Thus, are there actual means and methods of attaining a more enhanced kind of consciousness? Are there tools available that facilitate the expansion of consciousness into some kind of "higher" state?

Clearly there are. Indeed, there exist all manner of pursuits, regimens, and teachings that concern the development and evolution, in this lifetime, of our consciousness. Think of Buddhism or the many other spiritual teachings that promote, in one way or another, the cultivation of mindfulness and whose tacit inference is that there are levels of consciousness, that consciousness is mutable and that our inner world can exist in different qualitative states. There are, of course, also certain substances traditionally held to embody "spiritual" power that are deemed to enhance and expand consciousness. These are psychedelic agents such as psilocybin and ayahuasca. The latter of these is gaining much popularity these days, and there is much so-called ayahuasca tourism transpiring in Peru and other countries.

The former substance, psilocybin, is much closer to home (for most of us) and is found in various species of fungus long deified by those native cultures that used them. Such psychedelic fungi grow all over the planet, particularly in wilderness areas in my vicinity here in the U.K., as well as in Europe and North America. For this and various other reasons pertaining to the "quest for truth," I have spent the greater part of my adult life exploring these mushrooms, in particular, exploring the numinous realms of conscious experience that their active ingredient, psilocybin, can potentiate within the human psyche.

My personal independent research with these mushrooms has been, thus far, utterly fascinating and deeply rewarding. As to whether I have glimpsed the "meaning of life" and have had valid insights into certain age-old mysteries—well, that remains to be seen, as does the usefulness of such alleged insights in affording us a more healthy relationship with the biosphere and with one another—two issues that ought to rate highly in any personal growth endeavor. What I can say for sure is that my experiences with psilocybin mushrooms certainly *felt* profoundly significant, particularly in terms of their ecopsychological impact, and that I therefore felt obliged to spread word of such a remarkable natural resource. These mushrooms are really a catalyst that can galvanize new ways of thinking and feeling and can help retune the human race into harmony with the larger biospherical environment. If this sounds grandiose, then that is because the mushroom experience is so utterly compelling. An unleashed force exists there, some spiritual presentiment within the human psyche that the mushroom stirs into action. Consuming the mushroom is not like having a beer or dropping some party drug. The psilocybin experience can be life changing.

To study the roots of my long and winding psychedelic mushroom journey requires a trip back in time—all the way back to 1984. To re-create that era in your mind, know that it was the year that "Relax" by Frankie Goes to Hollywood got to number one in the U.K.; a BMX bicycle craze hit the U.K.; Carl Lewis won gold medals at the Olympic Games in Los Angeles; Madonna performed in a sexually suggestive way to "Like a Virgin"; Hollywood actor Ronald Reagan was reelected president; and Sir Bob Geldof's epic Band Aid project took off. There were few or no personal computers to speak of back then, no mobile phones, no DVDs, no MP3 players, and no Internet. But there were plenty of phone boxes, whopping great stereo cassette players, hefty digital calculators, and chunky digital watches. As ever, what we didn't know about, we didn't miss.

In 1984 I was young, naive, uneducated, and, like most people, had never really heard of psilocybin fungi. To be sure about it, I had an aversion to mushrooms and always avoided them if they showed up on a dinner plate. They were to be pushed aside and discarded like limp lettuce or overcooked cabbage. Mushrooms meant nothing to me whatsoever, and if I ever saw any fungi on a country walk, I was liable to kick them over. In those days, I was little more than an unemployed, malnourished punk rocker living on welfare and residing in the East London high-rise council flat of a friend, who shall herein be known as the Tall Guy. Clad in studded leather jackets and studded leather belts, we were in an amateur punk band—an extremely noisy and distorted affair. I think we were called Toxide or some other deliberately unsettling name. I would much rather tell you that I was the son of a diplomat living in trendy Kensington and that I was studying to be a classical musician of repute. Or that I was an ex-public schoolboy who, by the age of eighteen, had invented some new scientific instrument. Alas, there were no gold cufflinks, brogues, and fine educational pedigrees for my ilk—rather it was a case of scruffy old Motorhead T-shirts; mean, black Dr. Martens boots; and an avid interest in dog-eared Philip K. Dick books. Come to think of it, maybe this is how the psilocybin mushroom lines up its disciples. It settles not on orthodox and conventional people, but on those with some sort of persistent attitude of dissent. In retrospect, the mushroom must have seen me coming a mile away.

Living conditions for unemployed punk rockers in the early 1980s were tough. So tough, in fact, that one evening the Tall Guy and I were reduced to eating porridge around a candle because we had no solid nourishment and no money for the electricity meter. I recall that on one morning we even went out and stole milk, which, in those far-off days of yore, was left in bottles outside people's homes. For this misdemeanor I hereby apologize.

It was during this period of extreme economic hardship and sporadic delinquency that I went, one bright summer's day, to the local library. I am unsure why, but I started reading some big thick pharmaceutical volume. I found a section all about psychoactive drugs, which interested me. Some information about nutmeg stuck in my mind. Here was a readily available spice that was apparently "hallucinogenic." I also took out a book called *The Sacred Mushroom and the Cross,* by John Allegro, which argued that Christianity was based upon a mushroom cult revolving around the fly agaric, or *Amanita muscaria,* mushroom. Even if Allegro's book was little more than sensationalism dressed up in convoluted academic language, I did find myself intrigued by stories of "sacred mushrooms." This book (along with the nutmeg thing) was drawing me unknowingly toward the presence of the psilocybin mushroom. I had instinctively sniffed a trail, and a journey of sorts had commenced—one that would eventually lead to eschatological visions, sacred patterns, biospherical communions, and much more besides. The psilocybin mushroom was slowly but surely hailing me.

Having time on our hands and thinking of ourselves as maverick adventurers, we began experiments with nutmeg in earnest. The Tall Guy and I bought loads of the stuff from the supermarket. The check-out woman had no idea why we were buying up all their small plastic pots of nutmeg. She probably thought we were doing some major baking—because, in small amounts sprinkled onto rice pudding or cakes, nutmeg is quite tasty and provides a hint of exotica. Attempting to consume several heaped tablespoons, however, is an entirely different proposition. The best we could do was try to mix it with milk, pinch our noses, and then quickly down the foul, gritty liquid.

After a number of horrible stomachaches, retching sessions, and severe bouts of nausea, we eventually achieved a kind of strange psychedelic effect. The only thing I really recall about the experience was that I suffered a horrible sort of paranoia (the conditions we were living in were, as mentioned, pretty grim, and I think I became painfully aware of this fact). Nutmeg is not recommended. Actually, the pharmaceutical book I mentioned earlier stated that nutmeg was used by prisoners as a sort of cheap thrill, presumably because it was easy to get hold of. Good luck to them, I say. If an incarcerated person wants to induce searing stomach pains and paranoia and thus learn the hard way never to do it again, then so be it. As for me, I still get the shivers when I even as much as smell a hint of that foul spice.

Next up for inspection, and of more importance in my tale, was the fly agaric mushroom, as mentioned in Allegro's book (although, according to the recollections of the Tall Guy, we apparently also experimented in various ways with dried banana skins, horse chestnut bark, monosodium glutamate, dill, and even catnip eagerly unstuffed from a cat's toy). From what I could ascertain, these fly agaric mushrooms were the real deal. This was a mushroom with a long cultural heritage (despite the fact that it is a species usually listed as poisonous). Apparently shamans in Siberia had used the fly agaric mushroom and venerated its effects. These mysteriously dressed tribespeople spoke of superhuman strength, dreamlike visions, and the like. According to the many literary historical references I was reading, fly agaric fungi had the power to propel people into new dimensions of supernatural reality. I even read that Lewis Carroll was influenced by these shamanic mushroom stories and incorporated the ideas into his famous children's book *Alice in Wonderland*. Thus it was that I became fascinated with the notion of locating the fly agaric mushroom. After all, they grew in the U.K., so finding them out in the wild was a distinct possibility. With hindsight, it was as if the psilocybin mushroom was dangling this fly agaric mushroom before me like irresistible bait. My destiny was now firmly set.

Having concurred with the Tall Guy that nutmeg was obnoxious and to be avoided at all costs and that foraging for fly agaric mushrooms was the next logical step on our quest to attain a rewarding altered state of consciousness, we started visiting a lovely, large forest at Hainault, which is on the outskirts of North East London. Our first visits yielded nothing. Well, we did come across a wide variety of fungi, but not the exact sort we were seeking. I recall that forest very well. In my mind's eye I can still see the Tall Guy crouching down and examining a fungus and me feeling like we were brothers in some sort of fantasy story, a bit like children in a fairy tale, I suppose. I had the curious sense of some kind of bigger story or bigger picture. Anyhow, although we found a colorful and eclectic array of mushrooms, we failed to locate the legendary amanita.

I was not prepared to give up. After nutmeg's spicy diversion, the trail was definitely alive with a more compelling fungal scent. Thus, I repeatedly returned to Hainault Forest on my own. And then one day I found fly agarics! Lo and behold, dozens and dozens of them dotted the landscape, with their scarlet and white-flecked caps glaring brightly in the autumn sunlight! I brought a couple of carrier bags stuffed full of them back to the Tall Guy's flat. Which meant that I had to work out how best to ingest them. I think I must have tried every conceivable method as indicated in the various library books I had at hand. I tried drying them slowly, drying them quickly, mixing them with milk, grilling them, roasting them, toasting them, eating them raw, eating just the skins, and so on. Nothing ever worked! Well, the Tall Guy and his girlfriend threw up once, but we never, as far as I recall, got a memorable psychoactive effect. Unless of course I am still under their powerful influence thirty years on—which, although a canny notion, seems unlikely.

Despite my abject failure to elicit any psychological effect from the legendary fly agaric mushroom, I did read about a much more interesting mushroom species. This was the *Psilocybe semilanceata*, or liberty cap, as it is known in the vernacular (because of its pointy shape). Here was an apparently widespread species that most definitely had a reliable and robust psychoactive effect. I learned that similar species (with the same active ingredient—psilocybin) had been used in Mexico for millennia and that Britain's native species had been used from about the mid-1970s onward. In other words, here was a species of psychedelic mushroom indigenous to Britain that was, apparently, still having an ongoing cultural impact. Okay, so it might have been long-haired, flared, hippy-type people who had been out picking and consuming this U.K. mushroom since the 1970s, but it was nonetheless a significant psychedelic species. Effectively this meant that descriptions of the psilocybin experience were not confined to historical anthropological accounts but were being conveyed in contemporary academic books. I had, in other words, alighted upon a *local living mystery*. Needless to say, I was keen to locate and try out this alluring psilocybin substance. Somewhere, out in the wild green countryside, this beguiling mushroom awaited me. However, despite being keen, my initial searches proved totally fruitless. But I was a determined man. Something lodged in my mind, some deep inner need to find this mushroom and taste of its reputation.

Two years passed. In the autumn of 1986 I finally located the psilocybin mushroom in London's Richmond Park, which is now listed as a nature reserve and London's largest Site of Special Scientific Interest. I would like to say a word or two about this wonderful region. Although it is deemed a part of London, Richmond Park is so vast (some 2,500 acres) and has such refreshing wilderness patches that one can be forgiven for thinking that London is another world away. There are always large herds of freely roaming deer in Richmond Park; big old oak trees that look as if they have been lifted straight from the set of *The Lord of the Rings;* secret woods surrounded by ancient rusty wrought-iron fences; artfully sculpted gardens; towering sweet chestnut trees; large ponds; futuristic dragonflies; more than one thousand species of beetle; docile rabbits; horse enclosures; plantations; and vast swathes of ferns, whose dried remains appear like crispy bronze fractals every autumn. For lovers of nature, Richmond Park is a true wonderland. You can walk for miles and miles and lose all sense that a massive city lies somewhere around you. Certainly it is intriguing to realize that London was once like this all over. Strange as it seems, thousands of years ago Oxford Street, Leicester Square, and Piccadilly Circus probably all looked similar to Richmond Park.

So there I was strolling around the vast wild grounds of Richmond Park. It was autumn, and I knew there might be a chance that I could locate some liberty caps—or "magic mushrooms," as they are often referred to. I was searching for the mushroom in the open grassland areas of the park. These are patches of ground not interfered with by the park's various managers and that have what I call a "wilderness tang" about them. *Wilderness tang* is a term I coined that implies that the ground vegetation and localized area looks, and feels, wild—so much so that you can, as it were, taste that wildness, or at least feel a certain innervating something when you encounter it—in much the same way that a good mug of tea has a tang, which, to tea aficionados, will make them smack their lips and breathe out loudly with much gusto and appreciation. Or like satsumas—which can have a nice, sharp, fruity tang. These wilderness tang areas of Richmond Park that I am speaking of are, by definition, not mown and are not touched much by human hand. Such areas are somewhat akin to the shaggy mane of a lion. In other words, they are wild, unkempt, and, to my sensibilities, beautiful. As a chronic biophiliac (i.e., one who has an excessive love of nature) I confess to adoring wilderness tang and have immersed myself in large throws of it many times.

In searching the wilder areas, I eventually arrived at a small hill-top meadow a good few miles from the park's main entrance. To my astonishment, this meadow was adorned with hundreds of psilocybin mushrooms. They were everywhere! Although *Psilocybe semilanceata* is a small brown species when first sprouting, as they become dried by ambient wind and sunshine, they appear white and readily stand out among tufts of grass. There was another chap there picking them, and he confirmed what they were. I picked maybe a hundred or so and took them back home to Ealing, where I was then living. I ingested a dose of about forty specimens one evening a few days later. Everything changed from that moment on.

It would be a lie to say that my first full introduction to psilocybin was straightforward, that I slipped with ease into a transcendental embrace and became instantly engulfed in spiritual light. This was not the case. Far from it. About an hour after I consumed psilocybin for the very first time, I felt like I was losing my mind. It is amazing how naive a young man can be. You read about these long-revered fungi, about how they have been used for spiritual purposes for thousands of years, how they are deemed to be loaded with sacred shamanic power. You read about the colorful closed-eye visions people report. Jeweled landscapes are spoken of, or mythical cities and the like. Then there are stories of mystical union with the universe. Even the most academic books about psychedelic drugs are brimming with this sort of

extravagant reportage. It all sounds decidedly illuminating and alluring. And yet nothing can prepare you for what really happens once
millions of psilocybin molecules are coursing through your brain. If
you are taking an effective dose of psilocybin for the first time, it is
like nothing you have ever experienced before. *It cannot be imagined
prior to the event.* It is not like going to the movies. It is not like falling into a soft, warm, multicolored pillow. It is not like slipping into
a magical fairy tale. It is none of these things. These are all ideas that
we conjure up when we read about the psychedelic experience or hear
distant tell of it.

Until that point my only real experience with psychoactive drugs
was connected with alcohol and cannabis. Alcohol is easy to take and
essentially dissolves consciousness (although initially there may appear
to be a certain brightening of the mind—if one can call it that). It is
so easy, in fact, that my school friends and I used to readily drink too
much of the stuff at the age of about sixteen. This might sound daft,
but at that age and in the prevailing social climate, it was a regular
fun thing to do. Alcohol requires no inner preparation whatsoever—it
is an extremely primitive drug. For the most part, people do not have
their life transformed by alcohol unless it is in a negative way. Cannabis
is a bit more interesting. Cannabis can be mildly psychedelic but is
still nothing whatsoever like psilocybin. The same is true of ecstasy
(MDMA), which can take one to the threshold of a psychedelic experience but only hints at what psilocybin might be like.

With only my experience with cannabis (and nutmeg) to go on,
I guess I was expecting a simple transition to a psychedelic state of
mind in which I would perceive the oneness of all things. Perhaps
it would start with some nice colors? Or a warm glowing feeling of
transcendence? Not so. What was happening to me was horrible! As
the effects of psilocybin started to take hold, it was like my head was
becoming filled with noise and garbage. Or maybe it would be better

to say that *the mushroom revealed to me that my psyche was full of noise and garbage.* In any case, this was totally not what I had been expecting, especially given that I had spent two years enthusiastically on the trail of this legendary fungus. Yet here I was, caught up in some kind of rapidly escalating nightmare—as if what I had been long searching for was some kind of sick joke. If my psyche at that moment had been turned into an illustrative scene, then imagine a room crammed full of people all shouting different things really loudly. Rather than being transformed into a heavenly place, my youthful mind had been suddenly transformed into a madhouse asylum. A fiendish, hideous cacophony was overwhelming me, and I felt as if I would become trapped forever in that foul state of mind.

Other disturbing things were happening as well. I had, at that time, a number of astronomical photographic pictures on my wall, and they began to grab my attention. These pictures were of planets, such as Jupiter. I recall that Jupiter, with its fluidic whirls of color, suddenly appeared like a zany, bouncy rubber ball in some lunatic circus. It was like parts of my environment were mocking me. That, combined with the inner cacophony in my head, convinced me that I was going insane.

A classic response to this kind of bad-trip scenario is to go to bed and curl up like a fetus. That is exactly what I did. It must be an instinctive response when faced with any kind of unstoppable psychological onslaught. I had this notion that if I could cover myself up with blankets and sheets, then the mad, malevolent dissonance inside my mind might be assuaged. Unfortunately, this was not the case. Indeed, if you try to fight this sort of thing, it gets worse. If you try, as it were, to shut the door to the experience, the knocking gets louder. The eminent twentieth-century psychedelic guru Terence McKenna used to say that a bad trip is having to learn faster than you are accustomed to learning. Bad trips are not inside the mushroom. Bad experiences and frightful ideation are not part of psilocybin's chemical structure. What psychedelic substances such as psilocybin do is *amplify the contents of the psyche,* raising unconscious material into conscious awareness (the word *psychedelic* literally means "mind manifesting"). They show you clearly the underlying composition and deepest recesses of your psyche. They show you what you are and of what you are made. They reveal what is just beneath the surface of your conscious life—which will invariably be surprising to you and maybe even shocking. The human psyche is very big and very complex.

If the dark chaotic inner turmoil had continued for much longer, I would likely never have taken psilocybin again. But something happened that radically changed the course of my first psychedelic voyage. I called to mind something said by George Gurdjieff, whose teachings I had recently become deeply interested in. Gurdjieff's teachings chiefly revolve around the art and science of self-knowledge, with how to turn on a light within one's inner world. Recalling Gurdjieff's teachings and the feelings his teachings inspired, I was able to impartially observe my psyche; I was able to see the negative thought patterns within my inner world as clearly as I could see physical objects in the outer world. This meant that the psychological torment began to lose its grip on me as I studied it. Indeed, the longer I was able to objectively observe my inner turmoil, the more and more clear it became. And the more clearly I saw it, the less powerful it became and the more I became free of it. The erratically careering negative thoughts were akin to wild animals that lose their power and momentum once they are caught in the headlights of a car. In other words, my newly mustered, objective, conscious attention was like a powerful headlight that had just been switched on. This was one of my first insights into the power of consciousness when it is in a focused state and into how the dynamics of one's inner world will change through the bright, all-seeing light of consciousness.

As soon as this happened, as soon as my inner world became illuminated, the negative chaotic activity halted, then quickly began to evaporate altogether, leaving me in a state of extreme bliss, with waves of mystical energy pulsing through me, making me feel as if I had suddenly entered the realm of the gods. I shall never forget lying in that bed, breathing very heavily, each breath an orgasmic testament to some higher state of being. I felt as if I was enveloped in some ancient divine energy. It seemed utterly momentous to my young mind (I was but twenty-two). I also recall thinking that I was a reborn Native American of some kind. I could hear tribal voices, or at least I had the sense of a native tribal language deep within me. In retrospect, I think this was in all likelihood a result of my interest in Native American culture at that time. Or maybe it was a kind of spiritual archetype welling up from my unconscious, an archetype that was actually to emerge many more times in the following decades. In any case, that initial mystical psilocybin experience made its mark, and I was never the same again. I knew something that other people didn't. I knew there were realms of experience in which some bigger meaning could be grasped. I knew that we were part of a bigger picture and a bigger purpose. I knew what it meant to *wake up more*.

The next phase of the mushroom's influence began some six years later, at the Glastonbury Festival of June 1992. Primarily about music but with most artistic endeavors on display, the Glastonbury Festival is assuredly one of the most famous annual musical festivals in the world. This is especially the case if you are young. I had first "done" Glastonbury in 1986 (about four months prior to my first psilocybin experience), and it was a real eye-opener. Drugs play a key role at such festivals—or at least they used to. Back in the day, pretty much everyone was "off their heads" on some substance. To this day I vividly recall walking through fields packed with colorful people and hearing the earnest cries from an endless chain of drug salesmen advertising their wares: "Acid! Speed! Spliff! Acid, speed, spliff!" It was all very surreal and dreamlike, as if I were wandering around some weird manifestation of the collective subcultural British psyche.

I attended the festival again in 1989 and then later still, as mentioned, in 1992. It was during this latter occasion that I detected, and was drawn toward, a strong shamanic current—and once I was in this current there was no going back. With hindsight, this curious current must have always been there—it was just that I was not much part of it. The exact moment I got "swept up" was when I went to watch the Shamen play their set. The Shamen were a popular techno rave band at that time and were just then reaching the pinnacle of their career (some years later I befriended the main chap behind the band and even wrote a series of short fictional stories called "The Adventures of Lord Hempton" for their website).

I was very stoned and was standing right at the back of the large crowd of people that had gathered at the music stage where the Shamen were performing. It was late evening, and the band was using lasers. The performance looked cool and futuristic. At the end they played a lengthy track that featured a man talking. His voice was absolutely mesmerizing, as were the mystical, otherworldly topics he waxed lyrical about. The weird thing is that after the piece ended I was utterly awestruck, even though I could not recall exactly what this man had said. Somehow his words alluded to everything that I needed to hear—even though I was not really conscious of what it was that I wanted to hear. I just knew with absolute conviction that this man's quixotic assertions were the key to my immediate future, as if I had been exposed to an informational code of some kind that had triggered something deep inside of me. It was as if I were a nonlethal version of the Manchurian candidate, like I had suddenly been primed. But for what?

I raced back to tell my companions about what had just happened and to convey to them how incredibly inspired I felt. They just looked at me in a perplexed way. They wondered if I had been smoking too much dope. Regardless, the effect on me of the man's inspiring words lasted for days.

When I got back to London I immediately bought the Shamen's album *Boss Drum* and soon discovered the charismatic raconteur's identity. It was none other than Terence McKenna, who delivers an eight-minute speech on the track named "Re:Evolution" on the album. The band had played the self-same "Re:Evolution" recording of McKenna at the festival (I later learned that it was actually the first time they had played that particular piece).

McKenna—who died in 2000—was without doubt the greatest spokesperson for the judicious use of psilocybin that the modern world has known—so it was no surprise that I picked up on his rhetoric. What Timothy Leary was to the acid-dropping 1960s McKenna was to the shamanic fungus-wielding 1990s. He came across best in his lengthy talks—of which there are hundreds, if not thousands, to be found on the Internet. He was a psychedelic polymath, a turned-on Carl Sagan, a spellbinding bard of the highest order. He could weave together stories of the cosmic human journey that would enthrall and inspire. More important, he was stating in a cogent and convincing manner that psilocybin fungi were a valuable spiritual resource and that their visionary effects were of profound importance for the future of our species. For young people unsure of the value of the psilocybin experience and unable to really qualify its worth as an epistemological tool, McKenna's talks were a supportive nod, an intellectual thumbs up, a way of cross-referencing and validating certain transcendental experiences.

Despite the great esteem many people still hold for McKenna, it is clear that he erred in many of his speculations. This is particularly the case with his lifelong obsession with the year 2012 and what he called the "end of history." The notion of an eschatological event, or an Omega Point, as the Jesuit mystic Teilhard de Chardin called it, set to occur at the end of 2012 (as opposed to being a far-off event as Teilhard envisaged) was bound up with McKenna's time wave theory, the idea being that there is a mathematical fractal pattern governing the rise and fall of novelty in the world. While it is undeniable that the universe is forever conjuring up novel phenomena (such as solar systems, life, and consciousness, for example) and while it is certainly plausible that nature is teleological (as I myself have repeatedly argued), there is no compelling evidence that the ebb and flow of novelty follows mathematically determined dynamics that can be mapped out in advance. Thus, whenever McKenna would attempt to fit historical events into his beloved time wave theory, it would always seem rather arbitrary. Moreover, did it mean that other biospheres in the universe were constrained to follow the same developmental rules? How could such a theory apply everywhere? In any case, nothing untoward happened at the end of 2012, and it was basically business as usual on the cultural front.

McKenna also entertained something popularly known as the "stoned ape theory." The idea was that our distant African primate ancestors stumbled across psilocybin fungi after they started to venture out of the forest and onto the savannah grasslands. Under the influence of psilocybin, certain novel traits were inspired or facilitated—such as language and art. By means unknown, these new traits then became genetically hardwired. The theory is made explicit in McKenna's book *Food of the Gods,* and he also discussed it in many of his talks. While it is a fascinating idea, he never seemed to explain exactly how any genetic changes occurred. For evolution to occur, genetic changes have to occur. Human psychology is bound up with the cortex, and genes connected with the cortex must be affected if psilocybin is to have had a role in human evolution. I know of no way psilocybin could achieve such genetic modification, and I never heard McKenna detail such a mechanism.

Not all is lost, however. If we still wish to maintain that psilocybin (or a similar environmental psychedelic) had *some kind* of historical impact upon our species, what seems more probable is that mushroom use may have inspired artistic creativity and religious ideas in our more recent ancestors (which means genes don't need to come into it), an idea that author Graham Hancock promotes in his book *Supernatural*. Certainly it is possible, and thus the discovery and use of psilocybin may indeed account for the sudden cultural arrival of cave art and such. Until some kind of evidence emerges (such as fossilized *Psilocybe* spore samples within human remains), it is a moot issue.

Post-2012, in the McKenna debriefing era, I think it fair to sum up McKenna's pronounced shortcomings as the result of excessive wishful thinking. In other words, if McKenna was guilty of anything, it was in being too quixotic. He yearned for something spectacular to happen on a global level, an event of such magnitude that humanity would be pushed out of the rut of profane history and delivered to a new transcendental realm. That kind of idea is indeed wishful thinking and seems to absolve us of responsibility, as if we could regain paradise on earth by some means external to our own efforts and without radically changing our values and our conceptions about the world. It is akin to UFO fanatics imagining that one day "they" will come and that our meeting with "them" will transform everything, or akin to those who imagine that the Lord and his angels will descend from the heavens and bring justice and peace, or akin to the New Age idea that a "hyperdimensional portal" of some kind will appear, through which we will vibrate to some new level of being (whatever that means).

All these ideas represent sugar-coated wishful thinking, a sort of childish solution to solving the various problems of the world. It seems far more practical and probable that dramatic change will eventually come from *within us,* from within the collective psyche. We don't need to locate some "other" paradise or be swept up by some external eschatological force. The biosphere itself, Spaceship Earth, as futurist Buckminster Fuller termed it, is already an Eden and already contains everything we need to build a healthy, sustainable, egalitarian culture. We just need to realize this, stop pointing to the skies for salvation, and change our way of life here and now. This will not come instantly, but it can happen in the fullness of time. As the psilocybin-influenced comedian and raconteur Bill Hicks suggested, if we really put our minds to it, we could create heaven on earth and spend the future exploring the stars together. I reckon Hicks was spot on with that sentiment. Thus, we have to evolve ourselves in order to save ourselves. We have to effect cultural change according to our own inner efforts. Once the collective psyche has evolved and matured, it will be reflected outwardly in a mature culture. That is our only viable long-term destiny as far as I can discern.

McKenna can be readily forgiven for his overzealous eschatological musings because what ultimately led him to wax so quixotic was the mushroom. This is what psilocybin can do. The psilocybin experience can be so spiritually charged that one can go through a sort of personal eschaton. One can die to one's old self and feel ecstatically reborn. One realizes that life and consciousness are *ultrafantastic* and that we should be celebrating this and not be so caught up in things like money, war, and politics. There can also be an overwhelming impression that a principle of purposeful intelligence underlies all and everything, that human life is part of some grand, ongoing natural function. McKenna was keen to project this kind of psilocybinetic inspiration outwardly, and so was born his time wave theory, a means to hasten Teilhard's hypothetical Omega Point, to bring some temporally distant cosmic attractor right into the present epoch.

We can, of course, leave aside McKenna's eschatological fantasies because they were not the only thing he raved about. He had equal time for biospherical concerns and the need to steer human culture in a different and less materialistic direction. He made people question everything, and his voice and rhetoric were like a beacon shining forth among all the meaningless media that clamor for our attention. In any case, the bottom line for me is that hearing McKenna in 1992 helped propel me further on my psychedelic journey that had begun, rather shakily, some six years earlier. For this, I am grateful. I may now have outgrown many of McKenna's more fantastical ideas, but I still share his core love and high regard for the psilocybin experience.

Back to 1992 and my first exposure to Terence McKenna. Having bought and avidly consumed his lively and thought-provoking book *The Archaic Revival* in July of 1992 and being suddenly interested in exploring psilocybin once more, I decided to venture to Richmond Park at the very end of the following month. I was in luck. Even though it was a hot and sunny late August day, I managed to locate hundreds of specimens of *Psilocybe semilanceata,* the very same species I had picked so naively in the park back in 1986. In fact, that bountiful autumn of 1992 provided me with literally thousands of mushrooms, a wonderfully fortuitous abundance that never occurred again.

Compared with my situation in 1986, everything was different in 1992. I was older and wiser and no longer a grubby, dim punk rocker. I might still have had rebellious tendencies, but now I had the skill to verbalize any unorthodox points of view. Indeed, a few months earlier I had graduated from University College London (UCL) with a psychology degree. So here I was, an educated young man in the prime of life and ready for psychedelic action. At the very least I was in a position to more properly judge the merits of the psilocybin experience. To be sure, my final year university dissertation had been partly about the psychedelic experience—and I had received top marks for it. So I was basically all hyped up to explore the psychedelic edges of nature.

Spurred on by McKenna's quixotic musings, I saw myself as a kind of bold metaphysical adventurer fated to tackle the ultimate nature of reality by all and any psychoactive means necessary.

So it was that from the end of August 1992 to late November of that same year, I spent my time in the grip of what I would later call a "mushroom fever." It was a wonderful period of my life. I felt that I was investigating wild psilocybin mushrooms more systematically and more enthusiastically than any other British citizen before me. For a three-month period it was as if I had found heaven, as if I had awoken from a deep slumber into a reality that was both alive and directed, as though the world was the living text of some ongoing adventure story. It seemed as if I had uncovered a great secret that had lain buried in the English countryside, like a lost alchemical spell, a veritable philosopher's stone able to bond the human psyche with a greater entity that was all of life. True, I had always been interested in altered states of awareness, true even that this had led me to study psychology, yet I was never prepared for the explosive, vision-inducing power lying latent within a humble fungus. All my previous psilocybin episodes were nothing compared with what was to come.

Because I kept a journal at that time and documented my most astonishing experiences, I can reprint some of the material here to give a clear picture of what I went through and why the mushroom had such a massive impact upon me. In the "vintage" journal extracts that follow, I should point out that some sound decidedly naïve from this vantage point in time, while others are overtly mystical. Certain concepts like "Gaia" crop up a lot. While this deliberately poetic term (coined by James Lovelock for the self-regulating biosphere) was very popular in the early 1990s, it does sound a trifle dated. These days I prefer to simply speak of the biosphere and the naturally intelligent properties thereof.

Despite my acute embarrassment at much of their tone and style,

I still feel that these journal extracts can provide the reader with the flavor of the psilocybin experience as encountered by a fairly conventional young man living firmly within the city of London, and not out in some remote shamanic healing retreat or on some exotic island far from the hustles and bustles of modern life. Some of the writing was even done while I was still in the throes of the psilocybin experience, mostly written indoors at night. It is notoriously difficult to write while under the power of the mushroom, so an unconventional style is to be expected. It is truly a monumental effort to write in such a state—one has to wrestle free from rapture, then a pen has to be grasped as if it were a chisel, and only then may one carve out words upon paper (I had no computer or word processor in those far-off days).

But enough dilly-dallying. Here is one of the earliest things I penned at the end of August 1992. I was still bemushroomed and "glowing" when I wrote it. At first blush it might seem to be an account of a rather trivial incident, yet psilocybin has the knack of making even the most routine act feel epic:

You would not believe the complex flow of atoms, molecules, cells, and substances that surge about the alchemical surface of this extraordinary planet of ours. To grasp the awesome majesty of the biosphere, the living earth, in all its infinite glory, is a gift not granted lightly, but a gift that is nonetheless waiting patiently for each and every one of us if we but open our eyes and our hearts. In the meantime, let me describe a recent experiment that I myself have just now tried in the name of experience. Having bravely ingested a quite sizeable dose of fresh psilocybin, I then, after much other inspired activity, proceeded to analyze a certain specimen of organic life, namely an individual holistic-unto-itself kiwi fruit, originating from some distant land on the other side of the planet. In terms of seed dispersal, this was a momentous achievement for the kiwi plant that proffered up this particular fruit. I saw that such fruit is designed to be attractive, succulent, and phenomenologically rewarding, and in return the tree or plant that proffered it is given the possibility to produce further copies of itself through the dispersal of its seeds. It sounded terrific to me. A really tasty deal, in fact.

So there I was under the growing spell of psilocybin, with a genuine exotic fruit in my trembling hand. Throwing caution to the wind, I set about examining the kiwi fruit in more detail, turning it over and scrutinizing its rough surface. Looking closely, I discovered that its surface appeared reminiscent of furry animal skin. Plunging into the experience in even more detail, thus exploiting time to my own advantage, I began to fondle the exquisite creature. I was beginning to suspect that this was a form of intercourse with Gaia, for it seemed clear to me that this was part of her being in my hand. It was as if I had been a blind, blundering ape all my life, without any sense of the reality of the living biosphere. To be sure, like others I had had rare moments when one's consciousness briefly expands to encompass a larger field of reality, yet this time the experience was extended and deepened to the point of ecstasy.

And so it was that I continued to stroke and tease the kiwi fruit, anticipating the delight that lay ahead. The foreplay seemed to last an eternity. But the caresses and general tactile games could not proceed indefinitely. The time inevitably came when I had to bite into the tight skin of the furry being to commence the next stage of the organic communion. As the fruit sat passively in my hand, it was almost as if I could hear it, and this curious sensation seemed to infuse my soul with awe. The fruit was still alive, still a living part of life, drawing me nearer to an act of consumption.

Without bothering to peel the living gift, I finally bit into the fruity gene-laden cargo. That first bite made the entire world stop. *My psychedelically charged mind was opening like a flower as I was thrust ever deeper into the expansive living presence of the Gaian matrix. How fantastic, I thought, that we are woven into the fabric of the biosphere and that we engage in a constant interplay with all manner of other life forms. How extraordinary that energy can be transformed and sublimed in such complex, organic ways.*

To cap it all, there then followed a feast of epic proportions! Once bitten into, the fruit revealed a bright green luminescent interior fashioned with literally hundreds of seeds. I marveled at such astonishing evolutionary craftsmanship. Could these tiny seeds in the heart of the kiwi fruit really contain all the wealth of genetic information needed to produce yet more kiwi plants? Was I to believe that each and every dark speck embedded in the moist green flesh of the kiwi creature possessed such a rich store of information as to make an encyclopedia look "thick" in comparison? This was fractal reality with a vengeance, almost too brilliant to behold. I held within my hand a veritable powder keg of order to be subsumed into my body in order that a flow of organic evolution continue. We will have to keep this miracle to ourselves, you understand, lest the experience be stolen and redescribed by science in less, how shall we say, exotic terms. . . .

The psilocybinetic encounter was not over. Incredibly, I realized that I was about to eat the entire kiwi organism, every last morsel of it, without fear that it was a bad thing to do. Consider this carefully. This juicy configuration of matter, more exquisite and more softly beautiful than any manufactured device, was becoming transubstantiated into my body through a natural act of consumption. Such is the way of nature.

Eventually, the magic performance came to an end, and the kiwi fruit no longer remained. Indeed, it had vanished within me, eventually to become thought itself. However, the experience that I briefly describe here lives on in my memory, testifying to the wonder of the living biosphere. Nature's providence knows no limit if we but open ourselves to it and explore it. If every one of us could sense and feel the potential of Spaceship Earth, that it comes loaded with more than our dreams can imagine, then paradise would zoom into view over the horizon like the rising sun. Eternity awaits us, for time can be stopped. This is because experience is time. Through the effects of the psilocybin mushroom, conscious experience is magnified, time slows down, and we realize that reality is somehow infinite in depth. The psychedelic story did not end with the 1960s; rather, it has just begun. Naturally.

A week or so after the above account, I had another intense experience, this time involving powerful visions:

Let it be known throughout the land that I have experienced the best morning of my life, perhaps the best morning that a young male hominid could ever hope to experience. At 7:45 a.m. I ingested about thirty-five almost fresh, unprocessed, and thus legal (of course, for I am not one to abuse the law) Psilocybe semilanceata *mushrooms on an empty stomach. My body was thus geared up to surround and consume whatever I chose to provide it with to break my fast. And on this morning . . . oh boy!*

After about thirty minutes the subtle psychological shift in perception began. With eyes closed, I saw appallingly vivid visions that were almost too strong to bear. I saw multicolored "serpent-skin eyes," layer upon layer of gleaming eyes that appeared to cover the skin of some mythical serpentine creature. On reflection, I think they must have been eyes because eyes have a beautiful "sensate" quality about them, eyes reveal so, so much about a person; they glisten with life and signify sentience. I noticed that in the visionary state I still had a fovea-like visual area, that is, a centrally focused area of vision, and it was in this area of focus that I beheld the shifting pattern of these impossibly beautiful eyes.

I have to say that I interpreted these visions as being of some great serpent. Indeed, the eyes seemed to be its scales. I should stress that I was not afraid. During the last five weeks of experience, I have attempted to tread carefully, employing as much "objective" conscious attention as I have been able to muster, derived in all probability from my tuition in science methodology. At any rate, the visions now before me appeared to be a dazzling testament to the "truth." Even when I opened my eyes, I saw a dim afterimage of the fabulous serpent's tail slithering around the ceiling. Yet a voice told me to keep my eyes closed. I then saw spinning shapes, statuelike faces zoom up before me. I began to have an inner conversation with whatever the presence was. Having studied psychology, I know the clinical attitude to such phenomena, yet the experience was as real as real gets.

I felt somewhat like a child who was receiving instruction from a wise and ancient being. This being was not evil, despite its shifting serpentine nature. Like most people, I am not too enamored of snakes, yet this visionary serpent was a creature beyond any simple snake, seemingly an embodiment of Gaia, a huge organic entity wielding formidable wisdom and power.

A small and rather pathetic voice within me asked what was in it for people if we proclaimed this psychedelic Gaian reality. Still with eyes closed, I immediately saw a birdcage flung open, the birds inside flying free from their confines. This breathtakingly clear vision, which I interpreted as the freeing of souls, occurred so quickly, so spontaneously, that, as with other psilocybin visions I have had, I cannot infer that it was simply a product of my imagination. And even if we entertain the idea that all of this experience was somehow due to the unconscious, then that would mean that the unconscious is far bigger and far more full of intentionality than we might suppose. Something is going on in the psilocybin state that is radically different from normal conscious processes. It deserves serious enquiry. If the public and the science community were once interested in Freud's sex-obsessed theories about the unconscious, then surely the psilocybin visionary experience warrants similar attention? After all, some form of creative unconscious activity must be operating through the effect *of psilocybin, though on a level far beyond anything construed by Freud. Moreover, this extraordinary activity reaches conscious awareness, like the flowing of some new informative current.*

That the visions were serpentine must be connected with my current interest in the Mayan civilization, yet that does not detract from their significance. What I saw was absolutely not something my ego could have conjured up. The visions were beyond the typical products of the imagination, bearing a style and intentionality that bespeak of a deeper part of the psyche that commands attention and almost screams with significance. Because I am well aware of their religious nature, I surmise that serpentine visual motifs are a part of the lexicon of symbols within my psyche and that the "Other," whatever it is exactly, is able to orchestrate such symbols into a dramatic visionary dialogue.

After the visions had ceased, I wept tears of joy, this being the second time that mushroom visions have produced such a rare emotion in me. It is no small thing to cry with joy. One must be moved to do so. That the visionary trance state can do this testifies to the very real power of psilocybin. Some "higher" potential of the human psyche is clearly stirred into action.

It is interesting for me to look back on these early visionary episodes. Often I convinced myself that I was in communion with an *external* Other, which is to say some sort of intentional being or entity totally separate from myself. You commonly hear this kind of interpretation. Author Graham Hancock, for example, often talks about entities from other dimensions and such, which he infers on account of his ayahuasca experiences. I now favor a Jungian approach. I think all these "beings" and otherworldly sources of teachings and insights that manifest with psychedelics are part of the "higher self," and that the higher self is *an emergent aspect of the unconscious.* Which means that the Other is actually part of us. We should bear in mind that the unconscious is unimaginably vast. The human unconscious is not simply a static store of memories, but rather a huge organism-like network of information that seeks stability and integration (akin to a minimum energy state, perhaps). Within this undulating informational matrix are symbols, themes, ideas, schema, and self-organizing wisdom. What psilocybin seems to do is boost the natural integrative potential of the unconscious. Thus, information in need of resolution comes to the conscious mind, along with wisdom and tutorial dialogues. Whether through dreams or psychedelic reveries, it is the autonomous ability of the unconscious to yield up wisdom and uncanny tutorial insights that makes it seem like an external Other.

Here is another journal entry that involves visions:

At the very beginning of my blessed "mushroom fever" of last year, I refrained from closing my eyes. I found the outside world so delightfully transformed that it was enough to revel in one's visual surroundings. It was on heeding Terence McKenna's advice given in his book The Archaic Revival *that I first attempted to employ a technique with which to experience visions. McKenna had suggested that psilocybin be taken in quiet darkness with eyes closed. At first, I thought nothing of this recommendation, though I now realize that such advice was given in all seriousness out of respect to the mushroom's ability to initiate powerfully moving visions. One might assume that closing one's eyes would reduce the psychedelic experience in some way. Would it not be akin, I had thought, to the primitive, half-hearted attempts at meditation I had once tried? Would it not be . . . boring?*

When I first applied McKenna's technique, I was met with bizarre sights. I saw unexpected images, like green swaying palm trees, very clear yet strangely alien. These visions were also somewhat frightening, because the longer one remained with them, the deeper one plunged into the unconscious—or Gaian Mind, as McKenna was calling it. I learned that as the visionary trance progresses, the closer one is drawn to a powerful source of intentional information. Indeed, it is this intentional and communicative quality associated with psilocybin visions that makes the enterprise so intimidating.

Despite the fear one encounters in such an uncommon enterprise, one can exercise some control by instantly opening one's eyes. But that is to run scared. The visions demand to be met face on and accepted no matter how painful or intense they might be. Indeed, that psilocybin visions appear so alarming in their candor suggests that one should most definitely be in possession of a healthy, grounded psyche.

I vividly recall one of my earliest spectacular visionary experiences. It happened one morning when I had once more ingested fresh mushrooms on an empty stomach. I lay comfortably in bed and waited for the psilocybin to gracefully infuse my psyche. Sometimes, if one is really alert, the first psilocybinetic wave can almost be coldly analyzed as it washes over one's consciousness. This is a really fantastic moment. At a certain point, you are shifted into an animate, supernormal reality. With eyes open, one's surroundings may suddenly appear hyperreal and even sacred. Beauty can radiate from everything that one sets one's eyes upon, as though one had suddenly woken up more. Everything appears as if alive and in fluidic connection.

I lay in my bed, arms folded, feeling rather like an Egyptian mummy because my body felt rather heavy and dead compared with my spirit or consciousness, which was very much alert. When I eventually closed my eyes, I perceived a kind of dark Underworld populated with jeweled eyes. Then I began to descend deeper into this world, until I came face to face with a dark and threatening being, akin to some oriental gatekeeper of Hades, a bit like that evil-looking samurai warrior in the movie Brazil. So clear was this sight that I was taken aback and immediately opened my eyes. I looked around me for comfort, still afraid of that terrifying guardian lurking deep within my psyche. Then, like a brave adventurer, I *determined to face this being. After all, I persuaded myself, had I not a good heart, and was my conscience not clear?*

When I shut my eyes again, I began to recede away from the eye-populated Underworld. With a feeling of acceleration, I shot backward and upward until I emerged up out of a black hole in a vast expanse of snowy white ground. As the dark hole in the ground receded, I noticed, in the new "above-ground" scenery, a number of cheap and comical symbols of well-being, in particular, highly stylized, cartoonish "thumbs-up" signs. It felt great. More than that, I now felt in the presence of some Gaian-sized benevolent being, who was all around me. Then, and I do not say this lightly, it was if I ascended into heaven itself. Like a small child, I found myself in the presence of sacred beings that defy description. I saw spirits materialize before me, embodying themselves in flesh and blood. I saw Godlike beings "tinkering" with life forms. I felt convinced that I was witnessing the "Creators" at work.

When I finally opened my eyes, I wept. My soul had been moved by these visions. I had been carried to realms of wonder beyond imagination. And this knowledge, this divine power of the mushroom, known by native Mexicans for millennia, was now surfacing in of all places London, England. So, where on earth was psychological science in all this? Here was a phenomenon worthy of research, a tool for accessing the deepest depths of the human psyche. A tool even for accessing the divine.

On other occasions, the material of the visions would often be closely associated with items from my memory artfully juxtaposed to yield new meaning. It was as if the Other communicated with me in a language I alone would fully understand. For instance, once when I first closed my eyes, I saw with absolute cinematographic clarity a close-image "shot" of a hand holding a radio receiver, and I soon realized, with glee, that this was a cool expression of "contact." On another occasion, though this seems almost absurd to me now, I saw, again in high resolution, a kind of native peasant family having a meal. What struck me most was the fact that they soon began clapping, smiling, and rubbing their stomachs vigorously. Perplexed, I opened my eyes, only to realize that the vision was most likely indicating, in a rather humorous way, that it was good that I had consumed mushrooms.

I remember also that I would frequently see visions of ancient doors being opened, ascending stairs, or a multicolored serpent tail slither behind a slightly opened door. Always, upon reflection, it was clear that the visual images were highly symbolic, that they were a kind of dramatic visual language through which the Other would communicate its presence.

Alien motifs would also crop up in the visions. I would often see futuristic-looking people clothed in luminescent body-hugging suits getting in and out of advanced machines, or I would see what looked like the inside of advanced alien spacecraft. Another common motif, or theme, was that of the suspended animation machine, a clinically clean and white plastic-looking structure within which lay humans, usually a man and a woman.

In every case, whether earthly, heavenly, or alien, I can state with absolute conviction that these visions were not made by my ego. They were always so surprising, so intense, so spontaneous, and so rich in detail that it was rather the case that I was passively watching a film produced by something distinct from my ego and projected before me, moreover, a film whose meaning was not always immediately apparent but that required a few seconds of contemplation for the intent to be grasped, akin to the game charades. Once I had begun to experience such visions, they became perhaps the hallmark effect of psilocybin. During the visionary trance state, one interfaces with what feels like an ancient, wise teacher. If it sounds incredible, then that is only because the psychological power of natural psilocybin is incredible.

Again, this demonstrates to me that the unconscious has a tutorial potential. Indeed, many of us will have experienced such a tutorial effect in certain meaningful dreams—which we might reflect upon after we wake up. You can also "sleep on a problem" and may awaken in a state of knowing. Psilocybin seems to take this informative, creative potential of the unconscious to a whole new level. Even now, more than twenty years on, I can still recall many of those early visions. They would start up and have a life of their own. I would be both enthralled by them and terrified. Psilocybin visions feel like they are emanating from somewhere deep and ancient, as if one is accessing the dynamic source code of the human psyche, the very wellspring of all meaning and purpose.

Things on the mushroom front were not always intensely serious, however, as the following "live" extract—written during the experience itself—shows:

The banana. What a groovy name for a groovy fruit. Forget about kiwi fruit, for they are nothing in comparison to the sublime banana. I swear that I could write an entire BBC TV miniseries about them! Don't you dare peel a banana with careless forlorn again—for I have beheld much virtue in this seemingly simple fruit.

Grasping a banana while under the effects of psilocybin is like shaking hands with the plant kingdom. Smart primate meets Gaia. You can feel the fruit inside, like it's a caterpillar or larva waiting to break out of its yellow jacket. Astonishingly, fruit, before finally succumbing to entropy and decaying, lives for a brief period after having jumped the parental ship. Or at least it is the case that it can ripen. This notion astounds me. Cut off from its living parent tree, the banana nonetheless continues to develop and mature in a deliberate and functional way.

I like the curve of the banana. It reminds me of dolphins. Looking at it head-on, it appears uncannily like Tursiops, the bottlenose dolphin. Both look neat; both are sleekly curved. A big thought occurs to me as I continue to study the banana's curious five-sided symmetry. It is as though the banana is a supermathematical organic statement. In fact, I reason that this must be the case. The genetic code in the banana genome must code for both the proteins and the specific pentahedral structure of the fruit. Therefore, the banana is an expression of a mathematical formula. Which means I am about to eat a piece of natural mathematics.

It peels in a delightfully consumer-friendly way. This is just too much for a mortal man to experience. My first tug and three strips of skin conveniently unzip themselves, the flesh within looking like some alien creature. This fruit has clearly been designed by natural selection for the nimble-fingered hominid. It is so perfect that all it really lacks is a written instruction on its skin (in English, of course) to the tune of "Slippery—please dispose of with care."

Inside, the naked flesh of the stripped banana looks more alive than it did with its skin on. It is like a white larval bullet, a pupa living so slowly that we believe it inert, when in fact it is still transforming in a meaningful way. I take the whole flesh out, as one long integrated component. It looks like a pellet that has been squeezed out of some big creature, deposited in its trail, as it were.

I pull the banana flesh apart, and with the superconscious perceptual lucidity granted to me through psilocybin, the resulting rupture takes on epic proportions, as if some mountain had been rent asunder. I can almost hear the sound of the fruity flesh being torn apart. So white it is, and so rich in information, like some curious organic computer program.

I eat, entranced by the taste of this pure, unadulterated, untainted, additive-free piece of organic fabric. My, I had almost forgotten how good Mother Nature can be. It was like eating an energy bomb designed by a team of fruit engineers who had worked on its creation over millions of years. In fact, the banana proved so special that I ate another, and with the psilocybin coming free, the whole meal cost less than one half-pint of lager.

Despite such amusing laid-back experiences, the chief draw of the mushroom at that time was always its visionary power. Here I write more about serpent visions:

In the first six months or so of my heady mushroom venture, the serpent, or variations on this symbol, dominated my visions. Always, it was as if I were beholding some great and wise creature whose presence demanded respect and attention. Once, I remember seeing huge serpentine coils piled up upon one another and somehow turning as if they were the cogs of some organic machine. Then I found myself gliding toward a flexuous off-white mass, which for the life of me I could not comprehend. This rippled white stuff was everywhere, and I was being drawn into it, suffocating almost as it surrounded me. Suddenly, seeing this mass close up, I realized what it was. It was convoluted brain tissue. Spongy white cortical tissue, fold after fold of it. This was the immense brain of some mythical serpent related, I thought, to the biosphere. I felt that I was seeing a visual representation of the powerful intelligence of all life on earth, the "earth brain," as it were.

The scene then changed, and I found myself touring a building that was made of both artery-laced flesh and conventional material. Each room seemed to have a particular biological function. It was most bizarre. I appeared to be inside a kind of visceral architecture that was breathing gases, pumping oceans of blood, and digesting vast vats of food. In fact, visionary motifs indicating the fusion of man-made architecture with biological structure were repeated a number of times. I often perceived stately homes and palaces, or rather I would be gliding gracefully through such palatial places, and always the woodwork, such as the banisters, wall panels, and staircases, would be revealed to be made of the body of a living creature. To be precise, I perceived that these buildings were woven from the jeweled body of the serpent. Everything was alive, all was part of one coherent, constructive entity. And if I saw human figures in any of these scenes, they too were formed out of the transmutating body of the serpent. All the objects and entities in these scenes had the stamp of the serpent's hide upon them, in that a kind of pulsating grid of luminescent lines and scaly jewels pervaded every object.

On another occasion, I found myself being compelled upward along some dark space, destination unknown. Turning and twisting, my ascent seemed to be endless. Suddenly, my situation was revealed to me. With growing apprehension, I perceived that I was inside a kind of eerie lift shaft. Although I could not see where I was headed, the view downward disappeared into thick blackness. Evidently this was one infinitely long passage reaching upward. At some stage I felt as if I had been flipped over. I was at the top (perhaps, I mused, the top represented the future). There I saw incredibly vast structures that I found difficult to interpret. They were like bloody red biological organs of enormous dimensions, beating, pulsing, straining to grow and metabolize. They were rather sickly to look at, as if I felt the tremendous strain they appeared to be under. The organs, or whatever they were, began to split open like they were undergoing a kind of sticky, crackling, insectile metamorphosis. The sense of a struggle was disturbingly intense, so much so that my growing disgust stopped a proper evaluation of what I was seeing. The scene simply became too enormously gut-wrenching to view, and I ended the vision by opening my eyes.

Once I even saw the entire earth split apart, as if a mythical serpent, coiled up beneath the earth's surface, had suddenly burst forth and was rising upward. This vision was apocalyptic, like some multi-million-dollar epic movie portraying the end of the world. On the few other occasions when I divined eschatological events, I would see a colossal spinning vortex into which everything—all matter, all life, all information—was being integrated, a vast spinning spiral mosaic whose center appeared stationary and around which all else was revolving. In each case, the eschaton, while being all-consuming, was also radiant with sacred power.

I also recall a vision, at the peak of psychedelic ecstasy, in which I found myself floating in a decreasing spiral around the head of a enormous serpent in whose mouth lay a precious stone, gleaming with alluring transcendental light. The eyes of that serpent! Fierce, and supremely wise, they were fabulous! They shone with all-seeing sentience, their defiant gaze illuminating all that passed before them. I felt that I was approaching the Absolute, that the Absolute could only be depicted in such a way. For hours after that vision, whenever I briefly closed my eyes, I would see serpentine jaws opened, thinly curved fangs, pearly white, tipped with a drop of clear venom, a sparkle of light on each. These were symbols of power, faces of the Other as it is approached by the psilocybinetic voyager.

All this of which I speak is but one perceptual leap away. Beyond mundane consciousness lies a world resplendent with revelation, a vast landscape of potent imagery and self-organizing symbols, a realm only touched upon by my brief encounters. This realm is calling out to us. The mystery awaits.

In retrospect, it again seems clear that the serpent is an archetypal symbol of the deep unconscious. Like other commonly shared symbols from around the world, the serpent embodies a huge amount of information in terms of what it signifies and what it is connected to (things like the earth, wisdom, subtlety, power, fear, etc.). This implies that the unconscious operates in a language-like way, or at least there can be a language of symbols, and a kind of discourse between the "I" and the unconscious can take place.

Now to change gears somewhat and introduce a classic bad trip. Well, not just a bad trip but something that, at the time, felt far worse:

It is now some four weeks or so since I had what can only be described as one of the most unpleasant experiences of my life. Because these journal entries represent an honest, no-holds-barred account of the psilocybin experience, then I must here reveal the horrors that unfortunately occupy the flip side of the mystical experience. Let this be a warning, for I would wish it on no one to undergo such anguish, terror, and torment.

It is my conviction that these nightmarish trips are no one's fault but one's own. I was too greedy for numinous grace, and I paid the price. Although I had come "close to the edge" on a few occasions before, this time I keeled right over, into the fire, and, in some sense, died a horrible death.

At the time I took the fateful dose, my life situation was, to say the least, awful. Abandoned by a girlfriend, sick of my living arrangements, and completely inactive in any creative sense, I should have sought the virtue of patience until I was fit to attempt a return to the sacred realms that I had reached the previous autumn. But, as I say, greed prevailed; I wanted instant spiritual gratification, an immediate spiritual caress from the Other.

In my naïveté, I believed that a huge dose of psilocybin might wash away my melancholic stupor. How wretchedly wrong I was. To achieve a truly ecstatic experience, one's mind must be finely tuned, cleaned of psychological detritus, as though one's psyche were a pristine radio receiver set to pick up rarefied signals. This is the role of "set," so repeatedly stressed by the psychedelic pioneers of the 1960s. For me, however, everything was exactly as it should not have been. My inner world in turmoil, I was psychologically unfit to channel a heavenly experience. Even so, I went ahead, mistakenly believing that I knew better.

It was late evening and, unbeknownst to me, the time of the full moon. I remember taking two exceedingly large doses because after an hour or so, the first dose had not produced any discernible effect. In retrospect, I should have waited a little longer for that first dose to come into play.

The visions, when they first came, were poor, rather muddy, and unclear. Like an idiot, I tried to force visions to come, but there was just too much "noise," leaving me with only incoherent bits and pieces, a whirlpool of disjointed imagery. However, I did see one or two "solid" depictions. I saw futuristic-looking children and what appeared to be a long and winding tunnel through which they were traveling. I also saw images of people, plants, and places made out of a black rubberlike material. I interpreted this as meaning that all organic life was made from a universal "flexi-smart" substance.

Later, when the full impact of the two doses began to take hold, I saw staggeringly complex sights, most of which I am unable to describe. At one stage I saw images of humans in which veins and blood-red arteries were visible, rather like those pictures one sometimes sees in biology textbooks. These human forms emerged out of nowhere, taking shape before me as if they were spirits embodying themselves. I also remember passing through regions suggestive of the afterlife. I passed through a flotilla of floating entities of some sort, a realm pervaded with serenity and calm. Then I saw that these drifting entities, or souls as they seemed to be, merged into a fantastically colored machinelike pattern. This pattern, of enormous magnitude, was reminiscent of a rotating mandala, though the patterns within it were like whirling cogs, as if part of some immense mechanical system. It seemed as if I was witnessing some sort of spiritual recycling, in which millions upon millions of departed souls, reduced to an ineffable essence, were being absorbed into another system of being. It was an awesome vision, and it left me at a loss to fully comprehend it.

When, after some time, I opened my eyes, my room had transformed into a hideous kaleidoscopic onslaught of color, and I think that this marked the start of my nightmare. How far removed from the divine room I had experienced the previous autumn! It was horrible. I swore and struggled to my feet. The carpet appeared grotesquely cartoonlike, its ugly red color screaming at my senses. I felt sure then that I had awoken into an awful dream. I tore off my glasses in a futile attempt to escape the horrific visual data invading my visual cortex. But still the nauseatingly lurid hues swam about me, stifling me, choking me almost. I suddenly felt too big, like a giant lumbering around a ridiculous toy house. My clothes seemed preposterous, my reflection in the mirror an absurdity. I was a comical clown, trapped in a maelstrom of chaotic, disjointed perceptions. In my mind I heard the word Jekyll over and over.

I was overcome with such fear that I quickly retired to bed and darkness, in the naïve hope that I could escape the sickly "outsideness." Worse was to come. Indeed, the ghastly nightmare was only just beginning to gather momentum. As I lay there in bed, my mind was teeming with horrific thoughts. I began to lose all control. In trips before, I had always been able to maintain some semblance of control and will, yet now I was fast becoming a wholly passive creature, being tossed and turned in a malevolent sea of psychological torment.

Gradually, my sense of identity, my ego to give it a formal name, began to perish. Normally such a dissolution of the ego is experienced as an ecstatic release, a harmonious blending of oneself with one's environment whereby one merges with the larger Whole. Not so on this dreadful night. I was dying, at least in some symbolic way.

For perhaps an hour or more, I felt with absolute certainty that I was in some process of death. The darkness about me was alive with spite, malice, and destructiveness. All my surroundings felt overtly hostile. Suddenly I felt as though I was a captive explorer in the hands of murderous natives who were poised to tear me to pieces. I no longer had full control of my body. I couldn't move properly. Repeatedly, I tried to sit up, but found to my dismay that I could not perform any organized movement.

Thoughts of death. I am dying. No one to help you here. You have come too far, and now you die. The sound of rushing traffic outside the house leads me to feel as if I have suffered some fatal car crash, that I am lying terminally injured on the road. My body feels like dead, heavy meat upon a butcher's slab. I am convinced that I have suffered *a terrible accident. That thought will not go away. . . . At one point, I did manage to get up. Clumsily, I staggered about in the dark and somehow found the light switch. Too bright. Still the sick, garish swirls of cartoon color. My pathetic hominid body is shaking violently, hardly able to stand. I can do nothing, nothing at all. I turn off the light for the lesser horror of the dark. I make out the shape of my chess computer and realize with abject horror that I really am in a losing game, a game about to terminate.*

As my identity continues to crumble, I speak aloud, mumbling words that mean a lot to me, like the name of the woman who had so recently broken away from me. I am grasping for familiar concepts and ideas that give me my identity, that give me meaning, that keep me alive. I am even reduced to counting aloud and drumming with my hands to form a beat, something to focus on, some semblance of order to cling to, but this is useless too. Indeed, the oppression around me escalates. I am being annihilated by an external impingement of evil. Like a dwindling flame, my soul is smothered by a blanket of malevolence.

Once, and only once, the terrifying onslaught subsided. For perhaps fifteen seconds it ceased, and I gasped with relief. It was just the Other wrestling with me, I thought to myself. Just a test. And then it was back. To the death, to the bitter end. Someone help me. Too late . . . into the fire . . . utter annihilation. Who am I? This is beyond terror now. I don't know who I am. Overdose, like heroin . . . you've had an accident. I am no more than a dying animal. Remorse wells up inside of me. In my mind I ask forgiveness. It does not come. Merciless jaws of death, cold, inky black, consume me.

I do not recall what transpired next, though I later began to dream. I entered vivid hypnagogic dreamscapes. These were bewildering. I felt like a rural creature in The Lord of the Rings *or* Watership Down*. I became caught up in the telling of a tale. I was a character in the story, and as the story progressed it seemed that an act of creation was unfolding. This* *experience marked the beginning of a tremendous vortex in which I was a component. I remember my body making erratic movements as though I had become physically disabled. Strange guttural sounds issued from my throat. I felt slightly "off-key" or out of balance, like I was not in time with the world, offset somehow.*

The bizarre quasi dream continued, and the feeling that I was caught up inside a spinning creative vortex grew. This vortex was all around me; it was my reality, a cyclonic process rushing around and around. The first birdsong of dawn became integrated into this vortex. The vortex had left the dreamy regions of my psyche and had moved out into the environment. It was like some enchanting, self-perpetuating song or melody, gathering momentum as it spun itself out into the world, orchestrating itself into existence. Every external sound became incorporated into the musical vortex, each marking a new phase of the progressive, accelerating process. Then, in my mind, I heard, absurdly, the voice of some television news reporter. What exactly he was saying, I do not recall, though he was speaking in a noble manner, as if commentating upon some event of unbelievable consequence. Faster and faster swirled the vortex, and I felt that it should explode at any moment. I was utterly overcome with its transcendental mystery and power. What it all meant I have not the foggiest idea. What I do know is that it ended abruptly. One moment I was part of a spinning psychedelic vortex; the next moment I was lying in a rumpled, sweat-stained bed.

I have to admit that I cried a lot that morning. As I showered, I vowed to abandon my psychedelic quest and destroy all my written work. I had been pursuing a phantasm, I thought. It was a blind alley, leading to self-destruction and isolation. All my blissful experiences over the previous autumn were meaningless, spurious hallucinations, no more than a drug-induced psychosis. Clearly, I had a lot of thinking and soul-searching to do.

As the days progressed, I recovered, and the entire episode can now be put in perspective. It is clear that psilocybin should not be taken unless one's mind is free of worry, tension, and neurosis, and it is equally clear that one needs to be careful with dosage. One also needs to have a good life situation. One's immediate future should at least appear moderately rosy. When one is in such a positive frame of mind, then one will be open to ecstatic revelation.

As proof of these assertions, I recently gave some mushrooms to a female acquaintance, a free-spirited Italian girl who was eager to experience them. As I watched over her on a sweltering June day in the grounds of Richmond Park, my faith was somewhat restored. For about one hour, she was in absolute ecstasy, her eyes shut, yet streaming forth tears of joy at the visions she beheld. All she could report was that "It is all so beautiful!" I know how she felt. I had been to those realms many months before, and it is where I hope good fortune will return me in the near future.

A dark report indeed—but methinks it makes for a riveting read! Interestingly, this contention of mine that one should not take psilocybin if one's psyche harbors "worry, tension, and neurosis" can be challenged. As I write, U.K. researchers are currently looking into whether psilocybin can be used to treat depression. Research has found that after psilocybin administration certain parts of the brain become less active, parts connected with the usual sense of self. Depressed people spend inordinate and unhealthy amounts of time in circular thoughts about how "bad" or "worthless" they are, and it is this kind of mechanical mentation that psilocybin can jolt, nudging people into new ways of thinking about themselves. At least that is the general idea. Certainly it is the case that psilocybin can upset the usual associations that flow within the psyche. This is why everything can look new and unusual—because one does not perceive with tired old associations. For this reason it is hoped by current researchers that psilocybin can break old patterns of thought and thereby alleviate depression. But the doses employed will be much more moderate than those that I took prior to the above bad trip. Add to that the fact that patients will have a trained therapist to help guide them, and one can see that psilocybin may well prove to be a useful tool in treating depression. So what I really should have said is that one needs to be in good psychological health if one chooses to undertake solo research with psilocybin. This is especially the case with larger doses. Psilocybin is not to be messed with or trivialized lest you pay a hefty price. As they say, the poison is the dose.

Returning to brighter times, here is a fascinating example of a psilocybinetic synchronicity from 1993:

> Flouting convention, I had once again consumed wild mushrooms for breakfast and had decided to brave a visit to the British Library [note that this was the old British library housed in the British Museum before they moved it to King's Cross] while still under the mushroom's spell. So, I grabbed my speedy racing bike and set off through London's congested arteries [note that I in no way condone my actions here!]. As I zipped along, my perceptual system on full volume, I became acutely aware of the "tightness" of the road surface beneath my wheels. It was as if I had become the earth itself and could feel the taut strips of asphalt upon me, like it was a kind of constrictive casing. This sensation was most curious. I could literally feel what it was like to be bounded by concrete and tarmac, and, moreover, that a newly emergent aspect of the encased earth was set to burst forth like a chicken breaking out of an egg.
>
> I also began to notice the tires on all the belching cars around me. All that rubber. Endless amounts of the stuff. I asked myself: And whence does this rubber originate? Once again, the biosphere provides, rubber being derived from the extruded latex produced by rubber trees, or at least manufactured as a synthetic counterpart of natural rubber. With four-dimensional thinking, I realized that natural rubber, wherever it

should be used, whether in radial car tires, condoms, or Wellington boots, is still connected to the rubber-producing plant, just as books are four-dimensional extensions of the trees from which their paper is derived. Once more, I got that flash of insight in which I perceived the biosphere to be one huge organism reorganizing its body into ever more complex arrangements. Even the petrol in the automobiles around me was derived from once-living organisms—meaning that the biosphere can power itself on its past endeavors like a snake consuming its own tail.

While cycling, I also found that by briefly blinking [I do not condone my actions here!] a complete three-dimensional retinal image lingered in my visual cortex for some few seconds. This afterimage was an almost faithful representation of the reality, and it was strange to see it gradually blend into an equally colorful visionary dreamscape, like a photographic image of the real world morphing into a synthesized computer animation.

After what seemed like a marathon bike ride, I reached the British Museum wherein lay the library I sought. Crowds of people swarmed around the entrance. Could I feign normality? People, especially their faces, appear extraordinary under psilocybin, as though one were seeing someone's tribal heritage etched into his or her face, like those Maori people of New Zealand whose faces bear symbolic tattoos. Thus, one must constantly struggle not to stare too much at strangers while one is bemushroomed.

A ridiculous-looking crowd of Australian tourists were amassed in front of me, each a clone dressed in khaki shorts, wide-brimmed corked hat, long socks, and boots, as though part of a Crocodile Dundee appreciation society. Before entering the British Museum, I had to actually mingle through these odd hominids, and this proved to be a distinctly anthropological few seconds.

At last I was inside the museum, and I made my way to the library. Now, the main reading room of the British Library is a spectacle to *even the normal mind because it has a huge dome reminiscent of the dome in Saint Paul's cathedral (albeit without the ornate paintings and stained-glass windows). It is certainly not like your average local library. As I entered, I gasped in amazement. This was no library! This was a minicathedral unto itself! The centrally situated book-issuing desk was no less than a raised altar, presided over by a middle-aged African woman, whose noble face spoke of royal blood. And the acoustics! I became utterly entranced with the ambient sound. Because of the architecture, one can hear a stream of amplified sounds gently echoing around the dome. I was mesmerized by this acoustical phenomenon. My brain seemed to holistically process the varied sounds so that a kind of flowing music emerged. All the vibrations became patterned within my brain as one single composition. So, I sat down, enthralled by the spontaneous music of the British Library, a veritable symphony no less, of which I, with my supercharged perception, was the sole audience.*

The jacket of a middle-aged man sitting opposite me grabbed my attention. It was alive. And covered in serpentine patterns. Aha! Once again, the mark of the mushroom is displayed before me. The subtly hued, rippling, rainbow creases of this man's jacket were the stuff of living art. And I bet he didn't even know it. His garments should be on show in the museum outside the library, I thought to myself. After all, the museum is packed with holy relics.

As I sat there immersed in profound thoughts, a singular and most dramatic piece of synchronicity occurred, the nature of which still baffles me. A small balding man had quietly approached me and placed a book on my desk. He briefly nodded toward the book and then hurriedly left. Now, I had not ordered any book, and it is usually the case that should library staff bring a book to you, then it is because you have explicitly ordered it and have given them your seat number. And after the book has been delivered to you, it is customary for a copy of the book order to be handed over. In short, this staff member had made an error and had given me a book destined for some other reader. And what was this book that had found its way to me? Of the more than ten million books stocked by the British Library, which one should mysteriously and out of the blue reach me on such an auspicious occasion? Would you believe that it was none other than a book by Robert Graves, the very man who had first prompted Gordon Wasson to investigate Mexican psilocybin mushrooms back in the 1950s! *If it had not been for Graves's promptings, Wasson may never have gone to Mexico and may never have written his seminal psilocybin mushroom article for* LIFE *magazine in 1957 [note that this* LIFE *article was the chief catalyst for the West's interest in psilocybin mushrooms and that Wasson was actually the founder of ethnomycology, the study of the cultural use of mushrooms].*

I gingerly picked up the book. It was entitled 5 Pens in Hand *and was completely unfamiliar to me. I proceeded to skim through it, my mind racing to comprehend this strange turn of events. I thought that, because the book was right there in front of me, I ought to read at least some of it, or at least try to (reading can be difficult on psilocybin).*

I decided to read a transcribed talk Graves had delivered to university students concerning his famous book The White Goddess *and how he had come to write such a book. Graves recounts a series of remarkable coincidences that surrounded the writing of* The White Goddess. *These coincidences were so blatant and so frequent, says Graves, that he is reminded of a relevant witty story, which, for reasons of good humor, I retell here in its essence:*

DEFENDANT: *Sir, if you were to pass by a certain house at a particular time of the day and a brick should fall on your head, then what would you call such an event?*

JUDGE: *I should call it an accident.*

DEFENDANT: *And what, sir, would you say if the next day you should be walking past that same house at the same time when another brick fell on you?*

JUDGE: *Why, I should call that a coincidence.*

DEFENDANT: *And now, sir, if this exact same chain of events were to take place the next day also, then what would you call that?*

JUDGE: *Sir, I should call that a habit.*

Having told of the numerous "habitual" coincidences accompanying his writing of The White Goddess, *Graves goes on to tell of the fate that met the first two publishers who rejected the finished book. Both died not long after their refusal, one of whom was reputedly found hanging from a tree dressed in women's underwear. Graves wryly states that these two deaths were surely an act of Goddess.*

Like previous mushroom-related synchronicities I have experienced, this chance arrival of Graves's book possessed a kind of fractal depth. Not only was there a juxtaposition of meaningfully related events (in terms of a psilocybin connection), the very subjects of coincidence and synchronicity were involved also. Conclusion? Reality can be damn provocative.

Provocative indeed! I have often mused over the chances of that book turning up in front of me. There are many, many books that could have accidentally turned up that would also have appeared significant. Any book on mushrooms, any book by McKenna or any other psychedelic guru, and so on. That it was by Robert Graves (who nudged Gordon Wasson toward the secret psilocybin mushroom ceremonies extant in Mexico) and that it contained an essay about coincidences, well, it certainly seems more than chance.

While we are on the subject of synchronicity, I cannot fail to mention a very curious instance I unearthed involving the author Arthur Koestler. Many moons ago, when I first researched the history of psilocybin use in the U.K., I was sifting through all the news items about "magic mushrooms" in the U.K. press. Right alongside a magic mushroom news article appearing in the *Times* in 1981 there was a large picture of Arthur Koestler in conjunction with a short feature about him. The significance of Koestler is that he experienced psilocybin in the early 1960s but had bad experiences and thence severely derided psilocybin in his subsequent writings (he actually wrote an article condemning psilocybin in the *Sunday Telegraph* in 1961). However, no connection was made between the Koestler feature and the mushroom news item, although they were both printed on the same page. This was not surprising, though, as the link was tenuous and would only be known to a dedicated student of psilocybin history. A mere interesting coincidence, then, and nothing more. Two years later, printed right next to a *Times* story on the acquittal of a psilocybin mushroom possessor (which became a test case whereby the unprocessed mushroom was deemed to be legal to possess in the U.K.) was a short piece announcing the suicide of Koestler. This was a startling piece of synchronicity, given a decidedly fractal depth because Koestler had written two books chiefly about synchronicity entitled *The Roots of Coincidence* and *The Challenge of Chance*. He even ran a competition in the *Sunday Times* in 1974 to find the most interesting case of synchronicity. Indeed, a Koestler Foundation once existed that documented cases of synchronicity, although it no longer appears to be active. In any case, my psilocybinetic synchronicity certainly seems more than simple chance alone.

For what it's worth, my current take on synchronicities is that they indicate some kind of subtle, self-organizing aspect of reality. Whereas we are familiar with all manner of self-organizing processes—such as the formation of suns, spiral galaxies, water vortexes, snowflakes, life forms, and so on—I suspect that there are "higher" forms of self-organization, that there are, in fact, *currents* to the flow of reality that bring certain meaningfully related objects and meaningfully related forms of information together. Although I don't know how such integrative patterning mechanisms work, I have been forced to conclude along such lines due to the many profound synchronicities I have experienced over the years. It could be that reality has mind-like properties. Just as the human mind will collate and organize ideas and related information (which happens autonomously), so too might the larger reality process exhibit the same kind of self-organizing process—but with actual events and people being the elements that are being integrated.

Finally we have the following journal extract, which details an experience from 1993 that felt like a veritable flash of enlightenment. It seems a fitting metaphysical high note with which to end this chapter:

Seeking supernormal inspiration, I determined to visit the Royal Botanical Gardens at Kew in Richmond, south of the Thames, and do some perceptual fieldwork there. This glorious plant sanctuary provides a wonderful opportunity to confront some of nature's more exotic creations housed safely within Kew's splendid Victorian greenhouses.

Once I had arrived, I discreetly downed several mouthfuls of recently gathered mushrooms and awaited the dimensional translation of my perception. I was, it must be said, a little apprehensive, especially because I was in a public place.

The effects began to emerge while I was walking around Kew's vast and resplendent grounds. As ever, my senses were suddenly open to a surge of external reality as if I had woken up from the sleep of normal consciousness.

I came across a yew tree, upon which a sign declared it to have been worshipped as sacred in pre-Christian times. I carefully plucked one of its numerous reddish berries and began to almost stagger in awe at the dark seed sitting curiously loosely inside. I marveled at the natural design, for the seed looked as though it were the softly embedded occupant of a refined space vessel cunningly designed to deliver it to fertile ground, where its genetic legacy could be expressively released.

As I continued to stroll through the gardens, I came across some pine trees, whose sweet aroma welcomed my alert senses. Then I confronted an altogether different kind of tree, whose lofty green-leafed branches appeared mythically distinct. I furiously began to scribble the following notes, no small feat as it is well-nigh impossible to write during the full ontological throes of the psychedelic experience. Indeed, I had not done so for quite some time. At any rate, I managed the following:

A species of Fagaceae followed the pines, named Fagus sylvatica (the beech), with its smooth elephantine bark that is smothered with another display of naturally engineered genetic wizardry, namely lichen, testifying that this tree is freshly abrim with healthy biochemical processes.

As I sit once more under nature's psilocybinetic spell, I am convinced that a new science is called for, a science that views life anew under the perceptual lens afforded by the mushroom. For it is only through psilocybin's perception-enhancing magnification power that we are able to apprehend, in full, the sheer beauty of the biosphere, this luxuriant film of frenzied biological activity that surrounds the globe and from which we have been born. I therefore decree a new science—the science of psilocybinetics!

Such a science is to be dedicated solely to the observation of nature, in the field, with the aid of psilocybin, in order to write and record in the most literary means available those traces of her majesty that we are able to behold with the psilocybin-charged *naked eye alone. Thus, we should endeavor to build upon the previous body of knowledge collated by naturalists so as to give such knowledge a poetic finishing touch.*

A new empiricism then, improved upon by the object of study itself. Thus, nature experiences itself through its cortically endowed creatures—we Homo sapiens*—in the refined manner granted through the sublime perceptual effect of the psilocybin mushroom. It is as if a scientist peering at a slice of nature through a microscope were to eat a portion of that slice and thence find his empirical view enhanced. Pursued, such an intimate relationship with nature will assuredly yield infinite fascination and inspiration.*

After writing these words, I immediately had to relieve myself and did so in a manner most natural, that is, discreetly upon a magnificent species of holm oak, therefore once more bonding my body to Gaia. It was, I concluded, a fair exchange of substances: my recyclable urine in return for some of her beauty and splendor.

A number of daunting spectacles confronted me as I approached my ultimate destination—the King Kong-like "cage" of the tropical Palm House. My Goddess, it was incredible! I surely walked upon sacred territory! The fresh, chill October air invigorated me, birdsong cut through the icy surround, while a perfect blue sky loomed overhead. I sensed in that morning the mystical touch of eternity pervading all and everything.

Now, I knew as I approached the Palm House that within awaited the warm and humid atmosphere of its tropical flora. The air would be vibrant with life. But, under psilocybin, how would I be received into that bionomic unit? Would the caged creature within be sensitive to my unusual advances?

As I sat upon the steps outside the Palm House, an incredible landscape unfolded even there. Spiders scuttled across the seemingly monumental and "memory-laden" stone steps. I spied yet more lichen and other tenacious expressions of light-driven life. But I could not be waylaid! I had to venture within. . . .

What transpired within remains highly personal and largely incommunicable, bound as I am to the limits of the English language. Suffice it to say that I was under the impression that an uncanny communication of information occurred between myself and the tropical plant life. It was as if the dense green, slowly moving plant network around me was a place where occult aspects of the Gaian system "flowed" strongly, a good place to "tune in" to a larger field of intelligence. I must be somewhat coy here and state that I entertained this idea while under the effects of psilocybin, knowing full well that it would appear, in sober retrospect, to be a fanciful interpretation. Nonetheless, it really seemed as though the unfamiliar exotic plants were a living manifestation of intelligence, albeit of an almost static kind, somehow conducting a diffuse intentionality of some sort.

At first, a rush of "unfinished business" surged up from the depths of my psyche, and for perhaps half an hour I tackled these psychological obstacles until I actually managed to resolve them. I learned that without a stable, unblocked mind, one cannot achieve clarity and gain real insights. One's psyche must be cleaned of neurotic detritus and of all the worries and petty concerns that normally vie for our attention if one is to access new levels of being and understanding. And the only way to do this psychical cleaning is to engage in a prolonged period of active mentation, a process that the mushroom seems to aid.

Once my mind was free of distraction, I began to study the plant forms throughout the Palm House. I cannot begin to convey the living beauty pervading these dynamic organisms, these muscular green organs of Gaia, standing around me like benign light-munching triffids. I oscillated between an instinctual fear of being "noticed" by the plants— as though I were amid a den of vipers (many of the plant species were *poisonous) and that they knew that I knew—and a feeling of reverence for them. It was certainly the greatest display of vital energy I have ever had the good fortune to apprehend, a rich, diverse, living testament to naturally refined biomolecular engineering, far more impressive than any synthetic creation. It is as if psilocybin temporarily lifts a veil, and we see the miracles of life in all their infinite glory, a glory normally hidden to us perhaps because of our predominately utilitarian approach to nature.*

As for the unusually elaborate tropical flowers in bloom, well, I have to admit that observing them at close range was nothing short of perceptual intercourse, *a kind of abstract intellectual sex with plants to the point of unabashed rudeness. Indeed, I had to constantly check that my intimate perceptual encounters with these plants' sexual organs were going on unseen lest I be thrown out of the Palm House for botanical perversion.*

I perceived the complex colored intricacies of design in the various flowers (particularly the various species of Hibiscus) *with such depth and with such clarity that it was as if my mind was penetrating a higher dimension of the plant, as if my soul was being enveloped by the beauty that the flowers embodied. The closer I dared to look, the more alluring the flowers became, revealing a wealth of living, growing detail that appeared fractally infinite.*

The flowers seemed to represent great intellectual, or mathematical, statements that, through psilocybin, I could blend with, as if I were partaking in a higher perfected language that proceeded without the slightest hindrance or ambiguity. The sensation of being drawn into these floral designs through a resonance between the subtleties of design and my perceptions thereof was overwhelming to the point of ecstasy.

Forcibly freeing myself from the cunning grasp of the flowers, I next came across a decidedly unusual species of plant. What do I mean unusual? It was more like something futuristic, as though its particular genetic code were immeasurably sophisticated compared with other plants. At first I was convinced that it must have been artificial. Its many protruding branches all possessed a perfect new leaf unfurling at the very tip, and these appeared to be identical . . . and plastic. So, I thought, I had been taken in like a fool. This plant was obviously an example of those appalling pseudoplants one unfortunately finds dotted about banks and shopping centers.

Adopting the persona of Sir David Attenborough, I carefully grasped a leaf and made a minuscule incision, an action defendable on the grounds of empirical enquiry and, well, psychedelic suspicion. Immediately, thick white latex sap began to ooze out of the cut, and I realized with relief that it was the presence of latex infused throughout this astonishing (rubber) plant that was causing the plastic look of the leaves.

Here then was the origin of rubber itself. I suddenly began to conceive of rubber tree plantations as being contemporary biotechnological organs of the biosphere, their exudation of rubber being indispensable for our technology. And as the plaque in front of one of the Palm House's other rubber trees pointed out, it is also the case that synthetic rubber cannot match the qualities of natural rubber. Indeed, I later discovered that scientists had been unable to exactly synthesize natural rubber and that it has a variety of unique properties. Indeed, it is these unique properties that make rubber so invaluable to human culture.

I stood before the rubber tree as if I were before some holy output device for nature's inherent information-processing intelligence. I wondered at the complex genetic sequences of DNA that must lie buried within each and every cell of the rubber tree in order that it forge such a rare compound impossible to manufacture in the lab. And yet I realized that most of us are unlikely to conceive of items such as condoms as being the handy population-restricting extensions of the rubber tree. Nor are we likely to marvel at the rubber tree's extended presence in the motor industry (i.e., in the form of tires). With the enhanced perception granted through the mushroom, the plant kingdom, although normally operating behind the scenes, suddenly loomed up before me as if it were a dispersed alienesque organism symbiotically entwined within our mammalian species and our technology.

Next I met some coffee plants. A plaque declared the coffee plant to be one of the world's most important trade items. It also noted the reason why—namely that coffee beans contain the alkaloid drug caffeine, a stimulant of the human central nervous system. This obvious fact became a revelation to me as I studied the plant itself. Here was an organism, akin to the psilocybin mushroom already working miracles in my brain, also able to directly improve the function of my nervous system through a simple act of ingestion. I saw the process holistically. We natural entities, myself and psychoactive plants, were not in fact separate or rigidly bound at all. There was a continual chemical communication between organisms, a dynamic interplay in which substances mingle, flow, and interchange. Once again, I had that brief "Gaian flash" in which I perceived the biosphere to be a single coherent system, constantly stimulating itself into more and more integrated patterns of activity. Language-like combinations of elements such as carbon, hydrogen, nitrogen, and oxygen were being continuously churned up and organized over immensely long periods of time, as if life was effectively writing itself into existence.

I reached out and plucked a handful of beans from one of the nearest coffee plants. After all, why go looking for a coffee shop when fresh beans were on offer? Because the plaque stated that coffee beans were originally eaten raw in the form of a paste, I readily popped a few of the red beans into my mouth. Knowing that the lethal dose of caffeine in humans is somewhere in the region of one hundred cups of coffee, I ate about eight of the surprisingly tasty beans without worry. I then imagined my body slowly absorbing the caffeine and the subtle stimulation the coffee plant would then be granting me. Along with the mushrooms I'd consumed,

I was partaking in an endless dance of innervating organic alchemy.

Later, a moment came as I sat in hypercontemplation of life's mystery when I felt a perfect state of being wash over me. It was, I believe, a brief flash of enlightenment, a blissful state of mind when everything, absolutely everything, was as it should be. My psyche was charged with superconsciousness as glistening crystalline thoughts flowed into one another with mathematical precision and clarity.

I sat gazing at a small, shallow pool of water at my feet, in which I discerned a perfect reflection of the blue sky beyond the glass roof of the Palm House above me. As I considered this perfect and infinitely deep reflection, I thought it remarkable that light could be so reflected without loss of information. Then, a drop of water fell into the shallow pool from above, having originally condensed from the periodic fine sprays of water that serve to keep the greenhouse humid. This single drop of water temporarily shattered the perfect reflection of light, and instantly there appeared a series of expanding circular ripples that flowed out from the minute splash. These ripples flowed into one another, causing a series of unique interference waves that were eventually absorbed by the pool as equilibrium was restored. Once more the water was still, the disruption lasting no more than a second (the pool was very shallow—which allowed a very rapid return to calm). Yet the psilocybin allowed me to experience the process as being drawn out in time, as if the grain and depth of my perception had increased, providing me with more "room" to perceive. As the water stilled, the reflected light resolved into a coherent whole—but just as I perceived this coherent holistic reflection, another drop of water fell, creating another interference pattern. Again the rings were absorbed, and again the perfect reflection emerged.

I sat mesmerized by this process, particularly at the point when the whole image would suddenly resolve. I felt convinced that here, at work, was an important universal principle or universal process. This impression was very strong, though it was an intuitive feeling, as though the idea of interference waves temporarily veiling a perfect reflection was such a powerful metaphor symbolizing life and our quest for understanding that it would only be fully graspable at a much later time.

Each time the pool stilled, a holistic pattern of reflection seemed to "click" into being at a precise moment, rather akin to those stereo pixel pictures that appear, on first sight, to be merely random disconnected pixels, but that suddenly emerge as a coherent depiction of some object when the pattern is discerned. As the holistic pattern of reflected light coalesced again and again, I felt an ecstatic sensation of wholeness as if I too were merging with the whole picture. As interference melted away, all was revealed as connected, and this process left me awash with awe and exultation.

It was also apparent that the small reflective pool was formed from the drops of water, these same drops ultimately interfering with the reflective process. A self-reinforcing paradox then, like some cosmic dance of information that expressed the riddle of existence. Or was it all some imaginative trick of my intoxicated mind?

My conclusion on this matter, based upon similar experiences, is that the mushroom allows one to listen to nature (in all its forms) as if she were a powerful teacher, a notion commonly held by native peoples. Although such a belief might appear foolish, I have come to suspect that it contains some profound wisdom and insight that predates our modern Gaia theory, and further, that psilocybin fungi can be used to help us recover this wisdom.

Time passes, psilocybin is metabolized into inactive byproducts, and one finds oneself back in the profane world of sordid news stories, political shenanigans, religious bickering, gun fetishes, and ubiquitous advertisements selling the consumer dream. The psilocybin mushroom, temporarily at least, launches one into realms of experience both sublime and illuminating, and many would claim that such states of mind provide a valuable insight into the human condition, particularly with respect to our relationship to the biosphere and to one another. Indeed, the mushroom hints at some kind of future paradise in which we have realized what an honor it is be on this planet, a paradise in which we live in accordance with that realization. The psilocybin mushroom thus remains a remarkable natural resource to be explored by our culture.

2

Avalonia Psychedelica

～～～

Most people live in cities. Indeed, our numbers are now so huge that so-called megacities are emerging with more than two thousand people per square kilometer. Cities have a lot going for them. Shops, offices, public transport, sidewalks, restaurants, bars, clubs, sports facilities, schools, colleges, parks (if you are lucky), hospitals, fiber optic cables, telephone lines, libraries, and most of all, employment opportunities. In a strange and distinctly surreal kind of way, a city is a self-organizing meshwork of humans, concrete, and metal bound together by cables, data, money, business, and law. How long this volatile planetary growth can sustain itself is another matter. For now it is enough to know that cities are the biggest and most formidable physical structures on the face of the planet, growing and sprawling according to pressing economic and social needs. At night, cities can be seen from space, their vast swaths of electronic lights glittering like otherworldly jewels. Barring some kind of unprecedented population drop, cities of one kind or another are here to stay.

Despite their elaborate grandeur, cities lack a healthy connection with the rest of the biosphere. Not just a healthy physical connection, but a healthy psychological connection too. That is the price we have paid by becoming urbanized. Let us not forget that the rest of the biosphere supports city life by providing city folk with clean air and clean water. The combined ecosystems of the earth also keep the climate within a hospitable range as well as maintain the composition of the atmosphere. The globally active fabric of life likewise ensures crop pollination and the recycling of wastes. It is in accordance with this massive and diverse web of life that the human race has been sustained over the entire course of its history. The life-support system of the biosphere is akin to a stage that we have stamped about upon, our chests thrust out as we built our temples, our skyscrapers, and our monumental corporate brands. And while it may have seemed that we have always been able to stomp as we please, that we can mow down what we like, tear asunder what we like, reconfigure whatever we like, this cannot remain so forever. Indeed, with climate change it should be apparent to everyone that we are not innocuous "free-floating" players on an indestructible biospherical stage. The stage has cracks. The stage is not infinitely flexible. Seven billion people (and counting) cannot keep marauding about carelessly forever. At some point we have to acknowledge that we are indeed being supported by a stage, one that provides for all our needs. A worldwide "declaration of interdependence" with the rest of the web of life is therefore in order—but this sadly seems a long way off.

Our lack of biospherical awareness—which is to say our lack of consciousness about the larger life support system that sustains us—is particularly prominent in those people who deny any human-generated aspect to climate change. It is as if they believe that some sort of God Almighty must have made the biosphere and that he must have fashioned it in such a way that we can do exactly what we like with it. How divinely convenient. Thus, no matter what seven billion–plus humans do, no matter how much fossil fuel we extract and burn, no matter how much carbon we put into the atmosphere, no matter how much wilderness we decimate and turn into chopsticks and furniture, no matter how many synthetic chemicals we spill, no matter how big the oceans that we spoil, no matter what technology we build and how we use it, there will be no ill effects because the biosphere is infinitely flexible and will always bounce back to a configuration that supports human life. In other words, some sort of divine magic will conveniently ensure that we can do no real harm to our biospherical home. Whatever we do to the earth, there will be no price to pay and no karma. God, in his infinite wisdom, must have made things that way in our favor so that we could behave in any way we wanted to without fear that any balances would be upset. This notion brings to mind a kindergarten in which everything is made of soft rubber so that no harm can come to a child or the play area no matter how carelessly and belligerently the children therein behave.

Of course, reason cannot allow us to accept such a facile view of life on earth. Regardless of whether you believe that a deity made the biosphere, the fact is that all living things are connected and adhere to a specific kind of eco-logic that is inherent within nature's law and order. Indeed, the fate of all and any biological behavior will be determined by how closely it is aligned with this fundamental eco-logic. Behavior that makes good sense within the web of life will tend to persist. Behavior that does not make sense within the larger whole will tend not to persist. Well, senseless behavior might exist for some time, but it will not last indefinitely. What nature preserves and sustains in the long run (and long run means hundreds of thousands of years) is a matter of natural law and inescapable logic—and life is thus bound by it and must adhere to it.

Some things are good for the web of life; some things are bad. We know this for our bodies. If you continually smoke too much, you will, in the fullness of time, more than likely compromise your overall health. If you continually eat too much, you will eventually compromise your overall health. If you prevent blood from flowing to your arm, you will compromise your health. If you don't ever brush your teeth, you will compromise your health. It is not rocket science. Yet we seem blind to this same principle as it applies to the ecosystems and the total biosphere within which we are embedded components. We seem not to realize that we *cannot* do anything we please—at least not indefinitely. Especially not now, not with so many of us constantly gobbling up finite resources (the prescient 1982 cult movie *Koyaanisqatsi* ably conveys this growing realization). For instance, we cannot keep brushing all of our wastes "under the carpet," as it were. The biospherical carpet might be big and consist of strong fibers, but it is not infinitely big and strong—and nothing truly goes away. Everything must be processed somewhere along the line. At some stage, if we continue to behave in a manner inconsistent with the already established ways of life on earth, then our mess might well become impossible to rectify. Our continued healthy existence is subject to the same eco-logic that governs the continued existence of all other forms of life. If our cultural behavior does not make sense within the larger context of the biosphere, it will eventually be curtailed and pruned from life's web. There will be no malice in this—just the inevitable working out of natural logic.

Scale the biosphere down to a large garden. Now imagine what we have been like over the last few hundred years. We have learned how the garden works. Everywhere we looked in the garden, we found things that were comprehensible, and so we learned to harness all that sensible stuff to our own advantage. We uprooted stuff, manipulated stuff, extracted stuff, transmutated stuff, moved stuff, destroyed stuff, basically did what we liked to the garden. We found buried energy— fossil fuel—and used it to drive various machines that helped us maximize the garden's food production. We also made and fueled machines to make a seemingly endless supply of new products. In fact, there was such an abundance of fossil fuel and it was such a rich source of energy that we propelled culture forward at breakneck speed and totally transformed the layout of the garden so that regions of it bore little resemblance to how it used to look. We found that we could keep on improving our standard of living. So we grew and spread our numbers throughout every corner of the garden, our influence reaching to every nook and cranny.

And then what happened? Well, the garden eventually started to suffer and get sick under our relentless impact. Biodiversity was compromised. Many species vanished. Soil health was compromised. The ponds in the garden became contaminated with pollutants and untold tiny bits of plastic and thus became depleted of life. The gaseous composition of the garden's atmosphere changed, and the ambient climate changed. In short, our unchecked activity messed up a once pristine and biodiverse garden. What we sowed, so we reaped. All our actions had consequences. We should have heeded the old wise woman and the native tribesman who were waving from the very edge of the garden, where they had been banished. In a manner we thought twee and outdated, they said that we were but strands in the garden and that we had a duty to care for it. But we were so enveloped in culture and our own activity that we plain forgot that a garden existed at all.

To reiterate: apart from housing us and giving us gainful employment, cities have inadvertently served to alienate us from the rest of life's web. And because we are alienated from the larger web of life, we have failed to see that web unraveling. Or if we do see it, or we at least sense that something is deeply amiss, we simply tell ourselves that all will be okay. After all, the planet is massive. We are tiny in comparison. And the sun still pours forth life-giving radiance every day. Yet this negative impact that human culture is having on the biosphere's health is actually the single most important issue of our time. It transcends politics and the relentless bickering between nations. Climate change, undoubtedly exacerbated by humans, affects everyone. We are slowly realizing that all things are indeed connected—in ways we could never previously have imagined. Think of a company that dumps some chemicals into a river. If the chemical in question is black, we can see that it immediately disperses. The blackness gets thinner and fainter until eventually it has gone. But the chemical has not really gone, has it? It simply got divided into smaller and smaller parts, maybe even into individual molecules. But they are still there, carried out into the ocean, where they will invariably be ingested by fish and other marine creatures. And then they will become ever more concentrated inside the bodies of all the creatures that make up the oceanic food chain.

There is even a name for this insidious process—it's called biological magnification. So nothing really goes away or vanishes. As I mentioned before, you cannot sweep things under the biospherical carpet, *because all things are part of the carpet*. What goes around eventually comes around. If we start a fire in a tinder-dry forest, the conflagration might well recede away from us into the safe distance— but eventually it might be at our backs. Once you realize that human life is inextricably woven into the rest of life, then our actions—our cultural behavior, all the stuff we make, all the things we build, our energy policies, agricultural policies, and so on—all these things need perforce to make sense within the larger context that is the biosphere if we are to truly sustain our existence. As stated, only behavior that makes good sense within the larger biospherical context will be truly sustainable. That is the bottom line. I don't see how anyone can deny this. That certain people in positions of power *do* ignore such reasoning and steadfastly promote business as usual is beyond my ken. It just shows how out of touch with nature we have become.

The reasonable conclusion here is that if city life is to be sustained well into futurity, then it will have no choice but to become more organic and more attuned to the larger biospherical context within which it sits. Solar farms, green roofs, metabolic building surfaces, and maybe even nuclear fusion (which is clean and not to be confused with dirty nuclear fission) immediately come to mind—as they are more organic technologies in tune with the rest of life (and with the sun). As it stands, however, cities are akin to cocoons that seal their residents away from the very life-support system that maintains them and has always maintained them. To be sure about it, these days city dwellers may rarely venture outdoors. A drive to work, a day in the office, a drive back home—unless it rains heavily or there is a storm, you might not sense the existence of the larger biosphere. Maybe you might spy the occasional pretty summer cloud or delight in the sight of a vibrant spring bloom, but in the main you may be entirely oblivious to the wild, fractal-edged natural world that lies all around our refined, straight-edged urban world. Thus, the concept of Spaceship Earth and its various interconnected life-support systems might never occur to you.

Which is precisely where wilderness trekking comes in. My lengthy preamble about the nature of urban life was a cunning way to get the urban reader to willingly and eagerly leave behind the concrete and steel confines of the city and accompany me on a trip into the wilds, where the biodiverse face of nature is more apparent and where, perchance, the earthy psilocybin mushroom might await. As eco-author Edward Abbey has written (*Desert Solitaire,* 1968):

> The love of the wilderness is more than a hunger for what is always beyond reach; it is also an expression of loyalty to the earth . . . which bore us and sustains us, the only home we shall ever know, the only paradise we ever need—if only we had eyes to see.

I first began psilocybinetic ventures in the wild in 1995 and have never really looked back. Previous to 1995, I had always consumed the mushroom indoors. I may have gone outside while in the throes of the psychedelic experience, I may even have gone on a bicycle trip or a journey on the London Underground (activity that, again, I cannot condone), but I generally stayed inside and refrained from venturing into wilderness. In fact, the idea of "wilderness" seems strange in this era of megacities, particularly in the U.K. Unless you live somewhere like South America, Alaska, Siberia, or Canada, there doesn't seem to be much wilderness left. What I essentially mean by wilderness are those few remaining large areas of country-side where human activity is limited and where nature has more of a chance to "do its own thing" with minimal interference from us. Places that are miles and miles from the nearest house or road. In the U.K., such areas are restricted to national parks. Chief among these are the Lake District (England) and Snowdonia (Wales). These two areas have been the main locales of my psychedelic jour-neying to date. In terms of setting, they provide the most exquisite backdrop conceivable within which to take the mushroom. Indeed, I surmise that my psilocybin experiences in these glorious areas are what shaped my conviction that some kind of intelligence is inherent within nature (albeit an autonomous and unconscious intelligence). In this sense, I felt like a pioneer, accessing a hitherto unattested aspect of the biosphere that is not so evident in an urban environ-ment. Indeed, I learned that the eminent Greek philosopher Socrates was completely mistaken when he proclaimed that nothing of interest happens beyond the city walls.

My psilocybinetic trekking adventures started when I went, one day in 1995, to visit the Guru. The Guru is a very old friend of mine, a swarthy, hardy, generous, and totally trustworthy Maltese fellow who introduced me to the invaluable tutorial legacies of Gurdjieff (whose teachings, you will recall, came to my rescue during my first-ever mushroom experience), P. D. Ouspensky, Maurice Nicoll, J. G. Bennett, Jiddu Krishnamurti, Abd-ru-shin, and other teachers of the art of mindfulness and self-knowledge. The Guru is, I surmise, what the term *salt of the earth* was coined for. I first met him ten years earlier at Speakers' Corner in Hyde Park, a curious place where all manner of lively philosophical, metaphysical, and religious debates go on (or at least they used to). He was not a speaker but would get involved in the heated conversations that took place there. He struck me as possessing subtle wisdom, and I think that the first conversation we ever had concerned Gnosticism. Some evangelical Christian woman had earlier been warning me that Gnosticism was the work of the devil—despite my protestations that the Gnostic gospels (that I had recently discovered) seemed overtly spiritual and connected to some really existing higher psychological reality. This Christian evangelist was also adamant that the miracles in the standard gospels were literal. But the Guru, I learned, was of the opinion that the feeding of the five thousand with just a few loaves of bread was not to be taken literally but was really referring to "morsels of wisdom" such that everyone who listened to Jesus's teachings was "fed." Like me, he was also interested in the Gnostic gospels and claimed that these alternative accounts of Jesus's teachings were replete with profound psychological insights. In any case, the various views of the Guru struck a chord with me, and so I ended up eagerly meeting him at Speakers' Corner pretty much every Sunday for a year or so. Often what he said would elevate my youthful mind, making me feel very inspired indeed. Listening to him wax forth on spiritual matters was like drinking from a sweet effervescent fountain.

On the occasion in question when I visited the Guru, I for some reason told him that we ought to go on a spring camping trek. I was not sure where exactly, but I said I would look into it. After all, we both had tents and basic camping gear. Browsing some travel books in a bookstore, I immediately fell in love with pictures of the Lake District. It seemed unbelievable to me—for here were mountains that

I was totally ignorant of. Loads of them too! The pictures gave the impression that the Lake District was a sort of mini-Switzerland. The mountains had strangely evocative names like Scafell Pike, Skiddaw, and Helvellyn. I had no idea that there existed places like this just a few hundred miles north of London. The Guru and I simply had to go there. Little did I know of the grand psychedelic adventures that were looming.

As far as I recall we did two treks to the Lake District in the spring of 1995. I soon learned about the need for good equipment such as sturdy boots, waterproof coats, roll mats, and warm sleeping bags. We would camp in discreet spots and often trek across mountains to reach a new place to camp the next day (I was armed with a Landranger Ordnance Survey map, which I used to spend hours studying). We would also have a fire each night. This was, I think, the only questionable thing we did on such treks—although we took care to use only deadwood. Neither of us owned a car nor lived an excessive lifestyle, so one could argue that the burning of deadwood was part of our carbon quota. Of course, burning this deadwood meant that fungi could not break it down and recycle minerals—but I always concluded that our impact was pretty negligible. Although we would occasionally come across the overgrown remains of fireplaces from other wilderness trekkers, the impression we got was that very few people engaged in this kind of wild camping (which, I should add, is not legally permissible under most national park regulations in the U.K.).

After trekking around mountains and valleys for several days, the Guru and I soon fell in love with the Lake District. This was especially the case after we took mushrooms there. The first time we did this was on that first spring trek. I must have brought some with me, picked in all likelihood from London's Richmond Park the previous autumn. We were camped near Easedale Tarn, an area I wrote about in detail in the last chapter of my book *Darwin's Unfinished Business*.

We took mushrooms one morning and then, leaving our campsite behind, set off up toward the mountainous peak known as Sergeant Man. Just in case some ranger came across our campsite, I wrote a cunningly contrived note and left it attached to the front flap of my tent. The note was designed to thwart any attempt at interfering with our stuff. In bold capital letters the note proclaimed that we were entomologists from UCL, that we were engaged in an important field study, and that we would be back later. I doubt such a note was necessary—but this illegal wilderness camping was all new to me, and I did not want to take any chances. I wrote and left similar notes on a few subsequent occasions (albeit with creative changes to our alleged scientific occupation!) but soon realized it was unnecessary.

I well recall how it felt walking along that ancient rocky path as the psilocybin began to take effect. Everything in the immediate vicinity began to have an epic air about it. The path looked epic. The mountains on either side of us looked epic. The Guru's face as he followed behind me looked epic. I remember seeing a big black slug (common in those parts) that looked curiously like a fountain pen. Then I noticed that the rock faces on the surrounding mountains looked more than epic. They now had what looked like Incan iconography all over them. It was like we had been transported from England to Peru. The landscape seemed to exude monumental sacred power. This sacred energy, or whatever it was, was palpable, radiating from the rocks and the very ground on which we walked. Everything became intense—scarily intense, in fact. It was as if the Guru and I were fulfilling some sort of important mission, like we were characters in a mystical, dreamlike adventure.

On the way a strange thing happened that brought things back down to a kind of profane level. We came across a guy who appeared lost. He was an American. He was dressed in what looked like city clothes: plain trousers, a shirt, and a suit jacket slung over his shoulder. What struck me most were his shoes. He had on what looked like flimsy, cheap, casual plastic shoes. We were quite high up in the mountains, shrouded in rolling damp mist, and here was this fellow totally not dressed for the occasion. He would have looked more in context walking down Fifth Avenue. Nor did he have a bag with him—so he had no food or water. It turned out that this chap had been following some party of trekkers who had left the village he was staying at about three miles away. He had latched on to them—but he had evidently lost their trail. He actually asked us if we knew where there was a shop! There we were, miles and miles from anywhere, surrounded by mountainscapes, lakes, and boulders, and he wanted to know where there was a shop!

In my bemushroomed state, I felt very concerned about this man's welfare. It seemed so ridiculous to see someone so ill dressed and so ill equipped to be wandering high up in the mountains. Anyhow, we explained the direction in which he needed to go and wished him the best. Later that day, after we had returned to our tents, I actually trekked down into the village of Grasmere to phone the emergency services to alert them about this man. They listened to all I had to say and then made the decision, probably rightly, that it was not a problem requiring action—which was a weight off my mind.

After we left this curious fellow and continued our journey, the psilocybin experience kept increasing in intensity. I looked ahead and could see this path getting rougher and rougher. Being that this was my first trek in those parts, my map-reading skills were primitive and my faith in myself being able to find the way was lacking, to say the least. The path ahead was getting really rocky with strewn boulders all over the place, and with no worn turf it was difficult to see where it continued. I felt more and more uneasy. Here we were, high up in the mountains while under the influence of one of the world's most powerful psychedelic substances, and we were in immediate danger of getting lost.

Soon we were inevitably climbing up these rocks, and I had no idea whether we were still on the path. The feeling of being disconnected from the path and lost was overwhelming. Positive mystical feelings were fast being replaced by fear and terror! However, good fortune was on our side. A young trekking couple had caught up with us. I mentioned to them that it was difficult to make out the path— and the guy (I think he was Dutch) pointed out these small piles of rocks (called cairns) dotted here and there that actually marked out the route. Aha! And so it was that we learned that mountain paths are often marked out by miniature piles of rocks, especially where the path is in a remote place. From then on we would occasionally add a pebble or two to those useful and reassuring markers of the way.

Our spirits revived by being back on track, we continued our rocky ascent, all the while marveling at the incredible "realness" of everything. It was like we were dream characters undertaking an auspicious journey of historical proportions. Moreover, the higher we ascended, the greater the views became. Every twenty minutes or so we would reach a new vantage point, where bigger and bigger expanses could be seen, with more and more mountain peaks coming into view. It was awesome. The sense of a huge biosphere beneath our feet was astonishing. Emotions connected with immense size and power kept flowing through me.

Moving ever onward and upward toward greater mystical heights and even entertaining the idea that we might eventually stumble upon the lost city of Shambhala, I looked back and shot the Guru a long glance. There he was dressed in this amazing Peruvian-style sweater. Sensing the significance of everything, particularly the way friendships are forged and the kind of wisdom that can bond people, I asked him then how he had originally come into contact with Gurdjieff's teachings concerning the inner world of humans, this being the main influence the Guru had passed on to me over the years. He related how he had read *In Search of the Miraculous* (a classic book by Ouspensky about Gurdjieff's teachings) and how Gurdjieff's work had impacted him. There seemed to be a sort of thread there, like a spiritual current that moved through people, books, and events. In any case, I was glad to be there with the Guru. He was my trusted friend.

Later we reached a level area with fantastic views. I recall lying down on my back on the soft ground and feeling as if I were an ancient giant. More than this, I had a strange impression regarding the inter-connectedness of everything. The feeling of being "set" inside some larger thing, of being literally part and parcel of some larger fabric, or larger structure, was overwhelming. So much so that it felt somewhat claustrophobic, especially as I was acutely aware of my breathing. The felt realization that I was part of one solid, albeit fluidic, continuum became almost stifling. I felt so joined to everything else—in terms of my respiration, my body, the environment, and my perceptions thereof—that there seemed to be no space in which to really move. This was not a horrendous sensation, just uncomfortable due to its strangeness.

On one occasion that same afternoon, I also noticed an unusual kind of pattern evident in the air above the expansive landscapes down below me. There seemed to be some sort of mathematical pattern in the air. Not a bold pattern, but very subtle and almost invisible, like an ethereal skeletal fractal. At first I thought that maybe this was a real kind of hallucination—but the longer I observed it, the more I suspected that it was an objectively real aspect of the environment. In fact, I would later often perceive similar mathematical patterns in the roaring flames of our campfires. I later ascribed this pattern in the air above the expansive landscapes to water vapor. I got the sense that there are patterns within water vapor as it forms under the sun's hot rays and that, like the rolling hexagonal convection cells that manifest in water that is being heated, there are similar self-organizing patterns and structures in water when it is in its wispy, misty vaporized state. I have no idea if this is what I saw or not.

A little later, when we reached the highest point of that day's trek, I had a cigarette (I was at that time a tobacco fiend). This was while we were in the company of two other trekkers, the young Dutch couple who had earlier overtaken us and who were now attesting that the Lake District was one of the most beautiful parts of the planet. I had to agree with them. I declared that the poet William Wordsworth had said as much and that he was right to have been so enamored. There then proceeded an amusing debate about what I should do with the impending spent cigarette butt. The problem of whether the butt was biodegradable or not suddenly assumed great importance. As the cigarette inexorably burned down, I felt as if I was holding on to a time bomb, that something had to be done about it sharpish. I joked to the Guru that the situation was so serious as to warrant the summoning of a rescue ranger helicopter!

Later that night as we sat around the fire at the Den (this is what we christened our first-ever campsite), I wondered out loud to the Guru if it was possible that the psilocybin mushroom might grow out in these parts (recall that the ones we had consumed had originated from Richmond Park). After all, there were plenty of wild grassy areas. On the other hand, I thought that it would be inconceivable that they could grow in such an idyllic area. It would be too good to be true. I mean, we had instantly fallen in love with the Lake District. It was a Tolkienesque paradise compared to the city. There were waterfalls everywhere, majestic mountains, lush green valleys, gently winding streams, oaks, pines, juniper, colorful lichens covering the rocks, melodious birds everywhere—it was like a vast film set or outdoor art installation. No wonder Beatrix Potter had been inspired to create her wonderful illustrations for her children's books—the gorgeous landscapes of the Lake District that she visited in her youth are utterly enchanting (interestingly, Potter first garnered attention through writing a scientific paper about fungi—and she also illustrated some mushroom books). The idea that the mushroom grew in the Lake District would be the stuff of fantasy fiction surely? And yet I had this feeling—what I later dubbed my "psilo-sense"—that there were indeed *Psilocybe* mycelia growing under the very ground beneath our feet. Needless to say, we determined to return to the Lakes in the autumn to find out for sure.

So it was that in October of 1995 we first picked psilocybin mushrooms in the Lake District. They were everywhere! All the way up alongside the ascending two-mile footpath toward the Den, all around Easedale Tarn (a favorite haunt of Victorian walkers), and all along the mountainsides up toward Sergeant Man. To be sure about it, we found the mushroom growing alongside (and sometimes on) the very paths raved about by famous Lake District walker Alfred Wainwright, who famously wrote books about the best walks around the Lake District mountains. I had seen Wainwright on TV, with his trademark pipe and hat. I soon fancied I might like to become a sort of psychedelic version of him, and maybe sport a hat covered with a few choice fractal badges. I could even see myself giving advice concerning upon which famous paths the mushroom could be found. Thankfully I never developed this potential media personality!

Other trekkers in those parts would inevitably spy us stooping down and scanning the ground and were prone to ask us what we were up to. When I would boldly tell them that we were picking a brand of mushroom worshipped as sacred in Mexico, people were more often than not surprised and seemed to have no idea that such mushrooms grew there. I should point out that at this time it was totally legal to pick and consume fresh psilocybin mushrooms in the U.K. As long as one did not prepare them in any way, the law stated that no crime was being committed. This legislation was to change in 2005—but that is another story, which I will get to in chapter 4. Despite the legality back then, most fellow trekkers would talk for a bit and listen with interest about the spiritual experiences that the mushroom could afford, and then they would smile and be on their way. No one ever asked for more details so that they could investigate this resource for themselves. The impression I got was that the Guru and I were considered to be a bit "strange" for having an avid interest in psychoactive fungi. People simply had no idea how remarkable the psilocybin experience was. Instead of being considered a spiritual food with which one can commune with nature, the mushroom seems more to evoke notions of dodgy drug use and naughty countercultural behavior. Thus it is no surprise that this inspiring natural resource is all but ignored by mainstream people while being loved by countercultural types.

Mostly the Guru and I would consume the mushroom during the evening while lounging around a campfire. This became our preferred method of "communion." Typically the experience would start with a feeling of uneasiness. This is, I think, a fight or flight response of one's organism to the onslaught of psilocybin molecules as they infiltrate the neurons of the brain (psilocybin mimics the neurotransmitter serotonin). I soon began to refer to this brief period of uneasiness as a "retuning" process because it would usually be followed by a tremendous feeling of clarity, as if one had suddenly retuned to a new dimension of reality. Think of a radio and the jarring noise one gets when tuning between stations. Noisy static can suddenly be replaced by perfect stereo quality as a radio station is accurately tuned in to. This is what the psilocybin experience can be like in the initial stages. It feels like one has retuned one's entire being. Getting to this stage might involve some discomfort, but once the retuning process is complete, the resulting frame of mind and heart is utterly fabulous.

Being out in a wooded wilderness area at night under the influence of locally gathered psilocybin mushrooms is assuredly one of the greatest experiences available to a human being. I really mean that. This may sound strange—especially in these days of jet travel and organized adventures. One might think that doing the Inca Trail would be more impressive. Or making an ascent of Everest. Or snorkeling in the Great Barrier Reef. Yet nothing really compares to the wild outdoors psilocybin experience. A felt communion with an intelligence within nature blows everything else out of the water, because it is like finding your true self and establishing contact with an ancient wisdom, an integrating coherency, which binds everything but of which we are generally oblivious. A mere few seconds of this directly felt transcendental contact is beyond value. One may feel both blessed and touched. In fact, during one pioneering psychedelic evening spent up at a nifty vantage point high above the picturesque village of Ambleside, I was lying by the fire and said out loud "Porsche!" to the Guru. He looked at me strangely because he had no idea what I meant. I then explained that the fire we were enjoying and which appeared to my psilocybinetic vision to have sacred white pulsing embers at its heart was in the same qualitative league as a top-end car. In other words, when people think of a Porsche, they think of financial success and a special sort of rarely encountered ornate majesty embodied in a sleek, snazzy sports car. Yet for me, in my bemushroomed state, this seemed a joke. The real "Porsche," the real ornate majesty, the real wealthy privilege, was the sacred fire and blissful state of consciousness that I was enjoying. And it was all blessedly free! I was living the ultrahigh life—the real high life. Not speeding along in some flashy sports car dressed in expensive clothes and with my chest puffed up, but enveloped in the warming sacred splendor of Pachamama (i.e., Mother Earth), her generosity and magnificence warming every cell in my body and stimulating every facet of my spirit.

As I would lie there in such situations, reveling in the sheer glory of it all and wondering at how the universe was able to orchestrate such majesty, I would invariably find myself breeching certain time-less philosophical and metaphysical conundrums. Yet there was never any "final answer" as to how and why being and consciousness exist; rather, I would encounter layer upon layer of inspiring mystery. The only sure thing about the ultimate nature of reality was that it was not all accidental. Reality seemed to me to be infused with some sort of massive meaning and purpose—a vast, autonomous teleological wisdom, if you will—something I felt at the core of my being during most of my psilocybin experiences. Of course, that is the "psilocybin talking," as it were. That is the nature of its potential effect upon the human psyche. Certainly such experiences are true inasmuch as they really occurred—but you can never really *prove* that such felt insights really were insights.

Strange things happened on those early psilocybinetic treks. On one occasion while bemushroomed at the Den, we went out for a stroll late at night. We took this big, chunky lamp that I had (this was in the days before small trekking headlamps) and headed across the rocks and down toward Easedale Tarn. We came across a very curious sight indeed. We seemed to stumble upon a social sheep gathering of some kind. The sheep stood in a loose ring, and in the middle were two other sheep embroiled in what can only be described as an altercation. It was like something out of one of those Gary Larson cartoons, in which animals, out of sight of people, secretly behave in a humanlike way. There was no doubt in our minds what we were witnessing. It was a heated social scene of some sort, maybe a fight for dominance or something similar. One could sense the tension in that curious sheep gathering.

The big lamp I used during those early treks was the focus for a "trial" that I went through on another evening. This time we were camped lower down, on a small forested hill not far from Rydal Water, a picturesque lake between Ambleside and Grasmere. The Guru had retired to his tent for the night. I sat by the fire and was still very much under the influence of mushrooms consumed earlier. I saw that I had run out of water and so decided to venture down the hill to the river that coursed its way along the foot of the forested hill. It was a fair way, and such a chore was not a trifle, especially in my condition. But I had my trusty lamp, and so I gingerly set off down the steep forested hillside. As I entered the thick spread of trees and made my way down, I stumbled and clumsily fell on my backside. I also dropped the lamp. It seemed to happen in slow motion, and I saw it bounce a few times as it careered down the steep incline. Then the light turned off. I heard the lamp crash a few times way down below me, and then all was silent. I was left alone in total blackness. It was one of those starless and moonless cloudy, dark nights.

Although I could see nothing, my bemushroomed senses were on full alert. It was quite scary sitting in the dark like that. I was so far from the fire that there was no light whatsoever. And I was peeved that I had lost my trusty lamp. It was a good one—it gave great light. Losing one's main source of light was a bummer. So, as well as a growing sense of fear, I also felt foolish. However, I decided that as I was likely more than halfway to the river, I ought to carry on down and get some water—for at least I had not dropped my water canister. I could hear the rushing river down below me. So, fumbling on my backside, I slid my way down the slope and eventually came to the rocky bank of the river. It was still pitch black. Chagrined, I filled my canteen and then made my way blindly back up the slope, hoping that I would not miss the campsite.

I managed to make it back. How welcoming and warming the flickering glow of the campfire was! It was home. As I was sitting by the fire, glad to be back, an inner voice started up. Basically, as had happened on previous occasions, I began to have a kind of internal dialogue with some sort of "higher power." Nowadays I refer to this as the *higher self* and see it as the tutorial (and sometimes challenging) wisdom of the unconscious filtering through into conscious awareness—but back then I felt that it was the personification of Gaia, like I was a cub and that I needed to be "tested." Indeed, this inner voice dared me to go back down to the river in the dark. What? Was I crazy? In my psilocybinetic condition? Wander off, on purpose, into a pitch-black forest? No way!

The inner commanding voice continued to cajole and challenge me. I turned my head and saw that I would be venturing into inky blackness, the kind of uncompromising blackness that only a thick forest at night can harbor. I got to my feet. I could just about hear the river in the distance. With a sort of mathematical reasoning, I realized that as long as I put all my focus on the sound of the river I would be making a straight line toward it. And once I got to the river, as long as I turned 180 degrees about-face, then I ought to be able to head straight back up the hillside and not miss the campsite (as I had managed before). I should be able to do all that despite not being able to see anything and despite being bemushroomed. In theory, of course. But it was easier theorized than done (as ever, I would dissuade others from engaging in this kind of reckless activity).

I set off. I was exactly like a blind man, for I could see absolutely nothing. So I slowly felt my way along, all the while concentrating on the sound of the river. The sound of that river became my God, like a magnet that I was being drawn toward. As long as I concentrated on it, let its sound fill my being, it gave me inner strength and diminished the fear that was in the wings, poised to erupt and seize total control of my mind. Indeed, the fear was incessant, like it was bubbling just below my focused awareness. As I headed down into the dark, I had this terrifying thought about being lost at night in a strange, chilly black forest. How would one survive that? For sure, in a regular state of consciousness it would certainly be possible, but not while under the influence of psilocybin. It was inconceivable to become lost in the woods late at night. It would be a bad trip for sure. The notion of being lost in some sort of hellish madness from which there was no escape came to mind (such a scenario recalls the book *Lost in the Woods,* about Syd Barrett of Pink Floyd, who is widely rumored to have lost his mind from excessive LSD use).

This state of being lost, or fearing that one is lost, is worth going into more detail here because on several occasions while bemushroomed I have been well and truly lost. Even though the experiences were brief, they are revealing in that they embodied a significant psychological dynamic. For instance, once, in my mushroom fever days, I had determined to cycle all the way from North London to the Victoria and Albert Museum by way of Oxford Street. The psilocybin was coming on strong when I was about halfway along Oxford Street, heading toward Marble Arch. I knew that when I reached Marble Arch and then carried on toward Notting Hill, I would need to make a turnoff somewhere along the way and head toward Kensington. I forgot the precise route so decided to stop off at a bookshop that I passed to consult a map. I cannot begin to describe the complexity that bombarded my senses as soon as I set foot in that bookshop. The scene was awash with colors, sounds, and people. Straining to focus, I somehow managed to find the map section and located an A to Z of London. All the while the sensorial bombardment was growing in intensity. I then began to lose focus. What was going on? Where was I? What on earth was I doing? I seemed to be drowning in swirling, chaotic colors. Did I need medical assistance? Fear began to well up inside my psilocybinetic mind. I was well and truly lost. Nothing made sense. There was no direction, no path, no aim, no purpose. Again, what in good Goddess's name was going on?

Through an act of will, I mustered all my concentration and worked out the task at hand. I recalled *exactly* where it was that I was going and realized *exactly* what I needed to do. My whole being was now grounded upon a definite direction and a definite aim, which necessitated a specific sequence of acts that I needed to perform. Thus, I was no longer lost! Firmly back on track, I looked up the correct page in the A to Z book and was able to work out the route I needed to take. The route was right there in front of me. I could plainly see it and follow its course. The information had a kind of magnetic attraction to it, *like teleology was something you could actually grasp and pick up from the environment.* From being in a situation in which there was little sense and direction, I now was back on the way, like I had regained the Tao. Thus, about twenty minutes or so later I was in the museum marveling over Persian carpets and the like.

A similar thing happened on Dartmoor when a friend and I were engaged in a lengthy psilocybinetic all-day hike. Still under the psychological spell of psilocybin, I was trying to get us back to our tents but, for the life of me, could not work out where we were on the map. Until that point I had known exactly where we were going, and we had both had a fantastic day. Now I was filled with a kind of terror at the idea that we were lost. Nothing on the map made sense. None of the landmarks were recognizable, and it could have been any old random map that I was staring blankly at. The feeling of being lost was horrible, like being enveloped by an archetypal fear that has long haunted the human psyche. Eventually, however, I was able to focus on the situation at hand, used my compass to work out very roughly where we were, and reasoned that if we kept walking dead straight in a specific direction we would inevitably hit a long road detailed on the map. Basically, if the law and order prevalent within the universe was still functioning, then we would eventually reach that road! It would have to be so. It was a *mathematical certainty.* Thus, ten minutes later we hit the road in question, I was able to work out precisely where we were, and all was well again. Both this and the Oxford Street incident taught me how important it is to have an aim and a direction and not to give in to fear when one feels lost or is in danger of becoming lost. Indeed, Gurdjieff used to speak of this, stating that it was always important to have an aim of some kind—not a grandiose aim, but a small, practical, achievable one. Aims provide direction. Without a direction we can wander aimlessly—which is the essence of being lost.

So then, back to that pitch-black forest I was in. The only way to assuage the fear mounting up within me was to focus on the sound of that river. As I said, the sound of the river was my god, it was the chief focus of my consciousness, and I gradually got nearer and nearer to it, the sound inexorably increasing decibel by decibel. Eventually I reached level ground and the rocks. At this point I was holding my left arm straight out in front of me so that I did not bang into any trees. As I stepped carefully over the rocks beneath my feet, I could hear the river at full volume and realized that it was almost in front of me. Moving slowly forward, I found my outstretched arm moving downward. It seemed to have a will of its own. I reached out and . . . my hand landed directly on the lamp! By luck, the lamp had come to rest on a large flat rock a couple of feet from the river! Somehow, my hand had been led to it, like the lamp was the real magnet and not the river! I was amazed. How could this be? Those last few seconds my hand had really felt like it had a life of its own, like it was reaching out for something. And it came to rest exactly on the lamp! Even though I could not see it!

When I discovered that the trusty lamp still worked despite its earlier fall, I rejoiced! Let there be light! Now I could see the lovely river. Feeling like a celebration, I had an invigorating wash. Then, wiping my beaming face with the sleeve of my sweater, I turned toward the hillside and made my way back to camp. Needless to say, the next day I enthused about the venture with the Guru and, in subsequent weeks back in London, told my friends about the "magic lamp" incident.

The seeming ability to home in on that lamp (as opposed to its being a lucky accident) was echoed, in a mild way, years later. On one occasion when I was bemushroomed and had to leave the campfire to go back to my tent to retrieve something, I let a sort of instinct take over and recall observing quite clearly how my hand knew exactly where the required object was in my tent (which was pitch black inside). For the sake of argument, let us say I went back to get a spoon. In thinking about where the spoon was located, I might have had a vague idea. But some sort of instinct knew *exactly* where it was, so that when I pushed myself into the entrance of my tent I found my hand reaching out and expertly locating the spoon without any sort of fumbling and even before my eyes had time to adjust to the layout inside the dark tent. This was a very clear observation. There seemed to be a part of me, part of my unconscious, I assume, that knew stuff beyond my normal modes of perception and cognition and knew where things were located and the physical movements required to pick up those things. In a funny way, it was akin to the Force from the Star Wars mythos. Use the Force you must!

Other striking memories come to mind. One time when the Guru and I were trekking out in Snowdonia, we came across a field in which there were zillions of *Psilocybe semilanceata* mushrooms. I recall that afternoon's picking activity very clearly because it was one of the most beautiful spots to be foraging. Although it may sound somewhat archaic, the act of picking mushrooms is very enjoyable and reward-ing. Many Westerners are so used to buying things from supermarkets that they have lost contact with the biospherical source of their suste-nance. This is part of the price one pays for urban living. In fact, over the last few decades I have observed fewer and fewer people picking psilocybin mushrooms. It is like some lost folk art. Indeed, when I was a young boy I used to pick wild bilberries (also known as blue-berries) on the moors with my mother. How antiquated that sounds now in the age of supermarkets, when there is a pronounced separation between consumers and the food they eat. And yet this act of picking naturally occurring resources is one of the best ways of engaging with the natural world.

This mushroom spot in Snowdonia was the best. It was on the coast, so on one side of us were looming mountains, while on the other side was the ocean. The sky was blue, and the autumnal sun shone brightly. We spent an hour or so thoroughly enjoying the simple act of mushroom collecting. Who would have thought that vast sweeps of untended ground beyond cities and towns would yield a long-revered psychedelic substance that can afford a deep spiritual communion with nature? As I have said many times, were it not a true state of affairs, it would be the stuff of fantasy and science fiction.

Late that night I had a very powerful, albeit brief, mystical experience. Once again, the Guru had retired for the night to his tent. I was left trying to keep the fire going. This proved to be really hard because of the kind of deadwood on offer. Being an amateur pyrologist and having had by that time a good few years of experience in making and tending campfires, I had gotten to know the way different kinds of wood burn. Pine is always good because it burns well and leads to nice crystalline embers. There is even an occasional tinkling sound from the heart of a fire built from pine wood. Juniper is especially good because it has a wonderful aroma when burned. However, due to damp air, the wood on this night (beech) would not burn very well, and I constantly had to blow on the fire to evoke flames.

I recall staring down at the ground around me in the light from the fire. A dense mishmash of vegetation hugged the forest floor. This is a common sight, of course, the kind of thing you will, in normal perceptual circumstances, simply walk over. But with psilocybin, vegetation becomes infinitely fascinating. Well, to be sure about it, *everything* becomes more fascinating with psilocybin. The usual mechanical associations that go on in the mind are somehow obviated and super-seded by psilocybin. In this way, everything appears new, like you are seeing things for the first time. To cite pioneering psilocybin man Gordon Wasson (who famously wrote about the mushroom in *LIFE* magazine in 1957), objects beheld in the bemushroomed state appear as if they have come straight from the Creator's workshop.

While studying the vibrant green organic life beneath me, I was thinking about my book *The Psilocybin Solution* and how defeated I felt that I had been unable to get it published. I had gone through two literary agents—and both had failed to find a publisher despite good reviews from the various acquisition editors they knew. At the same time that I was dwelling on the difficulties of becoming a published author, I was also thinking about the fact that there appeared to be no new trees growing on the ground in the spaces between the already established trees. In other words, no seeds from the surrounding trees had sprouted anywhere from the layer of vegetation on the ground. It occurred to me that the reason for this was that the ground vegetation was akin to an interconnected carpet and that the only way a new tree seed could sprout was if the seed happened to be in a place where the dense organic context permitted such growth. Such a context would equate to a small opening in the complex biological network. I there-fore concluded that there were no new tree saplings because there was no space for them to take hold within that interconnected carpetlike pattern of life. I suddenly felt that this must be the case for my book, that it would not get published until it found the right context. It would have to quite literally "fit in" somewhere. And like the sporadic appearance of new trees in a well-established ecosystem, this might require some time to manifest. Although this seemed a good theory and was almost certainly correct, I can't say that I took too much sol-ace from it. Indeed, it is surely the lot, and even duty, of an aspiring writer to suffer years of rejection and obscurity. In any case, it seemed that the forest environment was explaining certain core principles to me by way of images and thoughts.

A bit later, I was staring into the fire and was thinking about the notion of eternity. I was trying to work out how it was possible for something to always have existed. This is known in the philosophy trade as the "first cause," and I have always been fascinated by such a notion. The first cause is considered to be the original kick-starter of the universe. The idea is that one can trace cause and effect further and further back in time until one reaches, say, the big bang. The first cause is the prime mover that initiated the big bang and all the subsequent chains of cause and effect that can transpire once time, space, matter, energy, and laws are in existence. As the first cause is not caused by something else, it must be uncreated and have always existed. Somehow.

Even the most hardcore atheists must admit to some sort of always existing thing—whether that always existing thing be a quantum potential or a quantum flux. Take your pick, really. Whatever view one has as to the ultimate origin of the universe, one will always have to invoke something that has always existed. The most seemingly minimal thing would be a *potential* of some kind, because even the so-called nothingness touted by some of today's physicists as lying at the "start" of the universe must represent a potential. Although it might sound as if such a timeless potential was simple, this is assuredly an illusion. Indeed, given that this potential turned into nothing less than the entire universe shows that "nothingness" is actually a tremendously significant "something" and not simple at all. Think about it. If everything—if all matter, all energy, all laws, and all forces—if the entire universe sprang out of some kind of quantum flux (or whatever), then that quantum flux must, in some sense, *represent a different form of the universe that it gave rise to.* There is no such thing as "nothing." "Nothing" cannot exist. By definition, only "something" can exist. Pure "nothingness" is an idea that is impossible. Even empty space is something because it contains space. Likewise, dimensions are not "nothing." Thus, to reiterate, there must *always have been "something."* And given that this "something" had the uncanny potential of turning into a universe endowed with the ability to evolve conscious minds, then this eternal, prime-moving "something" was highly substantial and of great import. The short of it is that there has always been a reality of some kind, an eternal principle, as it were, even before the birth of the universe that we are familiar with.

So there I was, trying to fathom how something could have always existed. The human mind is so subject to cause and effect and time that it simply cannot comprehend an eternally existing uncaused something. Try it—try to imagine something with no beginning, something that has always existed and that was not caused or created by something else. The mind boggles at this. If you really think about it deeply, you may even find yourself feeling a bit giddy, like you are touching the very edge of the mystery of mysteries. An eternal uncreated something. Such a thing cannot be grasped by our normal frames of consciousness. But I had an advantage on the night in question—for I had consumed performance-enhancing psilocybin mushrooms!

I seemed to be spiraling in on this mystery of eternity. It was the deepest I had ever been caught up in that particular metaphysical riddle. How can there be an eternal something, I kept asking myself? How can something exist that has no beginning and no end? How?! As I spiraled in closer and closer to the heart of this fascinating enigma, something very profound happened. For a split second, for the very briefest of moments, I actually grasped eternity! Somehow, it was as if I *became* that very mystery! I got the distinct impression that the only way eternity could truly be understood was to become it! I realized that the only real way to fully understand the deepest mysteries of existence was to become them, actually be them "from the inside," as it were. Or so it seemed.

No sooner did this extremely brief flash of "understanding" occur than I found myself spiraling back outward. I felt like I was traveling in a really rapid manner away from this deep center of "understanding." There was the feeling of unraveling faster and faster, and then the campfire came back into view, and I found myself right back down to earth, sitting by struggling flames in a Welsh forest during the middle of the night. It was a very odd sensation. But I was convinced that for that one single split second I had found a solution to one of the deepest philosophical-cum-metaphysical riddles that confronts us. The solution was to verily become the mystery, that if you become it you will understand it. I also felt sure that this was the *only way* of grasping other deep mysteries. Another way of putting this would be to say that certain things cannot be understood from the outside. Such as what it is like to be, say, a tiger. The only real way of fully knowing this would be to become a tiger. Actually, the same goes for the psilocybin experience. One can describe it in detail and even map a brain under the influence, yet these approaches will not be the actual experience itself. So in the same way that consciousness is fundamental and irreducible, so too, I think, are eternity and other age-old mysteries. The only sure way of grasping them is to somehow become them and know them from the inside. To live them and be them. Only then could you really know.

Another otherworldly experience I had in those pioneering treks also took place in Snowdonia. The Guru and I were once again on the coast, in the vicinity of Harlech, or at least within ten miles or so of that town. It was circa 1997. It must have been spring because I had brought with me an old supply of mushrooms gathered in previous years. Just before we arrived at a new camping area that had looked promising on the map, we had been on a typical long and winding ancient path that snaked its way over mountains and valleys. We had come back down almost to sea level and, upon leaving a forested area, had entered through a very old iron gate, the sort that requires one to stand inside a circular metal enclosure, close the entry gate, and then open the exit gate. After we had gone through this elaborate metal entrance, I joked to the Guru that it was, in fact, a secret portal of some kind, that we were being teleported to another dimension. Little did I suspect how apt that sentiment was to become. Anyhow, after we had set up our tents (in a discreet spot as usual so that no one would likely see us), I brewed up these old mushrooms that I had brought with me.

I should point out that while the mushroom can be eaten raw (fresh or dried), a mushroom brew will take effect more quickly, sometimes in as little as ten to fifteen minutes if you are sensitive. Interestingly, regarding the consumption of fresh, raw *Psilocybe semilanceata,* I have often mused how powerfully symbolic the process is. I have lost count of the times I have eaten freshly gathered mushrooms and noticed the soil on them along with fly eggs and fly maggots in their gills. As a culinary item, the fresh, raw mushroom is like rubbery, chewy dirt, about as undesirable a meal as one could imagine. And yet within this handful of tasteless earthiness lies spiritual bliss, the likes of which most humans are oblivious to. I have repeatedly marveled over this fact. It drives home the fictional nature of this story of life on earth that we are woven into, in that the mushroom is a kind of plot device that has been expertly engineered to embody all manner of symbolism. From a mouthful of what many people would call foulness incarnate (i.e., raw, unwashed fungi) can be delivered an experience of gratuitous heavenly grace, as Aldous Huxley called it.

The Guru was outside, taking in the sights as the sun gradually began to go down. There was a terrific view of the Llŷn Peninsula— which is a long, thin land mass that juts out westward from the coast of Wales in the direction of Ireland and beyond to North America. I recalled reading somewhere that Avalon—the mystical region associated with Arthurian legends—was based somewhere on the Llŷn Peninsula. Thus, it was not simply a mushroom tea that was brewing, but also a sort of ancient English mystique brewing in our minds.

The mushroom brew I made for the two of us was ridiculously strong. Well over three hundred mushrooms were in it, maybe even four hundred. I had once read somewhere that dried mushrooms gradually lose their strength over the years. That seemed to be a reasonable notion, which is why I boiled up so many, because some of the mushrooms were a good few years old. The truth, as I have since learned, is that the mushroom can retain its strength for considerable amounts of time—as we soon found out (bear in mind that thirty to forty of these fresh, diminutive *Psilocybe semilanceata* mushrooms can be an effective dose, able to induce spectacular visions behind closed eyes).

Later, the effects came on really strong. The first major thing that happened was that I was wandering around the vicinity, and as the psilocybin surged through my brain, I saw an ultrafantastic sight on some large granite rocks. In essence, I stood facing the most intensely powerful pattern I had ever seen. This was the same kind of sacred pattern I had perceived before and which I go into great detail about in chapter 5. All I can really say about it as it manifested on this rock face is that it was ultra-awesome. It radiated some kind of sacred energy. I am well aware how woolly this sounds, but it happened. Whether solely in my psilocybinetic mind, or I was seeing some normally hidden dimension of reality, or something objectively real was newly emerging there and then due to the right alchemical ingredients being in place, the fact remains that I saw this remarkable sacred pattern right before my eyes. It was utterly overwhelming. It was not a vision, not even a hallucination, as far as I could tell, but rather I was seeing a fabulous luminescent pattern covering the surface of those rocks. Bear in mind that these rocks, like most of the exposed rocks out in those wild areas, were covered in moss and lichen. So even with normal perception, granite surfaces are dotted with different hues and varying textures. But now the surfaces looked like a combination of spiral Celtic art, vividly colored hieroglyphs, and interconnected Islamic artwork—all rolled into one. But the pattern was not, as far as I could tell, familiar in any conventional way. So rather than seeing things that were not actually there, it seemed more the case that I was seeing the scene in a radically new way. In any case, the rocks seemed to blaze with psychedelic divinity. I was shocked. I felt like crying. Somehow, and in a way that still awaits a truly satisfactory explanation, I was interfacing with a higher-order reality. It was like I was being forcibly locked into place through the act of observing this indescribable pattern, locked into some higher dimension of reality, a dimension bursting with timeless myths and symbols, like I was in that moment of space and time close to the eternal source of all things. I kid you not; that is what it felt like.

I somehow removed myself from the sacred pattern and, both excited and humbled, rushed back to find the Guru. He too was under some sort of numinous onslaught. In the end both of us had to lie down in the meadow near our tents. I recall that the thistle plants in this meadow appeared hard to gaze at. They were really noticeable. Indeed, I was perceiving a kind of "sacred carpet" everywhere. Any area of ground that I looked at became part of this stupendously significant carpet. And the thistles were like an especially powerful part of that carpet. It was all too much. The sun was starting to redden as it sunk down on the horizon beyond the tip of the Llŷn Peninsula, or mystical Avalon, as it seemed. We lay there, each of us aghast at the transcendental psychedelic vortex into which we were being drawn. I was convinced that at any moment I would leave my body.

A little later I stood up and tried to grasp some semblance of normality. But everything felt weird, like I had totally left the normal world and was now in an alternative dimension. I once again had that stifling feeling, deeply aware of my somewhat labored breathing and how everything was part of one whole "solid" thing. As my usual sense of identity began to fade away, I started wondering about the contents of my pockets. Surely I could locate my identity by consulting those personal possessions? I got out my wallet and my keys. Nothing made sense. They were trivial items, mere props, with no real meaning. There was a bank card and other forms of ID. Yet, alarmingly, none of them really meant anything. In fact, they seemed more like toys. And so all I could do was to lie down again on the meadow and permit my being to dissolve even more. I had no choice but to surrender to whatever was happening to me. Which proved to be pretty much ineffable.

Eventually the most powerful psychedelic effects had passed, and we both managed to get to our feet. But even then the psilocybin was still working strongly. As the sun was nearly down and it was getting nippy, I prepared to make the fire for the night. I remember grabbing a firelighter from my tent and then, seeing the portable radio, exclaiming like a child: "music!" I turned on the radio and skipped back to the Guru, feeling my childlike essence emerging.

Lighting the fire proved to be incredibly difficult. Or at least it felt so. The Guru and I were crouched down by a small pile of kindling and were adding tiny twigs one by one in order to coach the fire into being. This is the way you light a fire in cold conditions and when the wood might have some dampness to it. You start ridiculously small, with a single small flame, and you feed in miniature twigs not much bigger than matches. One by one as well—because if you rush, you will starve the initial flame of air. Although this is always a very slow and carefully executed procedure, on this night it seemed to take forever. Years and years seem to pass by as we diligently attempted to get that fire to attain critical mass. And it seemed crucial that we do this because twilight was upon us and it was getting very cold. We had to have that fire! The fire was a kind of sanctuary that could protect us in our vulnerable state. One by one, in what felt like slow motion, we added miniscule bits of wood. I put a tiny bit in, then the Guru followed suit. Neither of us said a word. No longer feeling like a child, I now felt like we were two elderly tribal natives. We could have been aborigines, or at least akin to our ancient ancestors for whom a fire might have meant life or death.

Finally the fire was going well, and we could relax. By now it was fully dark, and the stars were out in full force. We seemed to suddenly both come back to earth at the same time. It was like a new lesser gear within the trip had suddenly kicked in. Normal reality was resolving itself. The Guru exclaimed how powerful the mushrooms had been that evening and what a strange trip it had been. I concurred. We then had a philosophical discussion about the meaning and significance of life. We soon alighted upon the idea of eternity. We both said that at times the psilocybin experience had somehow taken place in eternity. In fact, even at that moment, we still felt a lingering sense of eternity, that this part of the journey we were on was beyond the usual laws of space and time. I also recall thinking that the spot we were in, that whole area where the trip had taken place, was like a "Gaian arena." What I mean by this is connected with the sacred carpet perception I mentioned previously. It was like the carpet of life spread across the globe had electricity coursing through it (like an electric blanket) and that this electricity could concentrate at a certain location. When it did concentrate at a certain location, that area subsequently became more vibrant, more active, and more communicative in some way, like a stage set for some dramatic biospherical play. I really felt that. The only thing missing was a spotlight.

At some point in our philosophical discussion, we got to talking about modern life and all the cultural problems in the world. Many of our psilocybinetic discussions were like this. We would have these remarkable psilocybin experiences and then marvel about them in the immediate wake of their passing. We would invariably talk about the fact that we were lucky to be out in the generous wilderness but that we would soon have to venture back to the city, with its social strife and social friction. The thought of returning to civilization always bugged me and saddened me. Then again, I knew full well that context was everything. Our mushroom treks were so special precisely because of their rareness and the way wilderness can be contrasted with urban life. In other words, it was the dramatic change in environmental context that provided the contrast highlighting our spectacular experiences. Furthermore, outside of eternity, nothing lasts forever. Thus, coming back down from a powerful trip in which some aspect of eternity was felt is to reenter time and all that goes with temporal existence. It cannot be avoided. In other words, *all journeys must end*—although, of course, they may be individual sections of an even bigger journey of some kind.

While discussing the regular reality we had soon perforce to return to, along with the problems then existing in the world (which are seemingly always of the same kind), I concluded that the answer to everything was love. At that very moment the Guru pointed up to the heavens at a shooting star. We both saw it. It was a delightful synchronistic occurrence. We both marveled at that, and it seemed a fitting end to that day's long journey. The last thing I did before we ended the evening was to gaze out at the ocean toward America. I murmured to the Guru: "There are others!" I felt sure of this, that there were fellow men and women out in the world who would be sympathetic to this passionate interest of ours in exploring the mushroom's spiritual potential. As it happened, later that year I heard from, and met in person, an American fellow and a Canadian girl who were students at Schumacher College in Devon (an alternative college where open-minded ecological science was at that time pursued) and who avidly joined me on a psilocybinetic trek on the outskirts of Dartmoor the following year. So there were indeed others!

Among the many psilocybinetic wilderness activities I undertook that could be considered overtly reckless, or at least decidedly unwise, was the ascent of Mount Snowdon. I believe I was the first person to climb that mountain (the highest in Wales and higher than England's highest peak) while under the influence of a strong dose of the mushroom. Certainly, no one else should attempt such a venture, not because I wish to remain the only person to have done so, but because it carries all manner of risks. One could get lost, fall, or become disoriented, or whatever. The last thing one should be doing under the influence of a powerful visionary psychedelic is climbing mountains! Having said that much, I felt compelled in those heady days of yore to embark on just such an adventure. This took place in July 1998, and I was, for a brief time at least, in the company of the Tall Guy, who, you may recall, I had shared my impoverished punk days with back in the early 1980s.

We were camped not far from the Watkin Path, one of the chief routes up Mount Snowdon. As I recall, it was a really neat area—hidden from the path, but with some trees, a nearby stream, and plenty of dead wood for nightly campfire activities. Incidentally, the various wilderness camping sites I established over the years were arrived at after intense map studying, along with on-the-fly scouting when a potential camping area had been reached. I got good at this. On all the treks I ever did in the company of various close friends, a point would come when I would call a halt and ask them to keep an eye on the rucksacks. Then I would be off scouting for a suitable campsite. I usually found a good place. It was like a sixth sense. I could generally tell from the map if an area was promising. Once there, I could seemingly "sniff out" a good precise location. There had to be two (or occasionally three) flat areas for tent erection, dead wood in the vicinity, along with a nearby source of water—usually a stream.

Over the years I had the good fortune to camp in some of the most amazing spots. When you first arrive and set up camp, the surroundings are unfamiliar. Over the course of a few days, and particularly after psilocybin consumption, the area becomes akin to an organic palace. It is like being indoors, like one is the regal occupant of some ornate Gaianesque temple. Moss-covered rocks and boulders can soon become transformed into organically upholstered seats. Individual trees become familiar. Small trails are soon formed leading to a good place alongside a stream where water can be collected. After three or four days, such sites become a real home away from home. To be sure about it, they are more homely and more impressive than any manufactured residence, particularly as they are basically alive. I think that this is the closest one can get to the web of life—to be camped in some pristine ecosystem where biodiversity is apparent and where the resident individual organisms exude health, vigor, and vitality. Thus, it has been both an honor and a privilege to have camped in the most glorious wilderness areas of the U.K. that still remain and, moreover, to have picked and consumed freshly made psilocybin there too. That's better than any millionaire fantasy, or celebrity fantasy, or whatever. In fact, it beats any of the various fantasies that fill the contemporary Western psyche. Mansions and sports cars and huge bank balances do not grant one good relationships with others and with the larger system of nature in which we are embedded. Good relationships are everything, and money cannot buy them. Psilocybin can drive home this timeless truth.

The plan was for the Tall Guy and me to ascend Mount Snowdon together. We each ate a stiff dose of about sixty naturally sun-dried mushrooms and set off to join the Watkin Path. Now, it should be mentioned that I had not seen the Tall Guy for many years, and my deep interest in all things psilocybinetic was new to him. So these mushrooms he was eating were somewhat of a mystery. He had, by that stage of his life, allegedly consumed a number of psychoactive substances (along with the various foul concoctions we had cooked up some fourteen years previous), but this was, as far as I knew, his first major act of psilocybin consumption. In retrospect, I think I should have decreased the dose. But he was a big lad and fully grown up. Besides, he was with me, an experienced and trustworthy guide and companion!

The mushrooms seem to come on quite quickly, and I got distinctly nervous when I looked a few miles up ahead to where the Watkin Path disappeared behind imposing gray mountains. I pointed out to the Tall Guy that the effects would be really strong by the time we hit the foot of those yonder mountains. As they were smothered in rolling mist, this seemed really ominous. I think we both felt a sense of fear and awe about the spectacle that we were venturing into. Indeed, maybe I had bitten off more than the two us could chew? "Nonsense!" I told myself. Onward, forward, and upward!

Soon we reached a large boulder known as the Gladstone Rock. It had some kind of plaque on it testifying to something either achieved, or said, by the historical U.K. politician William Gladstone. By now, the psilocybin experience was upon us, and the Tall Guy was amazed at the changes in his perception, likening the enhanced view to boosting the contrast on pictures with computer software. I recall that he was finding our journey more and more overwhelming by the minute, while I was bounding about and ranting enthusiastically about the power and beauty of Gaia. Probably this did not give him comfort. Indeed, what were we doing out in the middle of nowhere, approaching the highest mountain in Wales with a view to climbing it while under the influence of a powerful psychedelic fungus? Were we nuts?

The next memorable thing that happened was that we reached the ruins of an old slate mine. It was peculiar, because the remaining pillars of one of the old buildings were configured like Stonehenge. This long-abandoned mine basically looked like an ancient ruined temple. The most striking sight, though, was a huge mound of quarried gray slate. It was covered in a thin "mesh" of grass. We both sensed the net-like quality of this organic grassy mesh. One could *feel* the tautness of the botanical net around the slate pile and that the slate was almost bursting out. Also, the grassy vegetation was gauzelike and almost transparent. It was a very striking sight.

By now the mushrooms were peaking in effect. We both had to sit down. I shut my eyes and began to have eschatological visions. The visual icons that manifested behind my closed eyes were common to me by then because I had seen similar visionary iconography over the preceding years, particularly back in my mushroom fever days. I was witness to an immense spinning vortex. It seemed as if all matter and energy, all things, were slowly spinning around and were gradually spiraling into the funnel-like center of the vortex. I sensed that absolutely everything was being drawn into this thing. It seemed to have a sacred character about it, and I interpreted it as a symbolic delineation of the Omega Point, as discussed by Teilhard de Chardin, a point in the distant future toward which the reality process was being inexorably drawn, a state of maximum coherency and interconnectedness, an ultimate oneness, if you will, a singularity not at the beginning of time but at the end of time.

When I opened my eyes, it became apparent that the Tall Guy was feeling a bit sick and was in danger of succumbing to fear. In particular, he was concerned that he might have a heart attack. That, of course, got me fearful as well. The entire dynamic of our shared trip changed at this point. It must be said that he was not too fit at that time. Even though he was only in his midthirties, he was not a well-seasoned trekker. I guess we had gone a few miles from camp by this point, and for the last mile or so we had been going uphill, so his nonoptimal physical condition was making itself known. Although we soon established that he was in no way in danger of having a heart attack, the bottom line was that he felt unwell, and the mushrooms were not agreeing with his digestive system. It was clear that he could not continue. We then had a discussion about what to do. I did not want to leave him. On the other hand, the objective of that day was to reach the summit of Mount Snowdon. So I asked if he would mind if I continued alone.

After a long discussion in which I ascertained that he was well enough, fit enough, and clear enough in his head to make it back to "base camp" on his own (as it was just a few miles away, and downhill), I set off alone. I felt a mixture of disappointment and also worry. Had he been in a worse condition, I would have gone back to camp with him. But he seemed okay, just not well enough to climb the mountain on that particular day and with those particular prevailing psychological conditions. I totally understand this. It was assuredly a great relief to him that he was able to readily opt out of the ascent.

Interestingly, he later told me of a strange synchronicity that occurred about ten minutes after we had parted. As he was setting off back down the foot of the mountain, a group of young trekkers passed him, led by a teacher or a scout. After they passed him, he (the Tall Guy) heard them shout out his name (i.e., Mr. So and So). He looked back in astonishment, thinking they were beckoning him up the mountain, but then realized that the leader of their party shared the same surname. In his acutely enhanced state of consciousness, the Tall Guy felt as if the very mountain was verily taunting him to come back!

Meanwhile, with renewed vigor, I was busy ascending the rugged mountain, confident that I could make the top despite my unusual mental condition. Once again, the path acquired a sort of spiritually charged aspect to it. The clarity of the rocks that I was treading upon was astonishing. Everything looked crystal clear and hyper-real. The only thing that was not clear was the actual way up the mountain because thicker mist was coming in, and I was approaching a place on the map where there was an important crossing of paths. If I took the wrong path, I would end up way off course.

As luck would have it, I met a man coming the other way. He looked very striking because he had a thick beard and a slightly aggressive air about him. In my mind I christened him the Bulldog Man. We struck up a conversation. Although I became fixated on the appearance of his hands, I heard Bulldog Man say that I was about to hit the important junction, and he pointed to it in the misty distance.

No sooner was I on this path than I was joined by a fellow solo trekker making his way up the mountain. He was a young Welsh chap, and we made the rest of the ascent together. Even though I was still very much under the influence of the mushroom, I managed to hide this from him, and I remember feeling somewhat chuffed that I could fake "normalcy" and conceal my perceptual astonishment, which was constant. It soon became clear that we were both lovers of the outdoors, and so we raved about the fierce beauty of wilderness and the joys of trekking. He also pointed out that when you were out in those parts, subject to whatever weather nature sends and with only your wits and your stamina to help you through rain and storms, it mattered not a jot how much money you had or what social status you held. The only thing of importance was that place and that time and how you dealt with the situation. In other words, inner strength and inner security were what really mattered—and this is what wilderness trekking and mountain climbing (even the minor mountain climbing we were engaged in) tended to nourish. It is as if such pursuits bring out one's essence, while all the false images and superficial ideas we have about ourselves fade away. A bit like the mushroom experience.

The summit of Mount Snowdon was a total letdown. Not only was it shrouded in thick mist so that the famous views were occluded, a large building was situated there that served the passengers from a train service that ran up the other side of the mountain. To me, all this was a travesty. It was hideous. Thus, I did not linger long on the summit. My friendly Welsh companion took a photo of me (which he later sent me), and then we parted company. Hours later I made it back down and, upon rejoining the Tall Guy at "base camp," was glad to hear that he had gotten back okay and had even had an enjoyable day.

On a few occasions I even undertook solo psilocybinetic treks. I did this twice in the Lake District and also camped one night in Richmond Park. Let me briefly describe the latter venture first. The time was early 1993 (a few years before I started trekking), and I had recently ended a relationship with a certain Irish girl. I felt compelled to break into a fenced-off forest in the park and to spend the night there bemushroomed. I had never done anything like that before, but it seemed a challenge, almost initiatory in a sort of shamanic way.

Having clambered over an ancient wrought-iron fence, I plunged deep into the wood so that I would not be seen by any park rangers or park maintenance staff. I constructed a fire and made sure I had enough wood to last the night. I consumed a stiff dose of mushrooms at twilight. Then I sat down and waited.

When the effects first came over me, I heard curiously distinct voices inside my head. This was a new phenomenon to me, but I was not too perturbed because I was able to study it objectively. The voices were those of mischievous children. They had one of the very thick accents found in Northern England, so thick as to be almost satirical. At some point I wondered if they were the souls of lost children. This made the whole thing seem sinister, like I was being set upon by the mischievous spirits of the undead (in retrospect, I think this was some bizarre autonomous manifestation of my unconscious, spun from media exposure and such). It did not go on for long, however, and soon I had lit the fire and was enjoying its warmth. This did not last long either, though, because I suddenly noticed what appeared to be eyes staring at me from between the surrounding trees (it was dark by this point). This was very scary, and I was convinced that wild dogs (or worse things) were prowling nearby and eyeing me. I then realized that they were not eyes but distant city lights that could just be seen through the trees. What a relief! It seems amusing writing about this twenty years later, yet at the time I felt abject terror. Clearly the mind can play tricks, and it is important that one be able to observe oneself impartially at all times. Fear has a way of getting out of hand if it is not clearly observed. The very act of impartially observing such psychological activity immediately changes the dynamics of one's inner world and can prevent fear from becoming overwhelming.

Later that night, with eyes shut, I enjoyed impressive visions of ancient Egypt. I saw what appeared to be the colorfully decorated walls inside the Great Pyramid of Giza. It was like I was having a tour of the artwork as it once looked. These powerful visions seemed to energize me, and I leapt up and made the fire bigger. I determined then to stay awake till first light. That became my primary mission—to keep the fire going right through till dawn. I also recall trying to break a really large tree branch. It was very bendy but would not snap. It seemed to become a symbol for corrupt ideas and dogma. So I had to snap it! I strained and strained, seemingly engaged in a fight with all that was old, staid, and insipid. But the darn thing would not break! I was huffing and puffing, sweat breaking out on my forehead, staggering around the fire like a wild man, determined to break that branch. Eventually I triumphed, and there was a loud crack as the branch split. Success! Ah, what I was secretly doing for the world, I thought to myself with a wry smile! And so it was that I stayed awake all night tending to the fire until, at last, the sun rose, and I clambered into my tent and went to sleep to the sound of the loudest avian spring dawn chorus that I had ever heard.

Trekking alone and taking mushrooms alone in the wilderness is undoubtedly very instructional because you learn a lot about yourself—your hopes and fears and the importance of other people in your life. You also get to see your relationship with the larger world of nature and the cosmos. Despite the learning opportunities that are here afforded, this kind of solo psilocybinetic trekking activity is impossible to recommend (like so many of my other ventures) on account of the inherent dangers. No one should follow my example on that score. I mention it only because it is part of my own idiosyncratic psychedelic journeying.

Of the two occasions when I took mushrooms alone in the Lake District, one stands out. It was late autumn 1996, and I had spent the whole day walking and had also managed to pick some fresh mushrooms. However, the weather was rough that day, with hard winds and intermittent rain. The sky was very overcast and looked decidedly stormy and ominous. The idea of a psilocybin trip during rough weather with a fire that might not endure was a none too attractive proposition. So I made a deal with myself. If in the early hours of the evening a star should appear from between the clouds, then I would take that as a good omen and would consume mushrooms—the hope being that more stars would appear, the clouds would disperse, and more clement weather would manifest. Well, strangely enough, after

I had pitched my tent at a favorite campsite near waterfalls and pine trees, I chanced to look upward and, lo and behold, a single star was visible in a small opening in the otherwise thick, gloomy clouds! This was like a nod and a wink from the biosphere! Thus, I consumed locally gathered Lake District psilocybin once more—only this time I did not have the trusty Guru for company.

One memory comes forcibly to mind. I sat near the fire and was contemplating the existence of my own consciousness along with the plant life surrounding me. I suddenly had a massive insight, like a significant revelation was being conveyed to me. I realized that the essential function of the human cortex was for "natural intelligence" to reflect itself. What I mean is that there is some kind of wisdom or intelligence within the totality of nature—within the laws and forces of nature and the creative consequences thereof—and that this intelligence, which is chiefly unconscious, can become conscious through the human cortex. In other words, there is an unconscious something that can know itself and wake up to itself through the vehicle of human consciousness. It was as if I sensed an ancient *will,* one that was inherent within the whole of nature in a pantheistic sense, but in a kind of "curled up" form, or a *hibernating* form, and it was very gradually unfurling and expressing its creative poten- tial through the evolving web of life, part of which is the advanced human nervous system and the conscious experience facilitated by it. Moreover, if one senses and feels the natural intelligence within the cosmos and one's deep connection to it, one realizes that *one must actually be a newly emergent form of that intelligence.* In short, we are effectively that which made us. Or more properly, *we are becom- ing that which made us.* Something hitherto unconscious and spread throughout nature is becoming wise to itself, as if a cosmic process of self-knowledge is underway. Whether or not this was a real insight, it occurred instantly within me like a momentous Gnostic flash.

The essence of this admittedly fanciful notion has stuck with me and seems to have become firmly rooted in my psyche. Indeed, in the eighteen or so years since that night, I have yet to abandon such a philosophical notion. In fact, I went on to write much about the idea, and so this is a fitting note on which to end this chapter and to begin the next—which is precisely about the concept of natural intelligence.

3
Natural Intelligence

The wild psilocybinetic treks outlined in the previous chapter undoubtedly inspired my ideas about the nature of the world. Indeed, they led to what I call the "natural intelligence paradigm," which has become a major part of my work. Such wilderness voyages can be contrasted with Terence McKenna's advice that the mushroom be consumed in the safety of one's own home in silent darkness. McKenna was wont to tell would-be psychonauts to disable phones and to make sure that they would not be disturbed in any way. He would then advise people to lie down in silent darkness, shut their eyes, and pay attention to the visions that are invariably catalyzed by psilocybin. This is wise counsel because it underscores the potential significance and tutorial nature of the psilocybin experience.

On the other hand, such a tutorial relationship can become apparent in other settings, especially those involving wilderness areas. Indeed, I believe that forests and remote national park areas (where you are unlikely to be bothered by other people) are some of the most rewarding places to engage in psilocybinetic communion. They are places where natural intelligence is readily apparent and can become even more apparent once the doors of perception are opened. This is because in wilderness areas the various organic life forms are generally far healthier than in the small patches of cultivated greenery in urban gardens and parks. Plus, you get the natural sound of rivers, wind, birdsong, and rustling leaves. You can also see the stars more clearly. In short, there is a special *quality* to wilderness areas (what I quaintly referred to as "wilderness tang" in an earlier chapter). As I say, I think this is principally because nonurban biological fabric is in better shape. There is improved genetic expression, increased biodiversity, larger interspecies activity, and therefore better overall health. In places where an ecosystem is left to develop under its own natural steam, there is enhanced vigor and enhanced life. Trees, for example, invariably look more alive and more vibrant. It is in these wilderness places hidden from towns, roads, and paths that the ever-flowing wisdom of nature can be more readily divined—not necessarily a conscious intelligence as we might know it, but intelligence in its most basic organic expression.

For good or for ill then, the chief fruit of all my various psilocybin experiences over the last twenty-five years is the natural intelligence paradigm that gradually formed in me as a result of various adventures undertaken far from the madding crowd amid mountains and forests. McKenna had his time wave theory (among a number of other unorthodox ideas), whereas my idée fixe has always been natural intelligence. What the mushroom gave me, or facilitated, was not a new invention or a new scientific breakthrough (although there have been cases of significant scientific insights being derived from psychedelic experiences—Nobel Prize winner Kary Mullis is a case in point), but rather a new way of understanding life, evolution, and consciousness. Thus far, apart from a handful of fans, this paradigm is either unknown or simply disregarded. Either the paradigm is plain wrong or there is something peculiar about the human psyche that prevents it from taking root. I shall have more to say about that latter possibility toward the end of this chapter.

Because it is my idée fixe, and because this book is about my personal journey, I feel compelled to delineate the natural intelligence perspective in some depth. Perhaps people in the future will look back on me as a victim of delusory animistic ideation. Or alternatively, as someone who had important insights that eventually became common sense. Either way, the natural intelligence paradigm is the "gift" I feel I received from all my eager research. I searched heart and soul for meaning and purpose beyond those forms of meaning and purpose promulgated by science, religion, and wishful thinking. I sought bigger game. I sought the full holistic truth—beyond dogma, beyond convention, beyond dead notions, beyond academic sound bites, and beyond what was merely convenient or sweet tasting. What I found was the essence of life as seen through new eyes, a sort of new breathtaking interpretation of something we usually take for granted. Again and again I saw life as an intelligence forged not from wires, chips, and electronic circuits, but from DNA, cells, and webs of bio-logic. It also became clear that this natural intelligence, this flowing organic wisdom, if you will, was pretty much unacknowledged by mainstream science (the process of evolution, for instance, is not considered to evince the characteristics of intelligence) and even circumvented by those keen to dumb down nature's creative acumen. Given the environmental degradation currently being dealt to the biosphere (and note that the biosphere can be viewed as a planetary network of sophisticated organic technology), it seemed a no-brainer that this attitude had to change. Psilocybin showed me that our appraisals of life and evolution were severely lacking and that a long-term future for our species depends upon a right understanding of what life on earth actually is.

As a way of exploring the notion of natural intelligence in more detail than the allusions to it dotted around previous chapters, let me here focus on intelligence itself, in particular the notion of *advanced intelligence*. For reasons I shall shortly explain, let me bring to the table the rather sensational idea that an alien intelligence has engineered the human genome. Not a mild intelligence or a passable intelligence, but a really sophisticated and powerfully alien intelligence, the kind of advanced intelligence you have to step back and gawp at. I bring this idea up because such hypothetical aliens would possess the same kind of attributes I accord to nature. In other words, the same kind of "power" and acumen is being alluded to. The chief difference is that the alien idea sees powerful intelligence connected to intentional aliens, whereas the natural intelligence paradigm sees intelligence and intention connected to nature (ultimately to the laws and forces of nature).

DNA-manipulating aliens is a kind of New Age idea and seems to be gaining in popularity. You hear about it a lot on social media websites. Similarly, a cursory look at YouTube reveals oodles of sensational films about DNA-meddling aliens and the like. What bothers me about this idea is that it may stop people from divining the often advanced intelligence underlying *all* life and not just human life. So I am arguing that it is a fallacious idea but can serve to bring the actual truth home. Let me explain.

The gist of the alien DNA idea is that at some point in the past advanced aliens genetically engineered the human race. Maybe this took place millions of years ago, hundreds of thousands of years ago, or even more recently. In any case, the idea is that this alien genetic tinkering explains our big conscious brains. In other words, human culture and human history is so different from the rest of life that it must mean that ultrasmart aliens made us, or at least changed the genes of primates in order to birth us. Conspiracy buffs and wide-eyed New Agers love this kind of thing. It has that "ooooh" factor that sells zillions of books and DVDs and attracts cult followers. People are wont to nod slowly and say, "Aha! Of course! Aliens engineered us to do their bidding!" Or something along those lines.

Without mincing words, I suggest that such a belief is unwarranted for lots of reasons. First off, science has now documented the human genome. Indeed, nowadays a huge and growing number of scientists are avidly studying genetics. We know how to map genes, how to compare the genomes of species, and how to link them all up. In fact, the modern study of genetics strongly supports Darwin's theory of evolution. All the evidence shows how the genomes of different species are related to one another through common ancestry. All the findings point to the fact that life is interconnected and that genetic changes (i.e., changes to DNA) occur over time. All the genetic facts so far discovered add up and make sense in the light of evolution. A good theory is one in which all the facts fit together. In other words, evolution is a compelling theory and accepted by most thinkers and academics (along with some religious spokespeople) because modern genetic findings (along with other evidence) support it.

Now, as far as I know, geneticists are not scratching their heads over human DNA. They are not mystified by certain genes or proteins that seem to be "out of place" or anomalous. Indeed, there are no genes that are out of place. There is nothing that sticks out like a sore thumb and that cannot be accounted for, which means that the human species is but one strand of the web of life, connected with other parts, made of the same organic ingredients, and, ultimately, no more conspicuous than crocodiles or mountain goats. Indeed, why not invoke aliens to account for crocodile genomes or mountain goat genomes? Not smart enough creatures? Then how about bonobo chimps, which certainly are social and smart? Or social insects such as ants and bees, which possess formidable swarm intelligence, evince complex communication capabilities, and build highly elaborate nests and hives? Why don't we hear about aliens engineering these other highly impressive creatures?

The bottom line is that somewhere along the line we share common ancestry with all other species. That explains why we have genes in common with other mammals (and even with plants!). And if you go back far enough, all life is linked to a single common ancestor. Thus, there is little reason to treat ourselves differently (at least not in terms of our biology). To say that we are somehow an anomaly and that we must have been genetically engineered by aliens is to fall into a sort of religious trap. One reason people couldn't hack Darwin's newly published ideas back in 1859 was that religious leaders had always claimed that humans were beyond all other creatures. Linking us to apes, as Darwin effectively did, would have seemed a crass, heretical, and unbecoming idea. It was taken for granted that the Lord made us in a divine feat of spontaneous supernatural creation, and therefore many thought Darwin a dangerous fool for suggesting that we shared a common ancestor with extant species of ape. Of course we didn't! We were God's chosen people, made by an exacting hand, and incomparable to hairy waddling simians, which, despite having certain gross similar features, were of an inferior caliber.

Suggesting that there is something "alien" about human DNA is akin to those historical conceptual follies born of dogmatic religious thought. It is a refusal to see ourselves as a natural expression of evolving life. More important, to think that way is, as I have pointed out, to totally miss the brilliance of other organisms. Why single out humans as being engineered by cunning aliens? Why not bang on about dolphins? Dolphins are very smart social creatures whose brains are relatively large for their size. Or what about the amazing ability of dragonflies to see through almost 360 degrees and fly upside down? Why aren't people waving pictures of dragonflies in the air, pointing to their remarkable design, and claiming that aliens must have engineered them? Or why not yell loudly about photosynthesis and posit such ingenious botanical behavior as an alien intervention?

The point I am making is that we would do well to reappraise, reinterpret, and get excited about *all of life,* and not just human life.

Indeed, it is precisely life itself and the larger system of nature that provokes the emergence and evolution of life that can be seen to have intelligent characteristics. In other words, the difference between the natural intelligence perspective and the alien intelligence perspective is that the former sees advanced intelligence as being an intrinsic property of the whole of nature and not something located on an alien planet or in another dimension or whatever. In this sense, the "alien DNA" brigade are very much like intelligent design creationists (the latter see a supernatural force governing evolution). Both groups are enthusiastically barking up the wrong tree. Both groups fail to perceive the real wonder, the real mystery. And the real mystery is not us humans in particular (although we are blessed with conscious intelligence), nor the sophisticated visual systems of dragonflies, nor the ability of plants to eat light, but rather life itself, the genetic code itself, DNA itself, along with the remarkably flexible and constructive ways in which DNA can be expressed. Plus, of course, the specific laws and forces of nature that verily conjure up life and nourish it. The whole of nature and the unfolding creative potential of nature is what we should rightly be talking about and not "alien DNA" scenarios.

Thus, notwithstanding a few things like complex brains and the bacterial rotors raved about by intelligent design creationists, evolving life seems to be completely taken for granted. The genetic code is a good example of this, of how we have become dulled to something that is actually worth repeatedly pondering over. Codes are usually associated with intelligence. Think of other codes. Like Morse code. Or computer code. Or the codes used by military intelligence to transmit orders. All these codes are obviously the product of intelligence—in this case human intelligence. The genetic code, however, is natural. It formed itself on its own and is a natural outcome of the way nature is configured (in terms of nature's specific laws and forces). Before it finally manifested here on Earth, the genetic code was always a self-organizing potential of the periodic table of elements—inasmuch as the periodic table of elements consists of carbon, hydrogen, oxygen, and those other building blocks of which DNA is made. The genetic code sits alongside other forms of self-organization—such as the natural formation of suns, spiral galaxies, and snowflakes. This is what nature does. Nature is a system by which various exquisite structures and patterns will, according to the influence of natural laws and natural forces, fall into place once conditions are "ripe," so to speak. The genetic code is one fantastic example of this.

Yet just because the genetic code is natural does not mean that we should ignore it as if it were meaningless. Far from it. The emergence of the genetic code and evolving life demonstrates that nature has intelligent characteristics. What do I mean by this? I certainly don't mean intelligent characteristics derived from aliens or divine intervention. Nor am I implying consciously intelligent characteristics. I am suggesting that evolving life is an *unconscious intelligence.* Intelligence is an appropriate term to use here because it is connected with the specific kind of information processing underlying life—a kind of information processing embodied by DNA along with the genetic code that determines the meaning and expression of DNA.

Now, DNA has a relationship with proteins, proteins being the building blocks of all living things. The way DNA expresses itself is chiefly through proteins. You are made of proteins, and so is your cat or dog, along with any plants you may have. The difference lies in the type of proteins and their number, distribution, and arrangement. One can think of proteins as microscopic building blocks, or microscopic Lego bricks, that are coded by DNA. Under the influence of electrical forces and such, millions of these protein Lego bricks organize themselves into cellular tissue, organelles, and the wondrous machinery of life. How the fullness of this orchestration occurs is a mystery. Millions and millions of Lego bricks constantly arrange themselves into various coherent structures that link up with one another to form further coherencies, the whole lot tied together through chemical cycles and catalytic loops. So it is not just the Lego bricks that are important but the way they spontaneously self-organize.

Anyhow, for now let us focus on DNA. As stated, DNA is the way that these precise miniature Lego bricks are coded. The specific sequences of amino acids that are needed to make up useful Lego-like proteins are stored in DNA. Discrete sections of DNA equate to, or provide the code for, sequences of amino acids—which fold up on themselves into proteins. Thus, a gene is essentially a long string of instructional code that, when expressed, will form something akin to one of those Lego bricks with, say, four attachment parts (when I was a kid, the most common kind of Lego brick was one with four attachment parts). Another gene might code for a Lego brick with sixteen attachment parts. And so on. Evolution is about honing these protein Lego bricks through the trial and error variation of DNA, getting the right amounts of proteins, and creating and sustaining new proteins that make some sort of sense in the context of the others.

Despite relying upon unconscious trial and error, *it is still a very clever system*—particularly because sensible life-affirming changes to DNA are preserved. Indeed, this is precisely why I am asserting that life and the genetic systems underlying life represent a real kind of intelligence—not a conscious intelligence but an autonomous, unconscious intelligence that works on its own. It does not have foresight or emotions, but simply does what it does a bit like an ever-adaptable autopilot. It is intelligent because it is precisely clever things, clever routines, clever systems of bio-logic that are continually being selected and preserved by the hand of nature. This exacting specificity, this preservation and *honing* of smart behavior, is what makes evolving life an organic intelligence in action. It is a *system-based* intelligence and can only really be grasped by seeing both life and the rest of nature as one whole. The intelligence is not just in the changing DNA, nor in the various evolving strands of life, but rather in the whole system of nature that provides the self-organizing stuff of which life is made along with the laws and forces that shape it.

What I am mainly trying to get across, then, is that the process of evolution in which DNA is being edited in a smart, life-enhancing manner warrants the term *intelligence*. After all, the behavioral processes carried out by our minds or by modern robots are readily accorded some degree of intelligence. Our minds can process information in a clever way and lead us to behave intelligently and so too can robots with onboard computers process information in a clever way, allowing them to behave intelligently (an example of artificial intelligence). Which, again, drives home the key point. *With biological evolution we likewise witness information (strings of digital DNA code) being processed, manipulated, and honed in clever ways.* Only the timescale differs. Natural selection is the preservation of those genetic changes (i.e., changes to the protein Lego bricks) that make some kind of good sense. Such sensible changes will lead to better modes of living and more offspring. Genetic changes that fail to make some sort of good sense will be pruned away via death or failed reproduction. I attest that it is this *specific modification* of *specific information* that lies at the heart of all intelligent processes and which lies at the heart of biological evolution. Hence the term *natural intelligence* to describe and appraise it.

The conclusion of this approach is that the evolving web of life is an autonomous intelligence. The intelligence is not outside of life in some supernatural space or connected to conniving aliens but is intrinsic to life—intrinsic to the universe, in fact. The organic intelligence that is life does not think of the morrow (although certain kinds of foresightful biological systems can evolve—think of hibernation or the creation of fat reserves to help survive future lean times) but always operates in the living moment. Biological changes and biological behavior that makes sense in the living moment are what will be sustained. Thus, a new gene, or a new gene complex, will be selected and sustained if it leads to some sort of sensible behavior that facilitates the art of living. There is no love in this and no malice. It just is. As I summed it up in my early *Metanoia* film (viewable on YouTube), evolution is a naturally intelligent process that builds naturally intelligent systems of bio-logic. Life is quite literally a living, flowing, and ever-expanding wisdom (for a much deeper look at the metaphysical implications of this perspective, please refer to my book *Darwin's Unfinished Business*).

What many people find hard to conceive is the notion that intelligence can be a biological thing. After all, we usually think of intelligence as something connected with minds and not with evolving biological material. In the early days of the natural intelligence paradigm, this was brought home to me by something said by the late Edward Goldsmith. A well-known ecologist and founder of *The Ecologist* magazine, Goldsmith had read a very early manuscript of *Darwin's Unfinished Business* and had said that it was fine to point out the smart and clever aspects of the living world (such as bee language or the behavior of carnivorous plants) but warned me not to talk of bio-logic itself as being intelligent (what I really mean by bio-logic is the kind of thing you see inside a cell—genetic activity, specific chemical cycles, specific behavioral routines, and such).

Goldsmith's reservation stemmed from the aforementioned fact that we usually associate intelligence with minds and not with tangible "things." Or if we do infer intelligence outside of the (human) mind, then it is only in terms of an overt behavior of some kind, say termite-fishing by chimps, for example. When we see a chimp fishing for termites with a specially chosen twig, we invariably infer that some degree of intelligence is involved. But we do not usually see the chimp's hands or its hand-eye coordination as being types of intelligence, nor its muscular apparatus or its vascular system or its digestive system. Nor, of course, do we see the evolutionary process that led to chimps evincing intelligence.

According to the natural intelligence paradigm, however, intelligence is essentially a *process* as opposed to a *thing,* more like a *verb* than a *noun.* It is a process, moreover, involving the manipulation of information. We know our brains process information. This is done through nerve cells, or neurons, firing and sending signals to one another. But it is harder to appreciate that the bio-logic underlying a neuron is likewise a process. Indeed, all of life—whether a cell, a group of cells, a chimp's hand, or the part of a chimp's brain that governs hand movement—consists of processes involving specific physical and chemical activity. Such astute bio-logic is the intelligence I keep referring to. It is not like there is some vital supernatural force pulling the biological strings, but rather that bio-logic itself is an embodiment of intelligence, albeit unconscious. Life can thus be likened to a clever verb in action.

I can think of two good ways to get one's head more firmly around this expanded notion of intelligence. I reckon the second way is better, but the first way is worth dwelling on as well. The first way requires some visual imagination. Think of Einstein's mind as he contemplated solving a physics problem. Einstein, of course, is synonymous with intelligence. So imagine him sitting there solving a difficult problem. Imagine seeing inside his mind. Imagine seeing his ideas and thoughts, as they move, merge, and collate according to the problem at hand. *Imagine you could see his thoughts as objects.* Maybe a clever animator could produce an animation in which Einstein's thought processes were represented by the movement and interaction of various colored shapes. What we would be seeing with such an animation is intelligence represented in a tangible objective form, laid out in time and space as moving colored shapes and moving colored objects. In fact, it is entirely possible that something like this really goes on in our clever minds—namely, that informational objects (ideas and propositions and such) are interacting with one another, maybe even in a mathematical way connected to "shape" and "fit." My point is that it is not too difficult to see that intelligent mindful processes can involve informational "objects" of some kind and that these could be portrayed as such.

This is exactly what I think life is. We may call it biology, or biologic, and we may look down a microscope at cells and perceive highly organized molecular interactions, but I think what we are really seeing is a living, flowing wisdom, an intelligent process made manifest and objectified in time and space, rather like seeing the contents of "nature's mind" in action. In this light, various species of life are akin to hypotheses—being repeatedly tested to see how well they make sense in the context of the larger environment. Spiders represent one integrated set of hypotheses concerning the art of living (the arachnid approach to how to live and be), lizards another (the reptilian approach to how to live and be). Similarly, an oak tree embodies a deciduous strategy in the art of living; a yew tree embodies an evergreen strategy. Each species, family, phylum, and group of organisms represents a different set of strategies and solutions to the art of living, being, and reproduction, which is to say that each represents a different strand of natural intelligence—akin to smart ideas constantly being put to the test. The intelligence of lizards and spiders—their alternative clever ways of ensnaring insects (by way of a web or a darting sticky tongue) is objectified in their bio-logic, which in turn is an expression of their DNA. Thus, there is a natural intelligence to both their DNA and the biological expressions of that DNA. Life is ingenious and replete with wisdom—all of it, whether individual behaviors or the genetic machinery driving those behaviors. Life is a flexible intelligence forever in action, forever moving, forever changing, forever adapting, forever honing its skills and forever *proving* itself. In other words, life quite literally *learns* over time—it learns to metabolize, hunt, respire, photosynthesize, repair itself, and all manner of other shrewd behaviors. Each one of us, with our various biological functions, is a living testimony to such learning. Given that life learns the art of living over time and has learned to solve all manner of problems in the art of living drives home the reality of life's inherent intelligence.

The second and perhaps simpler and more convincing way to grasp the intelligence of evolving life derives from slime molds. Slime molds are not fungi but single-celled organisms that evolved 600 million years ago at a time when brains had yet to emerge within the web of life. One species of slime mold, called *Physarum polycephalum,* has recently been investigated in depth by scientists. *Physarum polycephalum* is yellow and, although it is unicellular, can be seen with the naked eye and can take on the appearance of a thin smear of slimy mustard. It is often found on rotting logs and could easily be mistaken for a yellow fungus. In 2012 researchers published a paper claiming that this slime mold displayed intelligence. They found that it could learn how to navigate a maze and reach food. What the slime mold did was to explore its immediate environment by sending out tendrils into all parts of the maze until it located food. Once it located food, it would retract all the "useless" tendrils and focus its body on the direct route to the food. It was also observed not to cover ground that it had already explored, meaning that it could sense the slime trails it had previously left. The upshot is that the slime mold can solve the problem of how best to reach food in a new and strange environment—even though it is unicellular and has no brain.

Unsurprisingly, perhaps, many researchers have heralded the slime mold in question as evincing a primitive intelligence despite being devoid of gray matter. There were lots of news stories about this. Even *Scientific American* ran the headline "How Brainless Slime Molds Redefine Intelligence." In other words, it appears to be acceptable to speak of slime molds as displaying a certain degree of intelligence when it comes to food acquisition. The word *intelligence* is being used to appraise a specific kind of purposefully smart behavior.

Given that the slime mold's maze-solving abilities are considered to be intelligent, it is really not beyond the pale to see all of life as intelligent. After all, when you think about it, evolving life is curiously like that slime mold. As a whole, life reaches out in all manner of possible directions (via genetic variations), and those directions that prove to be fruitful (sensible behaviors that lead to an improvement in the art of living and reproduction) become preserved and strengthened, while "dead end" directions (genetic changes that are harmful) will be pruned away (i.e., "retracted"). Which means that life is like a slime mold writ large. Or to put it another way, *the intelligence of the slime mold is a recapitulation of the intelligence of the evolutionary process that engineered slime molds.*

It is important to bear in mind, though, that the intelligence of a slime mold is severely limited compared with life itself. Life has learned much more than how to home in on a food source. Regarding the problem of sustenance, life has learned how to grow food (certain ant species cultivate fungus gardens, for example), how to make food from photons of light (photosynthesis), how to catch food in a silken web (spiders), how to store food (think of nut-burying squirrels), how to graze food, how to hunt food, and how to feed upon seemingly indigestible substrates (think of fungi and bacteria feeding on dead wood or bone). Life is patently not a dumb and mindless thing, but rather an embodiment of an ever-adapting intelligence, regardless of whether it is conscious or not.

Actually, the latter example above brings into focus the intelligence involved in the process of digestion, of how to effectively digest a potential food. How does a herbivore digest, say, grass (which herbivores feed upon) that contains cellulose and is really tough? And how does it thence redistribute any resulting high-energy molecules? Chewing alone will only break the vegetation into smaller bits. How do you actually reduce cellulose molecules into simpler constituents? It is an engineering problem, but one that life has solved (by way of symbiotic bacteria, as it happens). How come life solved it? Because, like a slime mold testing out all possible solutions, life is a natural flowing intelligence that will always find a way to a solution as long as a way exists and can be reached through biological means. To be sure about it, we can apply this same kind of reasoning to all and any other aspect of life we care to think of. Spread thinly across the surface of the planet, life is a smart "protoplasmic film," forever morphing and expressing itself through different creatures, whose skills in the art of living have been selected and honed by the larger system of nature within which this protoplasmic film is embedded. In short, nature is an intelligent system that provokes and sustains intelligent evolutionary processes, processes that engineer intelligent systems of bio-logic. Intelligence is thus apparent on many levels, from organisms to evolution to the various natural laws and forces that govern evolution.

If the reader is still dubious about the use of the word *intelligence,* its root meaning supports a more flexible usage. The root meaning is "to choose between" (from the Latin *inter legere*). This is exactly what happens with evolution. Of the many extant genetic possibilities, the ones "chosen" and preserved by the all-powerful hand of nature are those that make some kind of sense, just as the slime mold tendrils that are "chosen" are the post hoc sensible ones that have alighted upon food. This is the essence of trial and error learning. It may not be a conscious intelligence, but it is a real kind of intelligence nonetheless.

Having said all that, most scientists have yet to conceive that evolving life is a kind of intelligence. Whatever evolves, whatever marvel is witnessed in life—whether a smart insect, a smart fish, a smart plant, or any smart system of bio-logic—it will not be deemed intelligent, nor will the process that formed it be deemed intelligent. Intelligence is something we tend to reserve for ourselves, something connected to the human mind, and we steadfastly refuse to see it as a process that can manifest outside the mind in an unconscious form—unless, of course, that unconscious form is connected with some clever AI robot. So although we will readily "big up" the intelligence of the human mind and the artificially intelligent robots fashioned by the human mind, we will not see the actual physical brain itself (billions of highly organized neurons) as embodying its own kind of intelligence. Nor will we see the genetic processes underlying the construction of the human brain as embodying intelligence. Nor will we see the gradual evolution of such genetic mechanisms as an intelligent process.

As a case in point, although notable biologist Richard Dawkins openly concedes that the immune system is a "very ingenious" part of the human organism (in his book *The Magic of Reality*), he does not see the evolutionary process that led to the immune system as being similarly ingenious. Or at least he does not express such a sentiment. Think about it. Well, actually there are a couple of things to think about here. First off, you may often hear renowned biologists and naturalists talking about how sophisticated some biological behavior is or how smart some creature's behavior is. But they don't really mean to imply intelligence. That is why you don't hear mainstream biologists and naturalists speaking about intelligent design—not because it conjures up religious creationism, but because the word *intelligent* is simply not part of an evolutionary biologist's lexicon. So Dawkins's use of the term *ingenious* is more like a metaphor. But more important is the fact that, as I said, while science might well acknowledge how ingenious some behavior is, the evolutionary process that engineers the genes and protein machinery underlying it is not talked about in the same way. Or if evolution is talked about in such terms, it is metaphorical or poetical. Scientists don't literally think that evolving life is a kind of intelligence. If they did, it would be common knowledge by now and would be delineated in biological textbooks. Yet natural intelligence is unheard of. The slightest suggestion that evolving life evinces intelligence is invariably met with frowns and scorn. If you start invoking intelligence when talking about evolution, you are dismissed—either as an intelligent design creationist fanatic or someone prone to fanciful animistic thinking (interestingly, biochemist Leslie Orgel is famous for asserting that "evolution is cleverer than you are"—but I am pretty sure he did not mean it literally).

It is decidedly strange, all this, especially when you consider the sheer amount of orchestrated bio-logic that underlies and supports human intelligence. Think of an individual neuron, billions of which underlie our minds. Each neuron makes use of electrochemistry to send precise signals. That is synonymous with electricity and is just as impressive an invention as the electricity cables and electronic circuitry we ourselves have created. Moreover, a neuron will recycle the chemical messenger molecules that it uses to connect with other neurons in its vicinity. In addition, the neuron will derive its energy from internal mitochondria, which are symbiotic organelles that have their own DNA. Plus, the neuron can grow and repair itself. And that is just one neuron! Billions of these marvels of nanotechnological engineering coexist and are held together in a magnificent coherency within our skulls. More than that, the entire integrated neuronal system originally emerged from a single microscopic fertilized egg cell. Yet we think it all to be dumb and mindless stuff. As to the process that has shaped the human cortex and engineered these electrochemical neuronal systems, evolution is likewise considered devoid of intelligent characteristics—as is the entire system of nature that governs all and everything.

So how come scientists and creationists alike steadfastly think of evolution as being nonintelligent? What lies at the heart of that widespread attitude? It is probably because when thinking about evolution, we invariably call to mind "random mutations." How can random mutations possibly involve intelligence? If evolution is all random, then how can intelligence or wisdom be involved? Well, what many consistently forget is that random mutations are just one ingredient of evolution—and a lesser one at that. The main ingredient, the most essential and most interesting component, the feature most worthy of contemplation, is natural selection. It should be firmly committed to memory that natural selection is absolutely not random. To reiterate, the changes in DNA that nature selects and preserves are those that in some way or another enhance the art of living. It is this enhancement in the art of living that equates to skilled behavior—anything from better cellular metabolism to better locomotion to better eyesight in the dark to better control of body temperature. All of these evolved skills (and there are any number of examples) are intelligent to some degree (skill implies intelligence)— even though such intelligence is unconscious (or at least it is likely to be unconscious). To put it another way, nature selects at the end of the day changes to DNA that have *proven to be wise,* germane changes that lead to some measure of acumen in the biological art of living. Thus, natural selection equates to intelligence—even though this intelligence is autonomous and unconscious (as it is with slime molds). The only real difference between human intelligence and the natural intelligence of life itself is that human intelligence is conscious, has foresight, and is expressed in relatively short amounts of time compared with the evolving web of life, whose intelligence is unconscious and operates over much longer stretches of time.

If you still can't see this, then think of a series of selected changes to a genome; for example, the long series of DNA modifications that led from standard-issue land mammal feet to the sleek flippers of seals (flippers still have finger bones inside). Imagine it took fifty mutations occurring over half a million years to achieve this change. The entire sequential process—nourished, highlighted, selected, and preserved by nature—can be viewed as a naturally intelligent response to living in water.

But why, one might ask, is the paradigm of natural intelligence important? Why bang on about it? Why battle with orthodoxy and invite abject criticism from mainstream biologists and even intelligent design creationists? Well, there are a number of good reasons to embrace this new view of life. First off, I think it has truth value. In other words, I think it is a more apt way of appraising life on earth. For instance, the current "official" definition of evolution is something along the lines of a "change in gene frequencies over time." This is so lame. To consider the eye or the tiger to which it belongs as little more than a result of changing populations of genes is to totally miss the wonder, splendor, complexity, and engineering triumph that is a seeing tiger. It is akin to looking at a smartphone, taking it apart, and then declaring that it is little more than a collection of components whose number, size, and shape have changed over time since the original invention of mobile phones. Or it is akin to describing the development of automobile engines as a change in the frequency of engine parts over time. Where is the allusion to ingenuity and acumen? Where is the recognition of nature's engineering genius? Every part of a tiger, every cell in its body, along with the genetic mechanisms hidden deep inside those cells, all move and behave in a naturally intelligent manner. Such orchestrated bio-logic is a real technology, nanotechnology, in fact, and far more advanced than our own nanotech.

I am reminded of a definition of life I once heard from an academic biologist. I had joined a forum on the Internet, a quite popular one that dealt with evolution as well as certain philosophical and metaphysical issues. I had asked this learned academic chap if he was ever tempted to speak of organic life as a technology. For me this kind of liberal terminology was normal, but he seemed perplexed by my thinking. So I explained that if we had never seen life under a microscope before, then on first seeing it we might think that it was an advanced technology of some kind, especially given the amazing nature of genetic processes (check out a textbook or watch animations on YouTube showing genetic processes, and you will see what I am getting at). This academic chap was adamant that life was not a technological phenomenon but simply "stuff what does things." I quote him here as I committed his terse reply to memory. Although his bad grammar was doubtless tongue in cheek, I am certain he meant what he said—namely, that life is nothing more than "interesting stuff." Maybe he was thinking along the lines of snowflakes. As we all know, snowflakes form into complex and interesting shapes on their own accord. One could say that atmospheric water in the presence of sub-zero conditions becomes "interesting stuff what does things." I think that this is what he was driving at, that life was not a natural organic technology but just bits and pieces behaving in a curiously interesting way. Just appealing patterns.

Well, what can you say to that? Here's what I reckon. Life is not simply like a snowflake. *To be like life, a snowflake would have to actively maintain a freezing temperature even when surrounding conditions were warming up.* If a snowflake could do that, if it could build nanotech heat-dumping machinery within itself (out of highly organized ice crystals) and thence keep itself frozen when all around it was sunny and warm, then it would indeed be akin to a living organism—inasmuch as it would be able to sustain its structure and pattern by actively controlling the flow of energy through it. Of course, that would make it an ultrasmart snowflake, right? If we built a snowflake like that, if the world's best engineers crafted a self-sustaining snowflake whose core consisted of ice crystal machinery that enabled it to keep itself frozen even in a warm environment, it would make headlines in every newspaper around the globe. It would be the very epitome of intelligent purposeful design—and not merely "stuff what does things." For the "things" in question are in actuality skillful behaviors. Intelligent and wise behaviors, in other words. Which is exactly what living cells continually demonstrate. Smaller than snowflakes, living cells are chockablock with remarkably nifty nanotech machinery. Ribosomes, for instance. These organelles—which are responsible for converting DNA into the Lego-like proteins I mentioned earlier—are routinely referred to as nanotech machines. Which they are. Yet they never make the news headlines. Presumably because the majority of scientists think it is all just "stuff doing things" and nothing more.

There are even error-correcting mechanisms inside cells. These enable DNA translations to be checked so that mistakes are not made. So not only do we have a sophisticated genetic code being read out by nanotech machines, there are error-checking machines in operation too. There are also sections of DNA that represent "start" and "stop" in genetic translation processes. As I mentioned above, animations have been made that show some of this amazing activity. The imagery is quite stunning. If you watch such videos or read up on the processes portrayed, you will immediately see why I suggested to the aforementioned academic chap that life was an advanced technology. Yet we have taken all these findings in our stride, and no one raises an eyebrow. As ever, we take life and its ability to evolve totally for granted. It is like evolutionary scientists are saying: "Move on, people; there is nothing more of interest to see here."

The tendency to take life for granted and disregard its innate intelligence is detrimental in a number of ways. After all, the way we view life will determine how we live life. If we don't see the biosphere as a network of living wisdom, we will not likely seek to learn from it. Think of sustainability (a buzzword nowadays) and the fact that life has already learned this art. Life has persisted for more than three-and-a-half billion years. There are rainforest ecosystems that have sustained themselves for millions of years (I have been fortunate enough to have visited some in Malaysia). How do they achieve this? How do thousands and thousands of species maintain coherency for such an inordinate span of time? Venture into such rainforests and you will smell and hear the inherent biological health and vitality. Every creature in its allotted place. A mesh of interrelated processes with an inherent wisdom that has evolved to be like that—because it works. Indeed, if it did not work, there would be no long-lived rainforests. It is the hand of nature again, the "natural choosing" of behaviors that make some sort of sustainable ecological sense in the long run. So whereas it might make good survival sense to be wholly selfish and act in a thick-skinned way to everything else that lives in your vicinity, it makes *more sense* in the long term, and the payoff is greater, if you can *cooperate* in some way. This is the essence of long-lived ecosystems. Cooperation works and ensures sustainability. That is why there is effectively a division of labor in a rainforest and why there is an extremely complex tangle of relationships and feedback cycles. It also means that we should be attempting to follow suit. We would therefore do well to see ourselves not as the stewards of life on earth, as you often hear, but rather as potential *apprentices*.

Although natural intelligence and natural wisdom saturate the biosphere, we never seem to give them a second thought. To be sure about it, we think of the biosphere mainly as a set of resources. What can we get from this forest? What can we extract and extrude from this ecosystem? What can we take out of this ocean? How can we exploit the chemical-production capacities of these bacteria? Which crop genes can we shuffle around to improve control of the global market? How can we remove this lake or reshape this piece of wilderness? The biosphere is so big that this cavalier and blundering way of life of ours has continued unchecked for thousands of years. Now, however, our decimation of the planet is reaching a point of no return. Our behavior is compromising the very integrity of the biosphere and exacerbating climate change. It is simply impossible to carry on with business as usual forever. Something has to change in the way we relate to the rest of life on earth. Hence my call for a new view of what life on earth is.

Consider also our attitude toward fossil fuels such as coal, oil, and gas, in particular the way we take them for granted and rarely consider the role of natural intelligence in their origin. The entire industrial revolution was built upon coal. Later, oil was used as well, chiefly to fuel engines. The beauty of fossil fuels is that they will often gush out of the depths of the earth, and a lot of energy can be had from them. As Bill McKibben attests in his book *Eaarth,* a single barrel of oil yields as much energy as twenty-five-thousand hours of manual labor. That is why oil is so valuable and why half of the world's top ten biggest companies deal in fossil fuel. In fact, oil is so important that its price is tied to recessions. It is easy to see why this "black gold" is so central to our cultural operating system. It commands value and importance because it pertains to energy. Energy is everything. If you look at life, one of its chief attributes is precisely the control of energy. Metabolism, in other words. No metabolism, no life. So just as a carefully controlled flow of energy is absolutely crucial for all living things, so too does human culture depend on it. If we turned off the electricity everywhere on earth, how long would normalcy last? It would not be too long before total chaos set in. A carefully managed flow of energy underscores life and human culture alike.

Now, the thing to think about here is the origin of our energy. Regardless of peak oil and atmospheric carbon pollution, the fact is that much of culture still runs on fossil fuel. But how come it is available? How come the earth is "packing" it? While we may dimly know that coal and oil originate from ancient plants, our thinking doesn't go much deeper. This is where expanded thinking kicks in because it can facilitate an appreciation of the natural intelligence working behind the scenes (or *supporting* the scenes, as is actually the case). What oil really is, what oil really represents, is the quintessence of millions of years of naturally intelligent behavior. Plants photosynthesize, and this remarkably sophisticated method of feeding upon sunlight (as well as water and carbon dioxide) produces sugars and other stored plant products that are rich in energy. These energy riches get buried en masse and eventually become converted over the eons into handy deposits of oil and coal. An oil vein under the earth is like a vast battery that contains ancient sequestered sunlight, a battery made by naturally intelligent botanical activity that we have plugged into in order to fuel our energy-intensive way of life.

So what happens when you keep thinking through all this? What kind of bigger picture emerges when you join the naturally intelligent dots? Well, it is perhaps best summed up by architect and futurist Buckminster Fuller, who back in 1968 wrote the following in his book *Operating Manual for Spaceship Earth:*

The fossil fuel deposits of our Spaceship Earth correspond to our automobile's storage battery which must be conserved to turn over our main engine's self-starter. Thereafter, our "main engine," the life regenerating processes, must operate exclusively on our vast daily energy income from the powers of wind, tide, water, and the direct Sun radiation energy.

The gist of this way of looking at things is that the biosphere has wired itself in such a way that it can build upon its past endeavors and, ultimately, launch a sustainable human culture based upon renewable energy. The situation is reminiscent of the Ouroboros, the tail-eating serpent of ancient myth. The idea is that the serpent sustains itself by consuming its past handiwork (i.e., its tail). Useful work (like photosynthesis) is preserved in the form of energy-rich products, and these can be used to fuel future work. As Fuller attests, the prudent course of action is to use this handy biospherical legacy to create renewable and sustainable forms of energy. That would be the wise thing to do, the wise way to think about peak oil and the exacerbation of global warming by human-generated carbon dioxide emissions. We need to be using these last reserves of oil not to power new fracking ventures and new searches for oil but to power research into new clean technologies. Nature has provided us with what we need. The only thing we really lack is the right attitude, the right way to conceive of the biosphere. We need to realize that *we are the biosphere,* or at least we are a means through which the biosphere has become conscious of itself (more than this, we are the way the universe becomes conscious of itself). If this realization were to become widespread, I'll wager it would do wonders for our long-term future on board Spaceship Earth.

In my opinion, this is the psilocybin mushroom's most important virtue—its ability to reorient the human psyche to become more attuned to the wisdom inherent in the biosphere rather than simply its resources. Sure, we depend upon those resources, and we have to make use of them, but how we use them and how we think about them are actually more important parts of the interactive equation. As we are effectively natural intelligence in its latest expression, the sooner we realize this, the sooner we wake up to what we actually are and what duties we have been handed by the larger biospherical system that sustains us, the sooner we can begin to create an ecofriendly culture that will fit in with the rest of life and can persist healthily into the foreseeable future. To ignore that option, to keep taking everything for granted from the biosphere while failing to regenerate it, well, that is assuredly a recipe for a terminal disaster.

For all these reasons I submit that the merit of the natural intelligence paradigm lies in its ability to radically change, and improve, our attitude toward life on earth. Rather than seeing life as little more than "interesting stuff what does things," or "interesting stuff that we can exploit," or "interesting stuff that we can patent," we can instead see life as a living wisdom that we can learn from, share in, and even celebrate. Indeed, natural logic dictates that in order for human culture to persist and thrive, it must perforce fit in with this greater wisdom. This means a culture that is more organic and more ecologically regenerative. As yet, cities and technologies stand out like sore thumbs from the rest of life on earth. Much of a city consists of dead surface areas. Where are the road surfaces that absorb traffic pollutants or garner energy from passing vehicles? Where are the high-rise building surfaces that metabolize and make clean, fresh oxygen? More important, why aren't green roofs everywhere? Indeed, why are cities not overwhelmed with greenery and vegetation planted in all possible areas? Not only would this make for a lush urban environment able to stimulate both biophilia and fresh air production, it would also stimulate and nourish biodiversity—such as bee life, butterfly life, and bird life. For too long we have cocooned ourselves away from the rest of the web of life, divorcing ourselves more and more from the earth's ecosystems. The root of the problem is this notion that life is nothing more than a kind of accidental prop and that only we are truly smart. With that kind of perspective, with human intelligence the only kind of "advanced" intelligence, it is no wonder we have such an exploitative attitude toward the biosphere. We just do our own thing and to hell with the larger biosphere.

Actually, our usual notion of what exactly constitutes advanced intelligence shows how blinkered we can be. Think of SETI, the search for extraterrestrial intelligence. One search technique employed by SETI is to look at radio signals emanating from distant star systems and to see whether there is some nonrandom element—a sign of an advanced manipulating intelligence, in other words. If you have seen the sci-fi movie *Contact,* you will recall that Jodie Foster's character discovers just such a significant signal. In that movie, a repeating series of pulses are found to embody prime numbers—2, 3, 5, 7, 11, etc. This implies that an alien intelligence encoded the signal because a lengthy series of prime numbers represents a non-random mathematical language that any advanced intelligence in the universe would likely be wise to and would notice. The language of mathematics cuts through subjective languages. Extraterrestrials would be unlikely to send a binary encoded message in their native tongue because it would be hard to decode. But mathematics is universal, and so specific sequences of numbers such as prime numbers make for a far better message. At least that is the reasoning. Such an advanced ET intelligence could also have utilized the Fibonacci series instead of a prime number sequence. The Fibonacci series is a string of numbers in which each number is the sum of its two predecessors—such as 1, 2, 3, 5, 8, 13, 21, etc. If SETI scientists discovered a radio signal embodying the Fibonacci series, then a communicative alien intelligence would be invoked to account for its origin.

The interesting thing is that the Fibonacci series actually occurs in nature. For instance, the spiral-shaped seed arrangements in both sunflowers and pine cones embody it. It can also be found in the arrangement of leaves around plant stems. The reason for such botanical phenomena usually pertains to optimum spacing strategies and is a typical expression of naturally intelligent behavior. Yet SETI scientists are not interested in this kind of organic Fibonacci "signal." It is not what they are looking for.

I wrote an essay entitled "Psilocybin and the Concept of Natural Intelligence" (*PsyPress UK* 2, 2014) that mentioned the remarkable occurrence of the Fibonacci series in nature and how we essentially dismiss it:

This . . . is not received as evidence for natural intelligence, just as the ability of plants to nanotechnologically print out 3-dimensional leaves or the ability of spiders to spin webs are not seen as expressions of natural intelligence. . . . A radio signal from space is one thing, an earthly organism is another. And it is not hard to see why the latter is overlooked. We have an image in our minds as to what constitutes an advanced non-human intelligence. We want a being of some kind, an alien, with a definite form, perhaps even hominid-like. As with traditional conceptions of God, what we cannot seem to imagine is that intelligence is an inherent property of nature and that it flows throughout the universe. In fact, our very bodies are spun from natural intelligence. But since we take bio-logic for granted (until we get ill or face death) we tend to view bio-logic and the evolutionary forces which weave together systems of bio-logic as being devoid of intelligence. Which means that we look hopefully afar for signs of advanced non-human intelligence when it is actually all around us and, indeed, inside us.

So once again we ignore natural intelligence. We continually revere our own intelligence but deny intelligence, even unconscious intelligence, to the larger system of nature that engineered us. We may even rave over artificial intelligence (clever robots and clever computer systems), yet we do not get very excited about the natural intelligence that the AI community often attempts to mimic. Apart, that is, from biomimicry researchers, who, bucking the trend, are most definitely interested in natural intelligence, because their aim is to "consciously emulate nature's genius" (this is how the Biomimicry Institute describes its work on its official website). The bottom line, though, is that very few scientists (or philosophers) seem prepared to state that nature has intelligent characteristics. You could argue that scientists don't want to risk getting mixed up with intelligent design creationism or that they are still recoiling from centuries of unquestioned religious dogma and so are loathe to embrace metaphysically potent ideas—but I suspect something deeper is at work.

Over the years I have come to the conclusion that the persistent refusal to acknowledge natural intelligence is actually due to a conceptual blind spot. Just as there is a blind spot in the visual system (the part of the retina where all the "wiring" goes through), which we are generally unaware of, so too does there seem to be a blind spot in our conceptions of nature. Whereas we get very excited over the concept of an advanced alien intelligence (meddling with human DNA or not), we cannot sense that same kind of advanced intelligence as a fundamental property of life and the laws and forces of nature that serve to evoke life. When you consume psilocybin, however, the miracle of life really hits home, and you can perceive natural intelligence directly. The blind spot is obviated. Something as simple as a leaf can then be seen for what it really is—namely, a sophisticated and breathtakingly wonderful example of organic technology. Here, for instance, is a further extract from the same essay mentioned earlier, in which I describe ivy as viewed under the influence of psilocybin. With normal perception and normal conception, a common plant like ivy would not be given a second thought:

> As my friend pointed out, each individual ivy leaf, whether small or fully grown, was *perfectly* formed. No more than a few millimeters thick and a few centimeters long, each veined leaf looked polished. There was a healthy radiant sheen to them. And they looked printed. Well, not just printed in any old way, but at maximum resolution on the finest quality glossy inkjet paper. Indeed, we began to imagine how hard it would be to print out such a leaf using conventional printer technology. Sure, you could purchase high quality glossy paper and use high quality color ink. And you could even print on both sides of the paper. But all you would get would be a flat 2-dimensional simulacrum of a leaf. It might be glossy and radiant, it might even fool an unsuspecting observer, but it would lack the 3-dimensional biological complexity of a real ivy leaf. Even if you sandwiched some nifty wafer thin pieces of electronic circuitry between the two sides of paper, you could not hope to mimic the full complement of bio-logic inside real leaves. Living things have a highly organized molecular complexity about them impossible to simulate artificially.

I do not recall exactly how long we remained rapt in awe over these incredible ivy leaves, but we soon began to ponder further the ability of ivy DNA to print out innumerable perfect 3-dimensional structures. It became clear that we were privy to some kind of *organic technology* wielded by nature, a technology that for most of us goes unattested and unsung but which, through the aid of psilocybin, was becoming overwhelmingly evident. In order to produce leaves, the ivy organism had perforce to construct them one cell at a time according to some master plan held within its DNA. And it was indeed a kind of printing, albeit achieved with precisely orchestrated protein as opposed to paper and ink.

Although the term "printing" might seem to overly stretch the definition of what it means to print something, plants really do perform a kind of printing process in that they are endowed with the technological prowess to make hundreds, or even thousands, of identical leaf structures, each leaf packed with photosynthetic machinery. Just as a 2-dimensional leaf pattern can be repeatedly printed out on a computer's printer according to a digital file [or how a resin-based 3D leaf can be printed with a 3D printer], so too can a plant print out real 3-dimensional leaves according to digital DNA files residing in its genome. The two processes are analogous to the extent that specifically organized information in one form is being sequentially translated into another specific form.

So why do we have a blind spot? Notwithstanding the psilocybin experience, why are we unable to acknowledge natural intelligence? Why do we see ourselves as smart but don't grant smartness to the cortical bio-logic that underlies our smart minds? And why do we not grant smartness to the evolutionary process that engineered the human cortex in the first place? Maybe it is because we are practical creatures who, in order to survive in the world, need to view living things in a purely pragmatic way. After all, if we just sat round all day marveling at how amazing leaves are, nothing would get done! Indeed, psychedelic pioneer Aldous Huxley reckoned that the typical way humans look at the world is utilitarian, inasmuch as we look at the world in terms of potential resources of one kind or another; whereas, according to Huxley, psychedelic perception grants one access to a bigger and more real world. So it might well be that the human psyche has evolved certain "restrictions," conceptual blind spots, akin to taboos maybe, that prevent us from being overly dazzled by living things. Yet this blind spot, or taboo, is circumvented by the mushroom. With it we may suddenly see life for what it is and thereby sense and feel the natural intelligence that courses through all things.

There is also the problem of the human ego. This can be so big as to negate anything that might threaten its self-proclaimed lofty stature. We are surely the most big-headed species to have walked the earth. We idolize our technology; we build statues of people; we cheer for people in power; we wave flags to glorify our various groups; we are basically so self-absorbed as to be oblivious to other reference points. In other words, we live in a vain and anthropocentric world. Certain plants and certain insects are deemed pests, but never us—and this is despite the fact that we are the most ecologically destructive species on the planet. A city fox is reviled for raiding a bin, but our own raiding of the biosphere is overlooked. Similarly, a miniature insectile flying robot made by robotics engineers is acclaimed, whereas the real insect it mimics generates little interest in comparison. Technology must consist of machinery of some kind and must be made by us for it to be called "technology." The same applies to the notion of design—it is something we alone excel at, not nature.

On the other hand, we readily talk about *natural selection* (as opposed to human selection). This phrase is not even restricted to scientists. Darwin's great idea and his chosen terminology have spread far and wide and become popular parlance. Given that natural selection is now a wholly accepted part of our lexicon, I think it is perfectly feasible to talk about natural design, natural technology, and, of course, natural intelligence. What we need to take on board is that the processes our brains facilitate (our intelligence) are not wholly novel but are a relatively new expression of previous kinds of intelligence. In other words, with a small effort we can overcome the aforementioned conceptual blind spot and see that evolving life is an unconscious intelligence that has engineered brains that facilitate a new sort of intelligence with conscious foresight. That is what makes the human mind different from the larger "mind of nature." Whereas the intelligence of evolving bio-logic is rooted in the living moment (genetic and biological behavior that makes sense is preserved and sustained), conscious intelligence can see ahead and operates at a different speed and with different dynamics. But it is still part and parcel of natural intelligence.

The upshot is that we are natural intelligence in its latest ongoing expression. Through the medium of consciousness, we are nature perceiving itself. We are evolution become aware of itself. We are, in fact, the very cosmos in the act of knowing itself. That is precisely the kind of innervating realization galvanized by psilocybin. When the doors of perception are thrust open and cognitive blind spots diminish, we see that we are an intimate part of an astonishingly smart process, fulfilling some kind of important function. As a species, we just don't know it yet.

So there you have it. I have said my bit concerning my idée fixe. What made me say it was the mushroom, or at least what I learned from innumerable psilocybin voyages. At least I can spread the blame if accused of some kind of intellectual blunder. But I really think the time for the natural intelligence paradigm is upon us. I even like to think that in the not too distant future it will be perfectly normal to talk about natural intelligence when describing animal behavior, botanical behavior, genetic processes, ecological processes, and biospherical processes and even when discussing the significance of consciousness. Maybe the notion of natural intelligence needs to be stated again and again so that we get used to it. So let me be blunt. Life is a natural intelligence. Evolution is the methodology of natural intelligence. And so too do the creative laws and forces of nature embody natural intelligence. Such intelligence might be unconscious (presumably), but it is gradually and inexorably becoming conscious through evolved nervous systems. As I once overwhelmingly felt while bemushroomed, consciousness is the way this fantastic system of nature wakes up to itself and is reborn. Long may this awesome realization continue to unfold.

4
The Powell Report

⌒⌒⌒

One would assume that politics has nothing whatsoever to do with consciousness. One would think that politicians have no business policing the chemicals employed by neurons in the brain. One would think that grown adults would be able to alter or expand their consciousness in whatever way they choose as long as they do not injure or endanger anyone in the process. Even if there is some degree of potential health danger in such a pursuit, one would still assume that it would be deemed socially acceptable in the same way that potentially dangerous pursuits like rock climbing, snowboarding, and white water rafting are deemed socially acceptable. Alas, none of this is so. The last century has seen a politically driven "war on drugs"—or, to be more accurate, a "war on some drugs some of the time." In fact, the war is specifically against drug users (i.e., people) and not drugs. So it is really the "war on some people who use some drugs." This "pharmacratic inquisition," as some have called it, has seen an inordinately oppressive reaction by the establishment to those who choose to alter their consciousness through psychoactive substances. Drugs are dangerous, we are told. They cause harm. They are bad for you. Above all, they are *wrong and immoral*. Those who indulge in illicit drugs are dodgy and depraved citizens in need of harsh chastisement. No surprise then that there is apparently no such thing as illicit drug use, only illicit drug *abuse.* If you make use of illicit drugs, you are an abuser, not a user. To be sure, if you utilize illicit drugs, you are indulging in *criminal behavior.* Moreover, the psilocybin mushroom has been tarred by this legislative madness and is pretty much prohibited everywhere on the planet. Can you believe that? Almost everywhere on the earth, wholly natural *Psilocybe* fungi are subject to prohibition, their possession carrying criminal implications.

Certain other drugs, however, are totally licit and are part and parcel of the fabric of society. Take alcohol. Alcohol is so ingrained within Western culture that you are more likely to find a pub or a new liquor store in any given town or village instead of a library or an old church. Alcohol consumption is everywhere. Drinking beer or wine or vodka is pretty much de rigueur these days. We invariably chuckle and wink knowingly if someone starts to tell tale of a previous night's hard drinking. Those who choose not to drink are the odd ones out. Yet alcohol kills millions of people every year. For instance, a recent study published in *The Lancet* estimated that around one in twenty-five deaths around the world were attributable to alcohol consumption.* That is an astonishing and lamentable statistic. Yet alcohol is still advertised on prime time TV, where we see good-looking young people dancing the night away followed by a brief and almost subliminal warning to the tune of "please drink responsibly"—even though, of course, alcohol inebriation precludes self-control.

As for the U.K. in particular, where I happen to live and where heavy drinking is an extremely popular pastime, current statistics show that one million people per year are admitted to the hospital on account of alcohol. I dread imagining what hospital emergency wards are like late on a Friday night. Can you imagine all those drunken

*See www.thelancet.com/series/alcohol-and-global-health (accessed December 2014).

idiots staggering around zombie fashion and discharging verbal abuse and vomit? Not to mention all the domestic and street violence that stems from drunkenness. How many women, through the ages, have been beaten senseless by foul-mouthed, drunken husbands? How many children have suffered the belt at the hands of a drunken father? How many stylish whiskey bottles have been smashed ungraciously over heads? And yet alcohol is not even talked about as a drug! Even though, of course, it certainly is a drug—the definition of a (psychoactive) drug being a substance that alters the mind and behavior. Thus, to talk of drugs and alcohol is skewing things right from the start. That we do regularly hear the term *drugs and alcohol* shows that language has been corrupted according to certain social and commercial forces.

The drug nicotine is just as notorious and likewise kills in large numbers. Not on its own, though, because nicotine itself is not so dangerous. It is the method by which nicotine is obtained that is the problem—mainly by way of burning tobacco, which releases all manner of noxious harmful substances alongside the desired nicotine (one could imagine similar ill health effects if we obtained caffeine by burning coffee beans and inhaling the smoke). More addictive than heroin, nicotine-containing tobacco smoke kills some 6 million people worldwide each and every year.

As with alcohol, this kind of statistic seems curiously routine and does not raise an eyebrow. If, however, someone dies from MDMA (ecstasy) or someone overdoses on heroin, it is often big news. Spy bottles of booze and cartons of cigarettes in a movie star's house, and no one gives a damn. Spy a mirror, a razor blade, and some cocaine, though, and all hell breaks loose. In blockbuster films we regularly see DEA officers out to seize shipments of this popular white powder. Where is much of this lucrative powder headed? Why, Hollywood, the very place where they make such movies! That's because, like pop stars, people in the Hollywood movie industry have enough cash to indulge in heavy cocaine use. Yet cocaine use is still deemed sinful and immoral, while alcohol and tobacco use is considered routine behavior.

In the United States, the drug situation is peculiar indeed. How many presidents do we hear ranting on about the menace of illicit drugs? How many times have we heard the political cry of "zero tolerance for drugs!"? You would think the world was being driven into an early grave—not because of global warming or ecological destruction or relentless material consumption, but simply because too many people are smoking joints, snorting cocaine, or popping ecstasy pills. And yet recent studies in the United States have shown that *deaths from overdosing on legally prescribed painkillers outnumber deaths from heroin and cocaine combined!**

One wonders at the role played by pharmaceutical companies in all this. Obviously, they are complicit in the painkiller trade. It's big business. And with big business, human life takes a back seat to the dollar. In the U.K. not so long ago a legislative change allowed the drug codeine to become available without a prescription. This meant that any adult could buy it over the counter. As it is an opiate and is related to heroin, the sedating effects of codeine can be quite pleasant, and thus one can see why it is an addictive substance (ironically, the prolonged use of codeine can cause headaches—which may encourage a user to take more of it). As to the number of codeine addicts in the U.K., recent studies estimate that more than thirty thousand people are addicted to painkillers containing codeine. That's a sizable number and warrants concern. My point is not to bash codeine (it's an effective painkiller), only to contrast the problems associated with accepted licit drugs with those associated with

---

*See www.drugfreeworld.org/drugfacts/prescription/abuse-international-statistics.html.

demonized illicit drugs. It is clear that culture operates with double standards. The media and the government are quick to point a finger of disgust at illicit drug users but will overlook the bigger problems associated with licit drugs such as alcohol, tobacco, and painkillers, along with the faceless industry giants who control their manufacture and distribution. Something has been awry in the collective psyche for far too long.

So why, exactly, are some drugs morally acceptable while others are deemed pernicious and worthy of endless media condemnation? Why are the authorities so oppressive and so keen to threaten people who use illicit drugs? Especially given the fact that there is an insatiable demand for drugs—a demand, I might add, that is generally catered to by ruthless armed gangs. And in the case of psilocybin in particular, what is it about this substance that has made the authorities classify it among the most harmful of all psychoactive substances? The long-revered psilocybin mushroom is currently classified alongside heroin and crack cocaine. Right across the globe too. How on earth is this possible? How did something considered a sacred sacrament in Mexico come to be deemed exceedingly harmful and corruptive? Either I am a criminal of the highest order for writing *The Psilocybin Solution* and this book or the politicians and the authorities have completely misjudged psilocybin and are misguiding the populace.

Having pondered long and hard on the "war on some drugs some of the time" and having heard the same old stern nannylike moralizing coming from politicians year in and year out, my conclusion is that the establishment is stuck in an irrational mindset that harks back to some older era when pleasure was connected with vice and sin. We might think we have moved on from those repressive guilt-laden times, but this is not so. In other words, politicians who snarl and snap at illicit drug use and wish to oppress drug users are like those historical figures who had hang-ups about homosexuality and people of a different race and who went out of their way to persecute them. There is some sort of irrational fear or guilt over that which is unfamiliar and perceived to be a threat. There may also be prevailing religious notions that serve to support such persecution.

Needless to say, the irrational political will to prohibit the possession of popular recreational drugs is terrific news for the armed criminals who are currently in charge of their manufacture and supply. What could be better for drug lords than politicians asking for stricter forms of drug prohibition? The profits to be made from illegal drugs are so vast that it is customary for drug cartels to slaughter one another, along with any innocent people who happen to get in the way. No wonder then that at the height of his illicit empire infamous cocaine magnate Pablo Escobar had bribed and killed his way to a whopping personal fortune of 3 billion dollars. Even when he and his cartel were fatally taken down, other gangs were only too happy to take over the lucrative reins. In fact, according to research from the United Nations, the worldwide trade in illicit drugs is estimated to be worth some 320 billion dollars per annum, which is almost 1 percent of the world's GDP. The trade is right up there with oil and arms. And the bulk of the sales are in the United States, the very country where the war on some drugs some of the time is so forcibly waged.

We should also give pause to the various *industries* that profit from current drug legislation. As well as the alcohol production industry, lawyers and prison contractors also come to mind. As the eye-opening 2012 documentary *The House I Live In* shows, big dollars are at stake when it comes to the criminalization of large sectors of the populace (incredibly, fully 1 percent of the U.S. population is serving time in prison; many are there for nonviolent drug possession). Think of all those armies of people involved in well-funded sting operations who get to kick down doors and prosecute illicit drug users. Then there are all those lawyers and judges who make large hourly sums of money processing an endless stream of drug cases. Plus the privatized prison industry that requires an endless supply of inmates. The war on some drugs some of the time is thus big business to those on both sides. Legalizing drug use would spell an end to most drug gangs and an end to antidrug officers and antidrug bureaucrats. No one is in a hurry for that. It is easier to keep the status quo than it is to change policy. That is one thing that all politicians do well—keep things ticking over and thereby sustain their bureaucracies.

One of the worst aspects of all this is the unquestioned notion that drugs cause harm, and therefore it is in the public's interest that they remain illegal. This is part of the legal criteria of how drugs are classified. We should bear in mind that the default status of any psychoactive substance is that it is legal to possess and legal to use. All substances start out that way, and therefore throughout the greater part of human history illicit substances simply did not exist. In other words, a substance is not "born" illicit—but can be condemned as illicit through specific state legislation.

To prohibit the use of a substance (and thereby create a new population of criminals), the authorities have to set out specific criteria regarding what constitutes, say, a Schedule I substance (equivalent to Class A in the U.K.). As it is, Schedule I substances are deemed to be the most harmful and to have no medical application. Notwithstanding numerous published studies on the therapeutic efficacy of MDMA, cannabis, and psilocybin, such classification criteria might still sound reasonable enough. Regarding social harm as opposed to personal harm, if a drug were to make people run around smashing shop windows, then that would certainly be cause for concern, and we would want to restrict its societal presence. Or if a drug made people overtly racist, then that too would be cause for concern in a healthy society that prizes social peace.

Now, harms such as these can be measured. More than that, they should also be self-evident. So what is the actual situation with psilocybin? Leaving aside personal harms for a moment, what social harms are associated with it? I can think of none—at least no obvious ones. Apart from bad trips or the very rare case in which an underlying psychosis is triggered in a vulnerable person, I know of no well-established social harms caused by psilocybin. Which means that *the only real worry with psilocybin is some sort of personal harm.* In fact, it is precisely personal harm that politicians bang on about whenever they talk about psychedelics. That is the bottom line concern—that psychedelics like psilocybin can compromise personal health.

But hang on a minute. If something is potentially harmful to an individual, why on earth would that be a *criminal* issue? Obviously with the examples of potential social harm that I cited (window smashing and racism), there would indeed be criminal implications. But with regard to personal health, there can surely be no crime committed if one is only (potentially) endangering one's own health. Imagine a mountain climber who obtained some ropes, metal anchors, and carabiners from a dodgy online website as opposed to the usual trustworthy channels. Let us say that the gear thusly obtained was cheaply made and therefore a threat to the good health of the climber if he used it. Would we really want to kick down this climber's door and ransack his house for evidence that the individual was in possession of dangerous climbing ropes? And would we really want to send that person in front of a judge to receive a jail sentence or a hefty fine? For the betterment of his health?

Holding the notion of health in your mind, think also about this. Some mushrooms are deadly poisonous. There are a number of such species. One of the most prominent is *Amanita phalloides*. This mushroom is actually the one behind most mushroom fatalities (curiously, they look very dodgy when mature, with a creepy gray-green color). Yet they are totally legal to possess. Naturally, if some knowledgeable police officers were to intercept you carrying a bag of these, they would certainly warn you of the dangers. That would make sense and would be the right and proper thing for the state to do with regard to protecting your health—namely, inform you and educate you of the health dangers that portend. That is the only thing the authorities are obliged to do—because that is their function. They certainly do not need to make possession of *Amanita phalloides* illegal. Indeed, I know of no country that has legislated against deadly poisonous fungi in that way. Yet psilocybin mushrooms—which are *not* deadly poisonous nor even addictive— are nonetheless illegal! Mushrooms that can damage your health to a maximum degree are legal to possess; mushrooms that can potentially give you a whole new look at life and can potentially boost your well-being are illegal to possess. How crazy is that?

Here we begin to see that the relentless war on some drugs some of the time along with the criminalization of drugs users is a kind of scam, a corruption of reason, a fallacy based upon erroneous thinking and erroneous judgments. *Somehow a health issue, through political smoke and mirrors, has become corrupted into a criminal issue.*

I don't know when exactly this corruption first occurred nor why it occurred—the important fact is that it *has* occurred and remains unchecked. Worse, this wholly misguided approach to drug use seems to have gone unchallenged for the entirety of living memory. All through my life I have heard politicians bleating about drug use as if it were akin to child abuse. You'd think users of illegal drugs were all filthy, shivering, depraved wrecks. Yet pretty much everyone I have known in adulthood has used one kind of illegal drug or another. And I don't count myself as mixing with oddballs and miscreants either. I am talking about people I went to university with and people employed in all manner of respectable jobs. Yet all of them have tried cannabis, ecstasy, psychedelics, or cocaine at one time or another. These are not bad people. The average illicit drug user is simply an average person—basically you, me, and almost everybody else.

Let us pursue the health issues surrounding drug use, which ought to be the principal issue of interest to politicians. Take a heroin addict. Now, a heroin addict has to have daily fixes of heroin—in the same way that a diabetic has to have daily insulin injections. By "same way," I mean that each has an intense physiological need for those substances. The addictiveness of heroin is apparently so strong that little can stop an addict securing a fix. If you are hooked on heroin, then you absolutely have to have it, and unless you are in well-paid employment, you will likely have to steal five hundred bucks or so per week to feed your insatiable habit (unsurprisingly, a large percentage of crime is associated with heroin addiction).

Regardless of why people first get involved with heroin (and bear in mind that pop stars and Hollywood actors can get into it as well as those who are down and out), the bottom line is that addicts are physically dependent upon the stuff, and therefore they have a health problem pertaining to chemical addiction. So how best to help them? By treating them as criminals? By propping them before a judge and then throwing them in jail? How on earth is being subjected to a judge and then incarcerated with murderers and thieves going to improve the health of a drug addict? Or how will a fine and a criminal record boost their health? If anything, their overall health will assuredly be worsened. This applies equally to all users of illicit drugs. In other words, we really must face the fact that *all* drug use—whether simply recreational drug use or hard drug addiction—

represents a health issue and not a criminal issue. That we have been conned into thinking of drug use as a criminal issue and that we have accepted doors being kicked in and drug users being thrown into the back of police vans and later into prison is a shameful case of sociopolitical oppression. It is in the same league as witch hunting in medieval times or the criminal treatment of homosexuality in the last century (it is striking to note that the father of modern computing, Alan Turing, killed himself as a result of being hounded by the authorities on account of his homosexuality). It is cruel and unwarranted oppression, plain and simple.

If we genuinely care about the health of citizens, then the only role for the government is to inform and educate the public regarding the health risks of drugs (as well as control their manufacture and distribution—each drug ideally requiring its own policy). Going beyond that and criminalizing drug users in the name of their health is a perverse injustice. It is really quite astonishing that this still goes on every day (note that in 2012, fully one and a half million people in the U.S.A. were arrested for nonviolent drug charges). And don't forget, the criteria for making a drug illegal are chiefly connected with the detrimental effects it has upon health. Drug legislation has always revolved around health and safety concerns. Yet we have seemingly forgotten this in our fervent desire to demonize people. Thus, society pursues policies that are likely to compromise the long-term psychological health of illegal drug users even when the drugs themselves might not compromise long-term health!

This mixing of health issues with criminality can be made clearer by bringing to mind mountaineering again. Some years ago the death toll for those attempting to ascend Mount Everest was about one in ten. I think that may have gone down now due to raised safety standards among guides—but the current death toll for ascending K2 (another big mountain) is *one in eight*. One in eight is not good odds—not good odds at all. If you were to go up K2 with seven other people, the odds are that one of you would not return alive. Attempting to ascend K2 is thus an exceedingly dangerous behavior to engage in. Yet we don't criminalize such mountaineers. Nor do we get large groups of armed burly men to smash down their doors and stick them in jail. In other words, there is no industry based on the persecution of fearless mountain climbers.

Of course we don't do anything like that—mountaineers are adults, and it is their choice what they do. They know the odds, and they make their own decisions. That is what it means to be an adult. If you are an adult, you make your own mind up about things. After all, you are no longer a child. As a grown adult, you can vote, take out a loan, establish a business, start a family, gamble, and so on. And it is your business if, as a grown adult, you want to go up a mountain—or take a drug (or do both, as I once did!). As long as you are not harming anyone else, what business is it of the government what you do? As mentioned, the only responsibility of government officials—if they really care about it—is to provide people with up-to-date, impartial drug facts so that an informed choice can be made. That's it. It is not the government's function to moralize and point fingers at behavior they consider to be immoral. To be more specific, the sole onus of the government in this instance is to *gather information from science, because science can garner impartial data on the potential harms of drugs.* All else is hearsay, whim, and personal bias—something government officials have no right to engage in.

But what on earth would happen if drug use became solely a health issue and was not subject to prohibition, persecution, and criminal injunction? In other words, what would happen if drug prohibition ceased or, in a less drastic scenario, drug use was decriminalized? Would society fall apart? Would there be all-out anarchy and chaos?

In considering such possibilities, it would be good to look at experimental data. Not computer models, but real-world data. Imagine that we could run an experiment in some country where we decriminalized drugs for a number of years in order to observe the outcome. It might sound very unethical to conduct such an experiment, but at least it would yield real-world data and be more instructive than the bellowing and finger wagging of politicians and media pundits, who seem terrified of the notion of decriminalization. Well, strangely enough, this experiment has actually been done. For more than ten years *all* personal drug use has been decriminalized in Portugal. What happened? Is Portugal still on the map? Or did it burn itself out and sink beneath the sea?

Many papers have been written about Portugal's drug policy, and there are conflicting interpretations of the data at hand, but it turns out that problematic drug use has gone down since drugs were first decriminalized there in 2001. Let me cite a 2010 paper by Caitlin Elizabeth Hughes and Alex Stevens:[*]

> While general population trends in Portugal suggest slight increases in lifetime and recent illicit drug use, studies of young and problematic drug users suggest that use has declined. The similarity in general population and youth trends in Portugal, Italy and Spain adds support for the argument that reported increases in general population use in Portugal reflect regional trends and thus are not solely attributable to the decriminalization. Moreover, the fact that Portugal is the only of these nations to have exhibited declines in PDU [problematic drug use] provides strong evidence that the Portuguese decriminalization has not increased the most harmful forms of drug use.

---

[*]"What Can We Learn From The Portuguese Decriminalization of Illicit Drugs?" *British Journal of Criminology* 50, no. 6 (2010): 999–1022.

At the very least then, Portugal has not fallen apart since 2001. After a decade, Portuguese society remains functional. Even if overall drug use remains roughly the same as before, once decriminalization was set in motion, at least drug users are not deemed criminals and do not have to suffer the criminal justice system (the long-term detrimental effects of which are not measured in academic studies). The paper concludes:

> But ultimately, the choice to decriminalize is not simply a question of the research. It is also an ethical and political choice of how the state should respond to drug use. Internationally, Portugal has gone furthest in emphasizing treatment as an alternative to prosecution. Portuguese political leaders and professionals have by and large determined that they have made the right policy choice and that this is an experiment worth continuing. Portuguese policy makers suggest that adoption of such a reform requires time to develop the infrastructure and the necessary collaboration between the criminal justice and health systems. They contend that such reform, while not a swift or total solution, holds numerous benefits, principally of increased opportunity to integrate drug users and to address the causes and damages of drug use.

Lessons can be learned from other countries, such as the Netherlands, where certain drugs are decriminalized. A few years back I went to Amsterdam to attend an ayahuasca symposium (like psilocybin, the psychedelic brew ayahuasca is also prohibited in most countries). Knowing that cannabis was decriminalized in Amsterdam and openly used in coffee shops, I was sure that the city would be in flames. Yet the airport was fine. The public transport system was fine. The hotels were fine. The shops were fine. The streets were fine. The canals were fine. Everything was running fine. In fact, I later learned that there was *less* cannabis use in the Netherlands than in the United States. The same is true of Portugal—there is less drug use there than in the United States. How does that work? And why is the rest of the world not taking note of Portugal or the Netherlands? Why is the rest of the world so keen on oppressing drug users and making criminals out of them? Why does the United States—with some of the harshest drug laws—have some of the highest rates of illegal drug use? In short, why is the war on certain drug users still being fought when it clearly does not work, when the only real issue of consequence is health, and when certain countries have manifestly proven that decriminalization can work?

As I said before, I reckon a kind of scam is afoot. We have been hoodwinked into accepting criminal oppression when there is no crime and no need for oppression. All that is really required to begin formulating a sensible drug policy is objective scientific information concerning objective facts. We don't need politicians nannying on about corrupt youth and decadent behavior, and baying for zero tolerance and more severe forms of punishment. On the other hand, the absurd fact is that when objective scientific advice *is* given, the government is wont to ignore it. Take the case of Dr. David Nutt. Nutt is an interesting chap, as he was once the chairman of the U.K. government's Advisory Council on the Misuse of Drugs. As the name suggests, the purpose of the council is to furnish the government with facts and figures about drug abuse (note the annoying misnomer "misuse" once again). Nutt got sacked because he dared to speak out in an objective way about the relative harms of drugs. The government simply refused to tolerate such an impudent man bandying about scientific facts. However, Nutt's sacking may well have been a blessing in disguise as he soon became involved with an independent scientific committee that spread the same kind of telling facts and figures. No matter how much oppression goes on, no matter how hard traditional modes of demonization are practiced, in the end the truth, as they say, will out.

Operating outside the government, Nutt and his colleagues published a study in *The Lancet* in 2010 that once again looked at the actual harms caused by various drugs, including alcohol and tobacco.* In the study, a table is drawn with twenty psychoactive drugs, including all the well-known ones plus some lesser-known ones, such as GHB (a synthetic drug) and Khat (a psychoactive plant used in the U.K. mainly by Somalis and Ethiopians). These twenty drugs were rated according to various measures of harmfulness. No surprise that alcohol came out on top of the table with the highest measure of harm, ahead of both heroin and crack cocaine. Near the bottom of the table LSD and ecstasy were listed. *Right at the very bottom were psilocybin mushrooms, which were rated as the least harmful of all.* The researchers summed up their report as follows: "Our findings lend support to previous work in the U.K. and the Netherlands, confirming that the present drug classification systems have little relation to the evidence of harm. They also accord with the conclusions of previous expert reports that aggressively targeting alcohol harm is a valid and necessary public health strategy."

It is probably still too soon to know whether studies like this can get through the government's thick skin. Politicians are extremely adept at ignoring scientific data—or at the very least they pick and choose. Thus, as with many issues, social change can be very slow indeed. Drug legislation and the way we think about drugs in general changes inch by inch, decade by decade. But at least the changes have been set in motion. And bear in mind that no one clamoring for drug decriminalization wants a society full of people out of their

---

*David J. Nutt, Leslie A. King, and Lawrence D. Phillips, "Drug Harms in the UK: A Multicriteria Decision Analysis." *The Lancet* 376 (2010): 1558–65.

minds. What we are talking about is, in the main, a new attitude toward the recreational use of those drugs that are no more harmful than alcohol. Nor is it envisaged that children be given drugs.

The key notion to be conveyed then is that adult drug use is a normal part of being human and, as such, should be free from criminal associations and criminal accusations. Indeed, throughout human history psychoactive substances have always been used by human culture where they are available. We enjoy altered states of consciousness. Who, as a child, has not spun around and around in order to get dizzy? Why do children invariably do this? And why do we invariably like the various giddying rides at carnivals and fun-fairs? In each case, it is the love of altered states of mind and altered sensations. We humans are sensation seekers and are naturally curious about altered states of consciousness. It is therefore natural that, as adults, we should have an interest in psychoactive substances. As to their harmfulness, this is something science is best equipped to assess and something that the government can subsequently delineate. That, in fact, is the kind of thing that we taxpayers pay the government to do. Oppression and criminalization have no place in this undertaking.

Let me get very personal at this point. I reckon it is always good to be honest and speak from one's own experience. I am a pretty regular guy. In my younger days I used to live in shared houses where cannabis was regularly smoked. Were we wicked, immoral youths? Did we rub our hands together and cackle about how perversely decadent and demonic we were? After nights spent getting stoned, did we wake up the following morning on some street covered in someone else's blood? Nothing of the sort. We simply enjoyed the recreational virtues of cannabis and used it in the privacy of our own home in the same way people might use alcohol. Only rather than gradually becoming more and more drunk, we experienced a more exotic effect; as I recall, cannabis makes music sound more fascinating and pleasurable. More to the point, every one of us in the house in question had full-time jobs. It is not like we were slackers or criminals.

Sometimes I think I probably overdid the cannabis a bit and would feel tired the next day. Cannabis can also be somewhat addictive—in that you can get used to using it and can start to use it habitually (the same as with alcohol). But I think *serious* cannabis problems are the exception rather than the rule, and I never had any deleterious withdrawal effects from ceasing my use of it. In any case, even if serious cannabis problems were common, this is not an excuse to start being oppressive toward cannabis users and to treat them as criminals. As stated, drug use is, and always has been, a health issue. The sooner drugs are decriminalized and the governments of the world take control over their manufacture, supply, and taxation, the better (note that personal supplies of, say, cannabis or mushrooms could also be grown in one's own home). The war on some drug users some of the time is simply not sustainable in a modern democratic society where freedom, liberty, and the pursuit of happiness are cherished. The phony drug war must, eventually, give way to reason and a new approach based on health and the best way of educating people and minimizing harm. After such education, it is individual adult choice that must prevail.

So how do mushrooms fare in this long-standing political mess? After all, as should be glaringly apparent by now, mushrooms have not escaped the oppressive hands of the establishment. I once saw a film on YouTube that really brought home how crass the law is with regard to the possession and use of psilocybin mushrooms. The clip followed some American (or maybe Canadian) cops as they drove into a forest and arrested a couple of young guys who were out gathering fresh *Psilocybe* fungi. It was a nice-looking forest. The guys seemed like carefree students. On being arrested, they proclaimed their innocence.

After all, what could be more natural than picking wild fungi out of the earth? How could an organism that grows in the wild be an illicit object? How could a natural organic resource, an untainted piece of the web of life, be outlawed? By the end of the clip, however, they were proclaiming their guilt, stating that it was "wrong," what they had done. They had bought into the demonization and guilt scam. They had been hoodwinked.

In the U.K., the mushroom was once free of prohibition and criminal associations. Although pure psilocybin was deemed illegal, the U.K. law had it that the unprocessed mushroom itself was a licit object to be in possession of. Only the deliberate processing of the mushroom was illegal. Thus, an individual could venture out into the countryside and readily collect and consume raw *Psilocybe semilanceata* fungi without fear of the law. And this is what I, and many others, did for years on end every autumn. In any case, this was all done out in the wilds, far from the prying eyes of any law enforcement officials. In all likelihood the police had far more important things to attend to than magic mushroom aficionados (obviously this was not the case with the cops in the aforementioned YouTube clip).

Things changed in 2005. In the wake of the widespread open selling of psilocybin fungi (large tropical varieties such as *Psilocybe cubensis*), Parliament introduced a new bill in which fresh psilocybin fungi became illegal to possess and to consume. It is interesting to see how these changes to U.K. law unfolded—especially as I shall end this chapter with the Powell Report, a document I wrote and sent to Parliament in 2005 in the hope of keeping the U.K.'s indigenous psilocybin mushroom legal. Although I failed in my lobbying, the Powell Report did have the dubious honor of being mentioned in parliamentary debates a few times (it is even mentioned in the prestigious Hansard Records).

The severe change in the law came about because in the few years prior to 2005 large tropical psilocybin mushrooms were being openly sold in markets and shops. At first it was just market stalls. Then the sale quickly spread to high street shops. I recall seeing mushrooms being sold in tacky gift shops in Oxford Street. The mushroom trade even started to make newspaper headlines.

No one seemed to know much about the mushrooms—apart from the fact that they were psychoactive and sold well. Being a long time mushroom user, I felt people needed information about the history behind psilocybin along with knowledge about the importance of set and setting so that they could get the most from the experience. Psilocybin is powerful and, as such, needs to be handled with some modicum of care and caution. By rights, vendors had a duty to educate people as well as take their money.

In light of this, I produced a multimedia booklet explaining all about psilocybin in the hope that the people running mushroom stalls might be able to sell them. But almost all of them turned me down because it transpired that, for various legal reasons, mushrooms could not be openly sold for consumption. Of course, people were buying them to consume them, but legally the vendors could not admit to this and had to state somewhere that the mushrooms were not for consumption. In essence, the sellers had good money coming in and did not want to compromise their trade by offering media that mentioned actual consumption of the mushroom.

Despite there being little interest in my specially made booklet (although author Andy Letcher did cite it in his book *Shroom*), I was not too bothered by this burgeoning mushroom trade—at least not until I saw them being sold in the aforementioned tacky gift shops on Oxford Street. Imagine a cheap, gaudy gift shop selling plastic models of the Queen, plastic nodding bulldogs, and plastic police helmets for kids to wear. Real bottom-end tourist stuff. And then, at the back of the shop, they have a stack of *Psilocybe* mushroom car-tons. That is the kind of thing I kept coming across, because more and more shop owners wanted a piece of the lucrative fungal action. There seemed to be something disturbing about such an approach. Whoever the mushroom producers were, they were clearly going all out to garner as much money as possible and did not care where the mushrooms were being sold, nor did they care about giving infor-mation on set and setting to potential consumers. It was simply an unmonitored booming market. Bigger and bigger bucks were being made. By someone.

All this hit home when I met a fellow—I will call him the Swiss Priest—who wanted, at that time, to publish my book *The Psilocybin Solution*. He was the head of a quasi church in Switzerland that alleg-edly used the psilocybin mushroom as a sacrament. I mean, this was not a brick-and-mortar church; rather, there was an organization that called itself a church over which he apparently presided. He was also involved in the widespread commercial distribution of psilocybin mushrooms. He told me about the "producer." The producer was a Swiss man (or maybe Dutch) who was growing massive quantities of *Psilocybe* fungi in warehouses. Once grown, they were neatly packaged and sent to the U.K. The Swiss Priest apparently knew this producer. Intrigued by the source of high street psilocybin fungi, I enquired as to his particulars. Had this "producer" partaken of the mushroom? Was he a spiritual guy on a spiritual quest to enlighten the masses? Apparently not. Unbelievably, it emerged that the producer had never consumed psilocybin mushrooms—yet he was *selling* millions of them and raking in massive amounts of cash. This seemed to me to be some-what questionable.

Just before my book could go to press, the Swiss Priest was arrested and sent to jail—on account of allegations that his "church" was selling psilocybin fungi to people in countries where they were illicit (hence my book had to go through more rewrites and wait another six years before it finally found a publisher). I had warned him about such a possibility, but he always shrugged it off. At the same time this happened, the U.K. government rushed in a new drugs bill intended to make the possession of fresh psilocybin fungi illegal. Although the aim was to halt the open trade of psilocybin fungi, it also made possession of the U.K.'s indigenous *Psilocybe semilanceata* mushroom illegal too. This irked me. The notion that a natural piece of the English countryside would suddenly become forbidden was absurd in the highest degree—especially given the fact that the mushroom grew everywhere, including in parks and other land owned by the Queen.

In the wake of this bill's being announced, I did my best to dissuade the government from going down the draconian path of prohibition (clause 21 of the bill is the part that deals with the mushroom). This meant that for the first time in my life I got involved in lobbying—which is when you petition ministers to go against the passage of a new bill. It was interesting because I had to learn about parliamentary processes, how new legislation is proffered, processed, and either rejected or passed. Nothing less than the laws of the land were involved. This is very serious business, because once laws are passed, all manner of consequences become apparent. Whereas a new good law might enable culture to operate more smoothly, a new bad law might cause misery, havoc, and, of course, criminal oppression.

My chief argument was that the government now had a good opportunity to instigate some kind of carefully monitored and carefully licensed mushroom trade. In other words, they could set up a way of distributing the mushroom in a judicious and informed manner. And they could also carry on reaping millions of pounds in tax that had already been underway over the previous two years or so.

Unsurprisingly, the government chose not to back off or to amend the bill, so it was eventually passed. What follows is a copy of the original Powell Report that I sent to all those members of Parliament that were involved in passing the bill. I offer the report here, as I think the keen reader interested in the modern history of the psilocybin mushroom may find it of interest. Note that the various germane statements from Professor David Nichols and MAPS president Rick Doblin detailed in the report were garnered by me in an effort to introduce some much-needed scientific data into the debate.

The Powell Report
Drugs Bill—Clause 21

Some Germane Considerations for the Attention of the House of Lords

Prepared by Simon G. Powell, BSc, author and independent witness of current parliamentary events—11 February 2005*

A BRIEF HISTORY OF *PSILOCYBE* MUSHROOMS

The use of magic mushrooms is believed to date back thousands of years. Eight-thousand-year-old rock paintings in Tassili, Algeria, for instance, depict dancing shamans with what appear to be magic mushrooms sprouting from their bodies. Mesoamerican civilizations like the Maya and the Aztecs are also known to have utilized magic mushrooms. From studying the artwork and customs of these historical cultures, researchers determined that the mushroom was accorded a sacred status.

Despite suppression by invading Spanish conquistadors in the sixteenth century, magic mushroom use continued in secret in and around Mexico until being rediscovered by ethnomycologist Gordon Wasson some fifty years ago. Under the guidance of a native Mexican shaman named Maria Sabina, Wasson took part in a religious ceremony in which magic mushrooms were consumed. Wasson went on to introduce the West to the visionary realms potentiated by the mushroom in his various writings. Since that time, we have learned that hundreds of magic mushroom species grow throughout the world. Millions

---

*This document contains background information and highlights the key issues at stake. It also contains testimony from professional experts that calls into question the assumptions driving clause 21. The document has been prepared in a user-friendly and informative way that will not tax the reader.

of people are now familiar with their various psychological effects.

In the U.K., there are a number of psilocybin species to be found in the wild. The author attests that he has located specimens of *Psilocybe semilanceata* throughout the whole of the Lake District, the whole of Snowdonia, the whole of Dartmoor, the Devonshire coast, the Welsh coast, as well as London's Richmond Park and Hampstead Heath. In short, psilocybin fungi are prevalent within the U.K.

The fresh mushroom is not listed in the Misuse of Drugs Act 1971—whereas coca leaf and opium poppies are listed (along with cocaine and opium). This means that the mushroom itself was never intended to be a controlled "substance." Similarly the peyote cactus was not listed either. One assumes that both the mushroom and peyote were not listed because of their long revered history and their relatively benign nature.

DEFINITIONS

Psilocybin, the mushroom's active ingredient, was originally classified as a "psychedelic" in the 1960s. *Psychedelic* means "mind manifesting," and the mushroom does seem to amplify subconscious and unconscious aspects of the mind. Nowadays the mushroom is often referred to as "entheogenic," which indicates that it can generate a deeply spiritual experience. The term *entheogenic* is in contrast to the term *hallucinogen,* which many scientists in the field regard as inaccurate. As leading expert Professor David Nichols (*Pharmacology and Therapeutics* 101: 131–81, 2004) explains:

> What are hallucinogens? This term was originally coined because of the notion that these substances produce hallucinations, an effect, however, that they do not ordinarily elicit, at least at typical dosages. Thus, that name is a misnomer.

Many different names have been proposed over the years for this drug class. The famous German toxicologist Louis Lewin used the name phantastica earlier in this century, and as we shall see later, such a descriptor is not so farfetched. The most popular names, hallucinogen, psychotomimetic, and psychedelic ("mind manifesting"), have often been used interchangeably. Hallucinogen is now, however, the most common designation in the scientific literature, although it is an inaccurate descriptor of the actual effects of these drugs. In the lay press, the term psychedelic is still the most popular and has held sway for nearly four decades. Most recently, there has been a movement in non-scientific circles to recognize the ability of these substances to provoke mystical experiences and evoke feelings of spiritual significance. Thus, the term entheogen, derived from the Greek word "entheos," which means "god within," was introduced by Ruck et al. and has seen increasing use. This term suggests that these substances reveal or allow a connection to the "divine within." Although it seems unlikely that this name will ever be accepted in formal scientific circles, its use has dramatically increased in the popular media and on internet sites. Indeed, in much of the counterculture that uses these substances, entheogen has replaced psychedelic as the name of choice and we may expect to see this trend continue.

EFFECTS

The first Westerner on record to deliberately consume the mushroom was ethnomycologist Gordon Wasson, who took part in a sacred mushroom ceremony in Oaxaca, Mexico, in 1955. Wasson later wrote about the ineffability of the experience in the following way (quoted in *Plants of the Gods,* by Schultes and Hofmann, 1992):

Here let me say a word about the nature of the psychic disturbance that the eating of the mushroom causes. This disturbance
is wholly different from the effect of alcohol, as different as night
from day. We are entering upon a discussion in which the vocabulary of the English language, of any European language, is seriously deficient. . . . For hundreds, even thousands, of years, we
have thought of these things in terms of alcohol, and we now have
to break the bounds imposed on us by our alcoholic obsession.
. . . With skill in our choice of words, we may stretch accepted
meanings to cover slightly new feelings and thoughts, but when
a state of mind is utterly distinct, wholly novel, then all our old
words fail. How do you tell a man who has been born blind what
seeing is like? In the present case this is an especially apt analogy, because superficially the bemushroomed man shows a few of
the objective symptoms of one who is intoxicated, drunk. Now
virtually all the words that describe the state of drunkenness,
from "intoxicated" (which literally means "poisoned") through
the scores of current vulgarisms, are contemptuous, belittling,
pejorative. . . . What we need is a vocabulary to describe all the
modalities of a divine inebriant.

Despite the difficulties in adequately describing psilocybin's
effects, a few basic observations can be made. Colors can appear much
richer. Time may appear to slow down—sometimes dramatically so.
Profound thoughts and insights may come to mind. Things in the
environment may appear to be interconnected and part of some large
pattern, as if everything were moving in a coherent, fluidic way. Even
the most common object may appear fascinating (it is possible that
these kinds of psychological effects occur because the usual associations we have about the world no longer prevail, and we are thus seeing the world as if for the first time). Hallucinations—the seeing of

an object that does not actually exist—are very rare. It is more the case that the world is perceived in a novel way. The House should also note that the mushroom is not addictive. Nor has the mushroom ever fatally poisoned anyone (the lethal dose of the mushroom is so large as to be impossible to consume).

PREVALENCE OF USE WITHIN THE U.K.

Wild magic mushrooms have been gathered and used in the U.K. for thirty years or more (Oxford academic Jeremy Dronfield has even speculated that our ancient ancestors utilized the mushroom for religious purposes). More to the point, in the last sixteen months or so various exotic species of *Psilocybe* mushroom have been sold at market stalls and such, the trade having spread from countries like the Netherlands. It is, of course, concerns over this trade that have prompted clause 21. As for figures for mushroom use in the U.K., a Home Office Report from 2000 (www.homeoffice.gov.uk/rds/pdfs2/hors249.pdf) stated that an estimated 1.5 million adults in England and Wales had taken magic mushrooms (these mushrooms would most likely have been picked from the wild or been cultivated in imported grow kits). Moreover, the report stated that "magic mushroom use is assumed not to be problematic." Indeed, there were no reports of mushroom-related hospitalizations in the section on hospital admissions.

THE IMPLICATIONS OF CLAUSE 21

The House need not be reminded that the illegalization of an organism native to Great Britain is unprecedented. Given that wild psilocybin fungi of one kind or another are prevalent throughout the British countryside, the implications of listing them as a Class A drug alongside heroin and crack cocaine provoke all manner of questions. Such legislation suggests a public health threat of epic proportions. Yet is there any evidence of such a public health threat? A cursory visit to any inner city area on a Friday or Saturday night will not reveal hordes of rowdy mushroom-using miscreants. Indeed, apart from various media stories about the trade in the mushroom, there have been no high-profile negative incidents.

Apart from the impracticalities of outlawing wild psilocybin fungi, the proposed move will make criminals of a large part of the population. From what was said in parliament during the bill's second reading and during the Standing Committee stage, the greatest fear seems to be that the mushroom presents a danger to the mental health of certain susceptible people. Upon what scientific information has this judgment been made? If we assume that the majority of mushroom users are healthy persons (and currently not criminals), then is it sensible to instantly make criminals of them on the grounds that an inferred minority of users will not be suited to the mushroom's effects? If harm reduction is one of the prime functions of the government, then how will banning the mushroom serve to reduce harm? Steve Rolles of Transform (personal communication) agrees:

> If you have mental health problems, then using hallucinogenic drugs, in fact any recreational drug, is obviously a bad idea. But what about the majority of people who don't have mental health problems? It is like banning peanut butter because a tiny minority of people are allergic to it. Surely people who have problems with drugs or mental health should get the help they need. Those who don't have problems (the vast majority) are unlikely to develop problems, are not a problem to others, and are not the concern of the State beyond being provided with accurate information about risks and being encouraged to make responsible lifestyle choices.

Neither group should be the concern of criminal law unless they harm others.

To be sure, the concerns over mental health issues are debatable anyway as the following exchange demonstrates. The exchange consists of a response [via email] from Professor David Nichols, president of the Heffter Research Institute, to comments made by Caroline Flint, MP [member of parliament, akin to a senator], regarding psilocybin mushrooms. Note that Caroline Flint's comments were prompted by a letter she received from me via my MP, Tom Cox:

Caroline Flint: "Mr. Powell refers to the relatively low health risks associated with magic mushroom use. However, magic mushrooms, like LSD, are highly hallucinogenic."

Professor David Nichols: "What does that mean? Highly hallucinogenic? Is being 'highly hallucinogenic' inherently dangerous, and if so why?"

Caroline Flint: "They are particularly harmful to those with mental illness or with an underlying mental health problem and can precipitate psychosis. Users are also vulnerable to self-harm whilst under the influence."

Professor David Nichols: "There is no evidence that hallucinogens produce mental illness in anyone not predisposed to it. That is, persons who experience the onset of psychosis would likely have suffered it in any case; hallucinogens may expedite the process. LSD is most problematic in that regard because it also activates dopamine pathways in the brain, the same transmitter that is believed to be involved in psychosis. Psilocybin does not activate dopamine pathways."

Caroline Flint: ". . . and, like LSD, those misusing mushrooms may experience negative flashbacks."

Professor David Nichols: "Hallucinogen persisting perceptual disorder (HPPD) as far as I know is only consequent to the use of LSD. I am not aware of documentation that mushrooms cause flashbacks. This effect could well be related to sensitization of brain dopamine systems, a well-known phenomenon, which could occur with LSD but is unlikely to occur after psilocybin because of differences in their mechanisms of action."

Caroline Flint: "Mr. Powell also refers to the recently published Dutch Report, which concludes that mushrooms are not physically harmful to healthy subjects. The report does at least concede that taking magic mushrooms can be very harmful to those with existing heart conditions."

Professor David Nichols: "There is no inherent reason for heart problems after hallucinogens unless someone already has a heart condition and they have an experience with mushrooms that causes stress that precipitates a heart attack. Hallucinogens do not interact with the receptors that control blood pressure or heart rate, and any cardiovascular problems are only related to stressful events; taking a hallucinogen is not inherently stressful. Thus, anyone experiencing heart problems after hallucinogens is already 'a heart attack waiting to happen.'"

Caroline Flint: "However, the report does not tell the full story; it does not address their effect upon worsening of mental health conditions or the potential for self-harm whilst under the influence."

Professor David Nichols: "Mentally ill persons should not be taking mushrooms, or any psychoactive drug at all. There is no evidence that mushrooms cause mental health problems in 'normal' individuals. The potential for self-harm occurs with alcohol intoxication or any drug that clouds the senses. How many alcohol intoxicated persons wreck their automobiles, often killing themselves and others? Alcohol intoxication leads people often to believe that they are completely in control of their actions, when in fact they are not. Mushroom intoxication rarely, if ever, produces such inhibition. Rather, mushroom intoxication is more likely to result in a state where the users are extremely conscious that they should not be out and about. Awareness is most often increased, not inhibited as it is with alcohol. Furthermore, alcohol is one of the most addictive and destructive drugs known to man, often producing lifelong dependence and personal destruction. Mushrooms are not in any sense addictive, nor do they injure the health of normal people. There is not a single documented case of death by mushroom overdose, nor is there a single documented case of mushroom dependence or addiction."

PSILOCYBIN THERAPY

As evidence of the benign properties of psilocybin, the House should consider the fact that there are three psilocybin therapy studies currently underway in the United States. These studies have been sponsored by the Heffter Research Institute (www.heffter.org) and the Multidisciplinary Association for Psychedelic Studies (www.maps .org) and have been sanctioned by those various officiating acronyms (like the FDA, the DEA, etc.), which exert strict controls over the use of entheogenic substances in the United States. Given the extremely draconian drug laws in the United States, such studies would be incomprehensible if psilocybin were truly dangerous. The studies are looking at psilocybin's possible role in mitigating the psychological distress of patients suffering from end-stage cancer; treating obsessive-compulsive disorder; and treating cluster headache syndrome. It remains to be seen what other therapeutic applications psilocybin has.

THE FUTURE OF THE MUSHROOM

Should the law remain as it is, psilocybin mushrooms are unlikely to gather more than a small consumer base. After all, a fresh fungus is physically unlike commercially bottled alcohol and lacks the "allure" of mass-produced illegal laboratory drugs such as cocaine or branded ecstasy pills, for example. Which is to say that the inherent characteristics of a fungus do not lend themselves to any kind of mass market appeal. Pills, powders, and bottled drugs like alcohol are, regardless of legality, "consumer-friendly," whereas a mushroom is the very symbol of "unrefinement." Similarly, the effects of the mushroom are not to everyone's taste. The mushroom cannot "drown one's sorrows." Rather than decreasing self-awareness and self-knowledge as alcohol invariably does, the mushroom affords an increase in awareness. For reasons peculiar to our culture, the majority of people seem to prefer a "quick fix," a "fast buzz," or simply to get blind drunk. By its very nature then, the mushroom does not appeal to this rather reckless side of the human psyche, and hence over the last thirty years or so mushroom use has remained a fairly low-key activity.

Having said all that, it is prudent to examine the current mushroom trade. At the moment, the trade is entirely self-governed. It would arguably be better that the trade instead be regulated and licensed. It would also be in the public interest that information of some kind be given to consumers. This, I would surmise, is a sensible way forward, and I would hope that the House can dwell upon this constructive possibility. The regulation and licensing of the trade suggests intelligent control, a policy difficult to criticize whatever side of the political fence one sits.

LAST WORD

I would like to point out that I have produced this document independently and at the behest of no one but myself. Thus, I do not speak on behalf of mushroom traders or mushroom distributors (although I hope I speak on behalf of many mushroom users, who are perhaps less able than I to commit their views to paper). However, I do admit to having a vested interest in these issues (more so perhaps than other concerned persons). As the bulk of my personal experiences with the mushroom were incontrovertibly spiritual (for want of a better word), the proposal that this natural environmental resource be criminalized carries with it an unmistakably dark air of oppression. And it is for these reasons that I recommend the House either to reject clause 21 until proper scientific evidence has been gathered or to amend the clause such that the *Psilocybe* mushroom trade become properly regulated and licensed.

Thank you for your time.
Simon G. Powell, BSc
Please do not hesitate to contact me should you require further information.

∽

The following two addenda were included in the final updated version of the report that I sent to the House of Lords (the first version of the report went to the House of Commons, who were first to debate the bill). The first addendum contains quotes from the initial meetings of the Standing Committee, excerpted from the Hansard records, which are verbatim reports of parliamentary proceedings. The second addendum is MAPS president Rick Doblin's written address to both the House of Lords and the House of Commons.

Powell Report Addendum: Part One
Dangerous Hallucinations? Some Hansard Extracts

Drugs Bill—Standing Committee—final meeting, 3 February 2005

Dr. Brian Iddon: "We have just moved cannabis from class B to class C on the grounds of the harm that it presents to society, yet here we are being tempted to put fresh magic mushrooms into class A, along with psilocin and psilocybin, which are already there. I have a problem with that. The Advisory Committee on the Misuse of Drugs, which comprises scores of experts in the area, should consider that before any statutory instrument places such substances in class A.

Magic mushrooms do not produce any addiction, they are not considered to be toxic, and I can find evidence of only one death. We have also received the Powell Report. That is interesting. It gives the species of magic mushrooms—there are many—and the range of districts in Great Britain in which they grow. I shall not read it out, but I can tell the Committee that one quarter of a mile from my house there is a small wood near a school. The children there well know the months during which the mushrooms grow. A few silly individuals, silly because they are under age and their brains are still developing, trip up to the woods—[Interruption]. Yes, they trip. I shall leave it at that.

Psilocin and psilocybin have been compared with lysergic acid diethylamide. That compound is definitely a hallucinogen. We know that it can create in people a panic so great that individuals have been known to jump out of the window and kill themselves. There is no doubt that LSD is a dangerous compound. I do not advise anybody to take it. However, psilocin and psilocybin have been classed as hallucinogens, although they are compounds that produce psychedelic effects. The Powell paper coins the term "emphyogenic" [sic], meaning that the compounds give people a deep, spiritual feeling. That is precisely why the Aztec and Mayan civilizations in South America used those compounds in their religious ceremonies. I do not see many accounts of those people dying in large numbers as a consequence of using the compounds in the course of worshipping their gods. Therefore, I question whether the compounds are so dangerous that they need to be classified as class A under the Misuse of Drugs Act 1971. I hope that the Minister has some evidence to that effect.

Finally, I think that we are acting a little soon. We should gather more evidence, because not enough research has been done on many aspects of drug misuse. We also need far more research on magic mushrooms before we consider passing Acts of Parliament, as we are in the process of doing this afternoon."

Caroline Flint: "I am not a scientist, but I have looked into some of these areas. My hon. Friend talked about the entheogenic properties of these mushrooms, which literally means "the god within." In that sense, people who apply this term are talking about the effect of any drug creating an uplifting spiritual experience. I have had a letter or two from people who clearly refer to this experience they have when they are partaking of magic mushrooms.

"The harm of magic mushrooms may be disputed but, as far as I understand it, their hallucinogenic properties are not. Hallucinations are one of the main effects that make the drug user want to use these mushrooms."

Mrs. Gillan: "Just before we were interrupted, I was going to support the Minister. I, too, used the same tried-and-tested means as the hon. Member for Orkney and Shetland and went on to the Internet, because I needed to understand what we were dealing with. I found relevant descriptions of the psychedelic experience, as it applies to mushrooms, at www.thegooddrugsguide.com. In some cases, the effects are very alarming and include strong hallucinations, with objects morphing into other objects, and some loss of reality—time becomes meaningless and senses blend into one. [Interruption.] I think that that sounds absolutely terrifying. It is said that that experience is rare, but it involves an almost total loss of the visual connection with reality. The senses cease to function in a normal way and the loss of reality becomes so severe that it defies explanation.

"I hope that the Minister agrees with that description, knowing what the effects are on people who may have a disposition to mental illness. We are talking about the severe outcomes of taking such drugs."

Caroline Flint: "The hon. Lady is absolutely right that hallucinations are dangerous. There is an increased risk of self-harm, paranoia attacks, and highly disturbing experiences, because hallucinations distort people's sense of what is around them. Depending on where someone takes drugs that cause hallucinations, the dangers can be very serious."

Powell Report Addendum: Part Two
Statement from Rick Doblin, president of MAPS

TO: House of Lords/Commons
RE: Drugs Bill—Clause 21
FROM: Rick Doblin, Ph.D., president, Multidisciplinary Association
for Psychedelic Studies (MAPS, www.maps.org)
DATE: February 3, 2005

By way of introduction, I have a Ph.D. in public policy and also a master's in public policy from Harvard's Kennedy School of Government, where I specialized in the regulation of Schedule I drugs. I also founded (in 1986) and currently direct the Multidisciplinary Association for Psychedelic Studies (MAPS), a nonprofit research and educational organization that sponsors FDA-approved research into the risks and potential therapeutic benefits of Schedule I drugs such as MDMA, psilocybin, and marijuana.

PSILOCYBIN RESEARCH IN ENGLAND

MAPS has been working with several researchers in the U.K. on the design of a questionnaire to be filled out by purchasers of fresh mushrooms at numerous points of purchase around the U.K. The questionnaire will assess both the positive and negative effects of fresh mushrooms. We have completed the final round of critiques on the questionnaire and should be able to start implementing the data-gathering phase within a matter of weeks. The study should take about four months for data gathering and analysis.

We intend to present the results of the study to the House of Lords/Commons in the hopes that some direct data would be helpful in formulating government policy.

PSILOCYBIN RESEARCH IN THE
UNITED STATES

MAPS is currently cosponsoring with the Heffter Research Institute an ongoing FDA-approved study of psilocybin in the treatment of obsessive-compulsive disorder (OCD), under the direction of Dr. Francisco Moreno, University of Arizona, Tucson. Preliminary results are promising. MAPS is also independently sponsoring the analysis of case reports and medical records from about seventy-five subjects suffering from cluster headaches who have used psilocybin mushrooms (illegally) and discussed their therapeutic effects on an Internet website (clusterbusters.com), with this case report study leading to a clinical trial to take place at Harvard Medical School, under the direction of Dr. John Halpern and Dr. Andrew Sewell.

PSILOCYBIN RISK/BENEFIT ANALYSIS

While no drug is completely safe, psilocybin has a relatively low-risk profile. There are no significant risks of physical damage from psilocybin, to either body organs or brain. This has been well established in over forty-five years of research. For background information supporting this conclusion, MAPS has created digital PDF copies of virtually all the pioneering scientific papers published on psilocybin and has posted them on our website at www.maps.org.

The mental effects of psilocybin are generally well tolerated; are milder than the classic psychedelics such as LSD, DMT, and ayahuasca; and are not linked to flashbacks. Generally, users of psilocybin report enjoyable recreational experiences and/or enhanced understanding of themselves and the wider world. Not infrequently, users report having spiritual/mystical experiences. The use of psilocybin contributes either not at all, or positively, to the mental health of the vast majority of users.

It is possible that psilocybin can trigger mental instability in people prone to such problems. Even in mentally healthy people, psilocybin can present powerful psychological challenges with persisting negative effects lasting until the psychological material that has emerged into consciousness, in a manner somewhat similar to dreams, is addressed and integrated. While such negative effects in mentally healthy people are rare, they can occur.

In about 1 in 5 million cases (this is just a rough estimate), problematic reactions to psilocybin have resulted in suicide. Although it is impossible to know for sure, it's likely that the positive effects of psilocybin have prevented more suicides than the negative effects have generated.

COMMENTS ABOUT
DRUGS BILL CLAUSE 21

The widespread use of fresh mushrooms in the U.K., coupled with what seems to be a lack of evidence about any increase in harms as a result, suggests that more study should be conducted before any action is taken to criminalize fresh mushrooms. Prohibition has well-known negative consequences, such as the creation of black markets with associated violence around sales, and should be a last resort as a public policy option.

The questionnaire to be administered to purchasers of fresh mushrooms is a tool that could provide valuable information to the House of Lords/Commons. Given the absence of an imminent public health threat of a significant size, I urge both the House of Commons and the House of Lords to observe more closely the actual consequences of the availability of fresh mushrooms and ground its decision on data and facts, rather than hypothetical assumptions and fears.

☙

Well, there you have it. I recall mailing out copies of this report to all sixteen members of the committee who were to look into the soundness of the drugs bill and who were to decide whether to pass it. Through the Internet, I also listened eagerly to the live committee debates. When it came to their discussions about psilocybin, some of the rhetoric used was frankly ridiculous (as cited above)—at least in terms of knee-jerk fear-mongering. Never was there a clearer need for unbiased scientific research. The fear factor evinced by the supposedly learned committee stemmed from the belief that the mushroom was harmful—so harmful in fact that illegalization was the only valid option. Yet the mushroom had been commercially available for almost two years prior to the bill, and this had not been significantly problematic in any way. And before that the U.K.'s wild species *Psilocybe semilanceata* had been used by British citizens since the 1970s (again with no significant problems). Plus, there was the (nonproblematic) wide availability of *Psilocybe* spore samples and grow kits.

The most important thing, though, was that first fact, that there existed almost two years' worth of health data related to commercial psilocybin usage, the very thing the government was apparently so concerned about. The data were out there ready to be collated and examined, along with data related to thirty years of "traditional" mushroom use. How many people had died in those two years that the mushroom had been commercially available? How many people had been driven mad, or worse, out of high-rise windows? As far as I knew, there had been no news stories like that (or if there were, such incidents usually involved alcohol as well). Indeed, the only news stories were ones about the sale of the mushroom and not fatalities and accidents. Yet here were these elected ministers fearfully speculating without any objective data at hand. Worse, they seemed happy to simply have a quick look on the Internet to get their data! How could they possibly make an informed decision without germane statistics and scientific evidence? If the government had at its disposal various advisory groups whose job is to collect scientific data, then why did it fall on me, a regular citizen, to furnish them with at least a modicum of scientific information? It thus seemed that whim and hearsay were the chief ways to decide upon the law of the land.

This fiasco whereby subjective fear and a dislike for what is unfamiliar decides the criminal fate of hundreds of thousands of people (or more) drives home the point that the U.K. system of governance, as is the case elsewhere, is outdated and in dire need of an overhaul. What we call democracy is in many ways laughable. Ticking a box every few years might well be democracy in action, yet it is of the most minimal kind. It is like choosing whether a house should be painted dark blue, light blue, or very light blue. What about the internal décor of the house? What about furnishings? What about the roofing material? What about the kind of wood used for beams? What about the kind of foundations? What about the room layout? And so on. Choosing the color of the house from a few available colors is to have virtually no input at all into the way the house is made and the way it functions. The same applies to democracy. Simply voting every now and again from a few available parliamentary candidates is to have virtually no say in anything. Hence politicians can pretty much do what they like once they have been voted in and are hooked directly into the power structure of the country. If they want to change laws without making use of professional scientific research, they can seemingly do so with impunity. Worse, as the recent governmental scandals have revealed, many U.K. ministers can cheat the system, steal public funds, and be bribed with impunity as well.*

---

*At the time of writing about thirty MPs and Lords have either resigned or have been jailed for misrepresenting expenses. See http://en.wikipedia.org/wiki/MP_expenses_scandal (accessed December 18, 2014).

Even when drug issues are being debated by the ruling government and the opposition in the House of Commons during Prime Minister's Question Time, the result is often akin to a rowdy bun fight at a public school. People shouting and jeering like they have guzzled too much sugary lemonade. It is incredible to think that one is watching people paid to supposedly run the country. Soon enough you realize that an age-old game is being played out, a traditional skit of shout and counter shout. With this kind of theatrical system in place in which objective scientific evidence often fails to penetrate, it is no wonder that the war on some drugs some of the time has been waged for so long and why ordinary citizens are continually being demonized and persecuted for using psychoactive substances. Then again, maybe some of the aforementioned members of Parliament were right when they underscored the dangers of mushroom psychosis. Only the psychosis is not provoked in people who use psilocybin mushrooms but rather in those who have never taken them. With that thought, let us move on.

5
The Sacred Pattern

$\backsim\!\!\sim\!\!\backsim$

November 5, 2009, was a very special day for me, for it marked a welcome new bout of mushroom fever. Immediately prior to this day, my personal life was none too good. My *Metanoia* film had failed to make any real impact. My various books were still unpublished and were essentially languishing on my hard drive. I was selling all sorts of tacky ephemera on eBay to keep my head above water and was even busking in the London Underground for loose change. And my good friend the Tall Guy had moved abroad (having fallen madly in love with a Swiss girl, who, at that time, was *Metanoia*'s biggest fan). The only thing of positive note in the preceding six months was my invitation to Switzerland at the behest of a successful businessman—the Big Boss—who was a fan of my work and who wanted to meet me there at his holiday residence. That had been in August—but by November the buzz had worn off, and it was unclear what role, if any, the Big Boss would have in any future projects of mine pertaining to the natural intelligence paradigm or psilocybin. He certainly had the means to support new projects, but what plans he had I knew not. I was poor and lonely, and everything was uncertain.

I well recall the lowest ebb of this period. It must have been late October. I was walking around Bloomsbury, having just left the British Library, where I had been doing some research for a new writing venture. Even though my previous books had all failed to find a publisher, I had nonetheless decided to persist with the natural intelligence paradigm and write more material. I used to joke to people that as I had successfully failed to get my first few books published, then I should strive to maintain that kind of successful failure. To feel consistent. Indeed, I was getting pretty darn good at failing. I was, in fact, becoming an expert at committing years to various projects only to have the results ignored. I had even come across a saying from no less a personage than Winston Churchill that captured the kind of unflinching optimism I was wielding in the face of abject adversity. Churchill apparently said: "Success is the ability to go from one failure to another with no loss of enthusiasm." Nice, perhaps—but deep down I had the sneaking suspicion that this was a loser's credo.

As I was walking around the cold, damp streets, I found myself becoming increasingly down. I have never been suicidal—never—and I cannot imagine taking my own life. That is an abysmally hideous concept to me. Yet, I found myself being propelled into a real pit of despair in my mind. At one point, and it rather pains me to admit this, I found myself mentally composing a letter to the Big Boss. In it, I thanked him for taking a keen interest in my work—as no one else had seemed to care much about it. I imagined topping myself somehow and the Big Boss reading this letter. These were intensely morose and absurdly self-piteous thoughts to have entertained. The idea that other people go through this sort of ultralonely anguish and then do actually take their own lives is a terrible and deeply saddening thought.

Thankfully, through persistent mindfulness, the negative feelings of self-pity and self-despair passed as quickly as they arrived, and I began to feel intensely conscious of the living moment as I walked around the streets and shops. And when you are well and truly in the living moment—with all its live sights and sounds along with a strong feeling of one's own existence—then all is generally well. Indeed, self-pity is a particularly insidious aspect of what Gurdjieff called "waking sleep." Morose self-pity grips you. Your attention gets hijacked. You get pulled down and down. It's akin to digging a muddy hole for yourself, jumping in, and then wallowing around, all the while bemoaning how terrible things are and how horrible the mud is. But when you think about it, life's essentials are what really matter—food, shelter, and good relationships. As long as these are met, or can realistically be met soon enough, then that is all one really needs. I am reminded here of those bankers and businesspeople who, in despondency, hurl themselves off tall buildings when they lose their fortunes on the stock market. Were their actual lives in danger from an economic recession? Or just their life*styles*? The essential thing is *life itself*—being alive and kicking alongside everything else that is alive and kicking. Anything else is really just icing on the cake.

The fact that our inner worlds can become totally consumed by self-despair and that we may consequently suffer greatly from this was remarked upon at great length by Gurdjieff. He called this kind of thing *unnecessary suffering* (which contrasts with genuine suffering as with, say, bereavement). Unfortunately, we are loath to give up unnecessary suffering. Like heavy baggage, we lug our suffering around. Self-pity, chips on our shoulders, things to brood about, enemies to hate, unsettled grievances, broiling disputes, vendettas, and so on. These mechanical thoughts consume our attention; they burn up our precious consciousness and make us feel miserable and depressed. Yet even if we sporadically see these things very clearly, we may nonetheless refuse to give them up. Imagine you met a man carrying a big, heavy, spiky iron ball in his arms. You can see it is very uncomfortable for this man to be carrying around this large, unwieldy object. If you told him to drop it, to let it go, it would be peculiar if he refused on the grounds that it was "not as easy as that."

That is what we are like when it comes to our unnecessary suffering—we carry it around and cling to it tightly. The proverbial chips on shoulders are more like plants in that we may carefully water them every day. People who feel that they have been hard done by someone or by some group may brood and moan about it every day and even take such negative heavy baggage to the grave. Such prolonged grievances may even become etched into their faces. Consider then the concept of forgiveness. If we can really forgive, then we can let go and move on. But we are often loath to forgive. We carry grudges around in the form of hate and malice, and it eats us up inside. And the fact is that none of these negative thoughts or feelings is consciously driven— they just manifest in a mechanical way. We quite literally *find ourselves* subject to all these useless psychological machinations. In that sense we are our own worst enemies. But consciousness of the living moment, real, strong, vibrant consciousness of both one's inner world and the outer world, right here and right now, can set us free. This is the promise of all techniques of self-knowledge. Attention shifts from being mechanically consumed to being consciously directed.

A week after my brief bout of despair, I got an e-mail from the Big Boss. He asked me if I had read a certain book about psychedelic drugs by one D. M. Turner. He provided me with an online link. I checked out this book. According to the book's editorial note, this D. M. Turner fellow drowned in a bathtub, in all probability due to experimentation with the drug ketamine. I mentioned this to the Big Boss. He told me that despite this rather disturbing death, the man still had some interesting ideas regarding the nature of the psychedelic experience. I felt I could not be bothered to verify this claim and wrote back to the Big Boss, saying that, at the end of the day, regardless of all theories and all ideas, *it is better to go to the Source yourself.* By this I meant that the actual psilocybin experience itself can take you to the place where you may get some answers. After all, you cannot hand someone the truth—the truth is something that must be personally experienced. Certainly it is the case that the psilocybin experience is more powerful, more compelling, and more alive with spiritual power than any guru or text.

E-mailing these assertions to the Big Boss made me want to call my own bluff. After all, it was autumn, there had been a fair bit of rain, and it was about time that the mushroom made its annual appearance. Although I had made several visits to Richmond Park during that October and had come back empty-handed, maybe now I would have more success? It was also the case that I had not taken a strong dose of the fungal medicine for more than a year. For some time I had felt down, unhappy inwardly, ungrounded, and pretty much out of any "Gaian loop," as it were. Thus, with the rather formidable notion of "returning to the Source" in my head, I felt obliged to once again visit that great swathe of London wilderness called Richmond Park. It proved to be a wise move.

Within ten minutes of entering the park, I came across a shrew, newly dead by means unknown, and then, nearby, spied some brand-new freshly growing psilocybin mushroom specimens. I soon found quite a few more. Then, as I was walking through a small oak forest, an extremely large piece of bracket fungus fell from high up on a big, tall dead tree. It crashed noisily onto the ground about ten feet ahead of me. I warily walked over to take a closer look at this apparent fungal booby trap. I do not know what species this broken piece of bracket fungus was, but it was a pale white color on top, whereas its gilled underside was crimson red, like blood. The entire chunk looked remarkably like the internal organ of some massive creature, like a lung or a heart. It all seemed rather ominous to me.

By the time I left the park I had about sixty-five *Psilocybe semi-lanceata* mushrooms. Success! I was armed with one of the world's greatest resources. And it was free too. I realized with conviction that I would have to take a stiff dose. Many of the specimens were on the large size, so I figured fifty or so would work fine. Maybe they would even serve to get me back "in tune." In any case, as I returned home on the London Underground I began to wonder when I should take them. For pretty much the previous seventeen years, ever since the infamous mushroom fever of 1992, I had taken psilocybin out in the wilderness, usually accompanied by one close friend such as the Tall Guy or the Guru. It would be somewhat strange for me to take them alone indoors in the city of London. Then I began to worry about where I lived. What about Mrs. Landlady, the woman who owned the house where I was then renting a room? Would she be in that evening? Not that she ever bothered me, but I would have preferred to be in an empty flat. All these kind of worries tend to crop up immediately prior to psilocybin consumption. Because you know the mushroom is going to work. It is not a game.

The last question about privacy was answered when I got back and was on my way to the front door. As I arrived, Mrs. Landlady was leaving, and I knew she would be out all evening. I was also very hungry—meaning that I had an empty stomach, which is a prerequisite for a serious mushroom voyage. So I had no choice really. Circumstances were dictating the future. I would be taking the freshly gathered psilocybin within the hour—all the signs and cues were leading me to that eventuality.

Already my palms were beginning to sweat, and I was feeling a tad uneasy. If you are familiar with the power of psilocybin, it is no small thing to consume an effective dose—especially if you have not done so for a long time and your current life circumstances are not, how shall we say, glamorous or redolent in creativity and innovation. Taking a stiff shot of psilocybin is not like having a stiff drink or taking advice from a "stiff" therapist. Psilocybin forces you toward the

Source. You become a cub in the presence of Pachamama, you become forcibly exposed to a massive influx of tutorial information emanating from the unconscious. You awaken to the real world both within and without—and this makes the enterprise truly formidable.

The time: 6:30 p.m. Drum roll. I eat about fifty raw, large liberty caps. With coffee. Such a consumption of raw fungi, complete with soil and grit, is no less than a direct communion with Gaia. I realize that the whole ritual is like some symbol, or metaphor, played out in real time and in real space, almost like you are in a game or a story, where acts can be symbolic. In any case, nothing could be more foul to our refined culinary sensibilities than to eat raw and slightly gelatinous mushrooms—and yet from this seemingly base and impure act we may well obtain the highest conceivable spiritual bliss. In their wildest reveries, humans could never dream up symbolic scenarios like that.

About thirty minutes after ingestion I see something that makes me leap up off the bed (having spent all day wandering for miles around Richmond Park, I was in relaxed, supine mode). I was then just beginning to feel a certain something happening to my perception. This is an amazing period if your mind is still—that moment when you first sense that your perception is changing and is becoming more expanded and more acute. For a number of minutes I had been staring at my bedside lamp. It was suddenly starting to appear brighter and clearer than usual. It looked new. It looked like I had never really seen it before. So shiny and gleaming. Why had I never noticed this lamp before? Was it a new lamp fresh out of the factory or what? I had rented this room for more than a year, yet here was this lamp that looked like a brand-new object to me! And then I could not help but spy a pattern, *the* pattern, the pattern that connects, the pattern that binds everything. This pattern was on the lamp. I had, of course, seen this pattern before—and I have already described its appearance during my voyages around the Lake District and Snowdonia. But this was the first time that I had seen the self-same pattern indoors for perhaps seventeen years! It is one thing to see the pattern on rocks or around a fire, but it becomes much more amenable to contemplation and study when seen indoors in wholly relaxed conditions. So this time around I was able to study the pattern more carefully and in more detail. For me, the sacred pattern, whatever it is exactly, is the very signature of psilocybin and something that commands high interest in my ongoing psilocybinetic research.

Let me retrace a few steps. I leaped off my bed because I clearly perceived the pattern on the surface of the lampshade. And it had not been there before. Or at least it had not been perceivable before. This was *not* an illusion. If I moved around, the pattern remained there. It did not vibrate or flicker—it was self-evidently an actual pattern on the actual surface of the lampshade, just like a picture might be on the surface of a lampshade. Only it was not painted onto the surface; rather, it was part and parcel of the surface. How to describe this pattern then? This is difficult because there is nothing like it. The only descriptive words that come to mind are tattoo, hieroglyph, and web. It was also reminiscent of serpentine skin. The pattern was not of anything in particular nor did it have any obvious symmetry—yet it was extremely noticeable.

I was so amazed to see this pattern again, and with such clarity, that I raced to my computer to attempt to write down something about it. Having scrambled to get WordPad open (in my bemushroomed state this seemed like the quickest and easiest program on my PC to launch), I wrote one line but then realized with absolute conviction that I would recall everything of import later—so I didn't need to be typing things down excitedly. As I shut down WordPad, I suddenly saw the same pattern on the surface of my computer monitor. On close inspection it seemed to be bound up with the dust and the glass and the way the light was being reflected. But it was definitely there—like some serpentine, glazed, webby membrane covering almost everything.

All of a sudden I heard explosions outside, and I was forced to put my contemplation of the sacred pattern on the back burner. I mean—explosions? Blimey! Hang on a minute. Of course, it was November 5! In the U.K., this date is celebrated as Fireworks Night. It is a tradition that commemorates the rather nasty execution of a man—Guy Fawkes—who apparently tried to blow up the Houses of Parliament in 1605 because of a dispute between Catholics and Protestants. "Guy" is the name given to stuffed effigies that are placed on bonfires on Fireworks Night. For those who have never heard of Guy Fawkes, or who have never seen the movie *V for Vendetta,* the ancient song reminding U.K. citizens to behave themselves goes like this:

> *Remember, remember the fifth of November,*
> *The gunpowder treason and plot,*
> *I see no reason*
> *Why the gunpowder treason*
> *Should ever be forgot.*

So there I was with the sudden realization that about half a mile down the road from where I lived there would be a massive fireworks display in . . . in ten minutes' time! Good Goddess! Of course, I would simply have to go there. It would be a spectacle not to be missed. Or at least the felt presence of Gaia convinces me of this and urges me to make haste. Thus, putting all thoughts of sacred patterns aside, I had to make the supreme effort to put my boots on and to ready myself to venture out into the cold, dark November night. There was me thinking that I would have a relaxed evening—and now here I was donning boots and contemplating the rather intimidating idea of venturing outside.

Everything felt new—like I was doing stuff and seeing stuff for the first time. My bike, for instance. What a nifty piece of kit to have parked just inside the front door! As I set off on this speedy machine (don't try this at home!) the smooth road felt fantastic beneath my feet. It was like the first time I had ever ridden that bike. And the street lights were amazing. It seemed to be brighter on this November evening than it was in the daytime! Everything looked remarkable. The car lights—bright red beams everywhere on the busy road. The sheer reality of everything, the fact that there was all this existing stuff and energy, all orchestrated purposefully and moving purposefully, and that I was conscious of it all—all of this was almost too astonishing to be true.

As I approached Streatham Common, where the fireworks event was being held, the traffic started to get thicker and clogged up. The road was really busy. Despite my bemushroomed state I was able to weave in and out of the cars with expert ease and soon found myself at the end of the road facing the common, where huge crowds of people lined the pavement. It was all so well lit up by streetlights that it appeared to me as if I had arrived upon a perfectly designed Hollywood movie set. I almost expected to see some famous actors arrive upon the bustling scene.

I stopped by a traffic bollard, still astride my trusty bike and surrounded by other onlookers. I was pretty much opposite the common and had a good view of everything, so I stayed there for the duration of the event. Of much more interest than the fireworks were the people around me. It was a family event, and there were lots of local mums and dads with their children. I kept looking at all the faces, which were extremely well lit up under the many streetlights. Streatham is what is known in the U.K. as a working-class area. Poor people live there—myself included at that time. It has cheaper accommodations than most other parts of London. There is no London Underground station in the vicinity, so you have to use slow, packed buses to get around. It is not like Hampstead or Richmond, where wealthy people live and where you find organic food shops and classy fashion boutiques. In Streatham you get lots of cheap fried chicken outlets, cheap discount stores, cheap booze vendors, and gaudy betting shops.

Streatham is also home to a colorful variety of racial types. Thus, looking around me, I saw Nigerians, West Indians, Hispanics, Caucasians, Asians, and stacks of mixed-race children. Suddenly it felt as if I were privy to some sort of bioethnic display. Here before my wide-opened eyes and wide-opened mind was the family of humanity. Literally. I was surrounded by the human species in all their colorful diversity. Moreover, *everyone looked beautiful.* My perception seemed so clear, so free of the interference from the usual associations, that I could see how attractive everyone looked. I no longer saw the usual blacks and whites and browns—but just saw people, human people, all related to one another, all having common ancestry. When I was a kid, there was a pop band called the Family of Man. I recall they played really banal music. Yet here was the actual bona fide family of man, and there was nothing banal about it at all. I even felt that I loved all these people, this big family—that they were all my brethren. Sometimes you hear people saying that we are all brothers and sisters. Maybe it is more correct to say that we are all cousins, because one definition of cousin is the sharing of a common ancestor—and science teaches us that we do indeed have a common ancestor with everyone we might meet. Thus, by dint of scientific fact, we really all are cousins of one another. More to the point, psilocybin can facilitate the full-blown felt experience of this fact. Psilocybin has no time for racism or other shallow creeds.

I did not plan to have these kinds of perceptions about the human family—but that is what happened. I basically found myself in a state of mind in which I was seeing the true face of humanity and realizing with absolute conviction that we really are one family. I saw this. It was not a "nice idea" or a "nice thought" but a beautiful, undeniable truth broadcast straight into my psyche. I also saw that according to the number of mixed-race children on view they would likely come to the fore in the future. The future was not black and white and full of mistrust, but brown and full of hybrid vigor.

While I was marveling at the flow of racial bloodlines and the fascinating mix of faces all around me, a very strong thought, or voice, came into my head, as if planted there by some higher wisdom. The thought said that if you could not get past racism, if you could not accept other races as fellows, if you could not see through a physical face and sense the mindful human being underneath, then you had failed an important test. It was as if an ancient examination was still in progress, that by molding all these different racial characteristics within humankind, the naturally intelligent biosphere was putting all of us to trial, testing each one of us, checking to see how we relate to one another and how subject our minds are to harmful and unhealthy discrimination. Whatever the case, at that point I was overwhelmed by the attractive splendor of our species in all its variety and color. Everyone looked cool and attractive. I was loving it!

A large double-decker bus passed by, and I was confronted with something equally as extraordinary and equally as full of implications as the family of humans realization. On the side of the bus was a massive color poster advertisement for the disaster movie *2012*. Now, the fact is that I had seen this poster in many places. Down in the London Underground, for instance, there were big *2012* posters, and also a really huge one surrounding the IMAX cinema in Waterloo. Whenever I saw this poster I was reminded of a closed-eyes psilocybin vision I had back in 1992, which I related in an earlier chapter. To reiterate, this is what I wrote from that era detailing the vision in question:

Once I even saw the entire earth split apart, as if a mythical serpent, coiled up beneath the earth's surface, had suddenly burst forth and was rising upward. This vision was apocalyptic, like some multi-million-dollar epic movie portraying the end of the world.

Seeing this poster on the side of the bus gave me the strange feeling that I was somehow being connected to the past, like two different eras were linked by an uncanny psychological wormhole. Understandably, about a week later, I went to see the *2012* movie. While pedestrian and devoid of even a single Mayan glyph (it was just an over-the-top eschatological action movie), there was one particular scene that made me shiver. The earth had started to crack apart, and a guy was flying a plane up and out of the geological carnage, all the while surrounded by crumbling buildings and violently swirling debris. I had the distinct feeling I had seen a few seconds of these intense scenes during my 1992 psilocybin vision. But how could that be possible? How could I have seen clips of this film in my bemushroomed mind's eye some seventeen years previous? I admit to having no idea and can concede that it might have been a strange coincidence or even a strange synchronicity. But I am not alone in linking the content of psilocybin visions to clairvoyance. Fungi expert Paul Stamets writes in his *Psilocybin Mushrooms of the World* guidebook that he had visions of future events, in his case pertaining to the devastating effects of a flood. I confess that I am still bemused by the idea of being able to see the future.

After the fireworks had finished I set off back home, zooming in and out of all the stalled traffic. Back inside, I crashed onto my bed. Then I quickly got up and checked for e-mails. It was at this point that I received a new message from the Big Boss telling me that I was *right on target* about the idea of needing to go to the Source. How correct he was! How invigorated I felt! My perception was like that of some new genetically engineered species! My consciousness was so vivid as to be almost loud! Surely my superconscious beaming, bounding, brimming mind would register on a government satellite or something!

I thought then about my friend the Guru. Feeling much love for him and all my other friends, I realized I had to go and see him. But it was getting late in the evening, and I was not sure I had the inner drive to cycle to his house, which was about four miles away. It would mean another intense ride through nighttime traffic, but busier this time as there were a number of main street arteries to navigate. There were also some hills to negotiate.

I tried ringing him. He answered but, being old and a bit knackered, he couldn't hear me very well. "Okay," I shouted. "I will come visit." And thus I had to prepare myself for another epic cycle ride (again, don't try this at home!). Treating the cycle ride as a challenge, I gamely sped rapidly to the Guru's place. He lives in a rough neighborhood made up of small, bleak council estates. I can forcibly attest to the dodgy nature of the area as I had previously lived rent-free in his front room for a number of years. The street his place is on was home to car thieves and gangs of hooded youths. Sometimes the ambient hostility was tangible, and I often used to dread turning into the street when I lived there. People who reside in more pleasant neighborhoods have no idea what poorer areas are like. One time when I lived there I was writing on my computer when a newly stolen car was left abandoned right outside the window. A little later the car was set on fire—this being a sort of game that the local kids used to play. Which is to say that I sat about twenty feet away from a burning car. It can be difficult to write about natural intelligence amid incendiary urban conditions like that. Then again, I used to remind horrified friends and family that certain species of psilocybin mushroom enjoy being in the shit—they literally thrive and grow in the stuff. So I would look at difficult life circumstances as having the same kind of fertile potential. Again, this could be a loser's credo, but who knows?

I enthusiastically rang the Guru's bell, admiring the large, sprawling Japanese crab apple tree that I myself had originally planted outside his front window as a sort of organic shield against the flaming hostilities of the street. Once inside the Guru's house and having confessed my bemushroomed state, the first thing that struck me was how beautiful his untidy kitchen looked. The Guru, see, while being wise, is not at all bothered by household messiness. My mother would have had a heart attack if she were there to see the unclean state of his kitchen. There were bits of junk lying around, stains on the walls, and cobwebs in all the corners. Yet, to my wide open eyes, this shabby clutter had a subtle beauty to it!

I immediately pronounced forth upon the beautiful chaos before me. In excited and enthusiastic tones, I told the Guru that his overtly grimy flat brought to mind a science documentary that I had once seen concerning the decomposition of human corpses. This is a taboo subject, of course, the sort of thing one does not like to think about, let alone see actual film footage of. Intrepid researchers had filmed and studied the manner in which human corpses are broken down and recycled. This process is a real eye-opener. Such recycling is a true and necessary aspect of the biospherical system and can therefore be instructive. Moreover, to watch footage of a corpse being devoured by maggots and bacteria is not so awful if one watches with an open mind. In fact, when I saw this documentary, I actually perceived a kind of hideous beauty in the recycling process. This oxymoronic sentiment may sound disturbing—but the beauty lay in the naturally intelligent principles at work. The surface might look dead and disgusting, but the various specialist organisms beneath the surface that are busily and diligently recycling spent molecules are anything but dead and disgusting. The process by which dead life is converted into new life is really quite fabulous. Organic death is but a stage in a larger process. Patterns of life dissolve, and the fragments and parts become incorporated into new patterns of life. There is a profound splendor to this if one knows how to look. So it was that I likewise found beauty in the grime and decay of the Guru's flat.

Having ordered some coffee, I sat down at the Guru's kitchen table. He started to chat about this local young woman whom he had recently met in the local park. She had a new baby, and apparently she was going through a difficult time with her partner. The Guru was attempting to cunningly get the two of them back together by a carefully controlled process of book lending and book swapping (I think the book used was either by Krishnamurti or Herman Hesse). That is the kind of thing the Guru does—he helps people with their inner worlds and their relationship problems—almost behind their back.

While he was talking to me, I noticed something about the kitchen floor. Although it was well over three hours since I had taken the mushrooms, I was still getting strong perceptual effects. This became more and more evident as I stared at the floor. The sacred pattern was starting to manifest again, only much stronger this time. To be sure, the experience was so intense that it is etched into my memory. Whatever part of the floor I looked at, this pattern began to manifest. I would focus on one point, and then sections of pattern would appear like fractal serpentine scales around the focal point and then seemingly lock into place. And then the serpentine pieces would merge into one piece, and then the entire psychedelic configuration would start to spread out to the periphery of my vision. Thus, after a while the whole floor sort of froze into one large pattern. But it was not just any old pattern—it was a powerfully radiant sacred pattern. In fact, it was as astonishing as the one I had spied on the Snowdonian rocks more than a decade before.

What do I really mean by according a sacred status to a nonspecific pattern? This is extremely difficult to explain, as there is nothing else like it. It is like trying to explain what color is to a blind man.

I suppose I was prone to see it as a sacred pattern because it had an innervating and radiant quality about it. It was such an alluring pattern that the longer I looked at it, the more solidly it locked together. And it felt like I was being drawn into it. At one point it was even as if it "winked" at me. I have no idea how this was possible, but that was what it felt like. There was also some kind of physiological effect going on—like a feeding process—as if the pattern was a source of tremendously invigorating nourishment.

In any case, the pattern was full of sacred power and energy—or at least this is the only way I am able to describe the experience. There was an emotional quality connected to the perception of this pattern, an emotion so intense and so numinous that "mystical experience" inevitably comes to mind. I absolutely loved looking at the sacred pattern. It was like being immersed in waves of ecstasy, like pulses of divine energy were associated with perceiving the pattern. Whatever it was or whatever it represented, I had some kind of synergistic relationship with it. And, as I already mentioned, I had seen the same sacred pattern many times before, most notably out in the wilds of Snowdonia and the Lake District on rocks and the ground and such.

During my mushroom fever period of 1992, I also saw the self-same sacred pattern on an elephant poster that was on my wall. When I looked really closely at this poster, at the particles of ink, a pattern appeared and began to spread out. It was not really something new appearing but more like a pattern otherwise hidden in the physical surface of things, like it was always there but not normally visible. It is always a "divine" pattern that slowly and inexorably manifests, spreading outward and locking all and sundry into a single solid, interconnected coherency. And the perception of such is always accompanied by extremely intense spiritual feelings of awe and elation. For me this is the hallmark of the psilocybin experience and demands more research. Indeed, I would go so far as to say that the psilocybin experience represents the very edge, or forefront, of life's evolution, that nature is folding back on itself and coming to know itself in more and more profound ways through the vehicle of consciousness. Some might argue that space travel represents the cutting edge of the human story, but I beg to differ. The mushroom experience affords greater wonder.

A few days later I returned to the Guru's flat. I could not believe the kitchen floor. It was plain cheap linoleum. Functional, but dull and tawdry. Nothing sacred about it at all. And yet a few days earlier the floor had transformed before my eyes into a fabulous, multicolored, sacred serpentine pattern. This perplexes me even now. What, exactly, was the sacred pattern that I saw on that day and on so many previous occasions?

The following July I took another dose of psilocybin, somewhat bigger this time. Again I saw the sacred pattern, this time on the wall and also on Mrs. Landlady's kitchen floor. Writing this I know it may seem absurd that something as mundane as floor linoleum could repeatedly be the source of so much inspiration. Indeed, it sounds decidedly nuts. But as I stared at the pattern on this second occasion and tried to work out of what it consisted, it became clear that it was formed by the lines worn into the surface. Under normal perception these just look like random squiggly dark lines—because I checked the next day. So how can seemingly random disconnected lines of wear and tear become transformed into a hieroglyphic sacred pattern? Likewise, how can the surface of a mottled wall suddenly be transformed into a maplike hieroglyph? How can fine-grain ink, when scrutinized on the surface of a printed picture, transform into a fractal-like pattern that appears to be connected with other surfaces in its vicinity? And out in the wilderness, how can a granite rock smothered in various species of lichen and moss suddenly look like it is smothered in a sacred tribal pattern, which, upon closer inspection, extends onto the surrounding ground? How, indeed, can the ground, made as it is of various plants, suddenly appear like some sacred luminescent carpet woven by a divine weaver? In short, what is this sacred pattern that connects? What is this psychedelic psilocybinetic signature that can appear on the surface of anything and everything? Is it simply an illusion? No more than an enchanting artifact of chemically altered perception? Or is it something much more profound?

In August 2012 I had a chance to observe the sacred pattern yet again. This time I was able to really focus on it. Having just moved into a new flat (the first time I had ever had my own permanent, non-shared flat), I was keen to get properly settled in—and a strong dose of psilocybin was a good way of aiding this integration. I was also due to have a podcast interview the following week, so I figured it would be good to do that with some fresh psilocybin experiences to call upon.

The pattern was first noticeable on the bedroom carpet. It was very distinct. I knelt down to have a better look. The pattern was part of the actual carpet—an aspect of all the wear and tear. In other words, the pattern consisted of the actual three-dimensional surface of the carpet, and not something that was not there. This drives home the point that "hallucination" is a misnomer. What psilocybin does is alter the *way* one sees things. The longer I looked at the pattern, the clearer it became. Again, it had the quality of a serpentine tattoo or a serpentine hieroglyph. And there was something linguistic about it—as if the pattern exuded information and import.

I then saw the self-same pattern on the living-room wall. Inspecting the wall with great care, I could see that the pattern was made up of all the little bumps, or grain, of the wall surface. The notion of a membrane came to mind again. It was as if there was a thin crocheted membrane stretching taut across the wall's surface, like an informational veneer. This felt like a good description, yet it was misleading, because the wall's surface *was* the membrane, or at least the embroidered membrane was an actual part of the structured surface of the wall—even though, of course, we cannot usually divine this phenomenon.

Next, I saw the sacred pattern on my trousers. I was reminded of how Aldous Huxley waxed lyrical about the beauty he saw in the folds of his trousers. I felt the same kind of astonishment about the patterns on mine. Again, the pattern was connected with the material surface, with the detailed wear and tear.

Evincing a sort of scientific curiosity, I then tried to look at something with a more bland and less "rugged" surface to see whether the pattern would emerge there as well. So I looked at a new cushion whose surface was smooth and plain. Well, from a distance it was smooth and plain, but as soon as I studied it up close, a pattern began to emerge from the detail in the threads.

A large *Tron* poster on the back of my front door beckoned me. This proved interesting because I was reminded of my experience with the elephant poster back in 1992. First off, I saw no pattern. Then I looked more closely, and the sacred pattern appeared yet again. At first it was in the miniscule creases and crumpling of the poster. Then it appeared in the ink patterns, in the fine grain of the paper, and in the color differences. Once I spied it, it began to spread out, and I could see that the pattern was in everything, like everything was part of a single fractal surface. Indeed, the fractal analogy is quite useful because nowadays it is common to see three-dimensional fractals, and one can well imagine what it would be like if individuals were literally woven into a three-dimensional Mandelbrot set (the Mandelbrot set is an infinite series of numbers that can be viewed as an iconic fractal image with infinite depth and complexity). The fluidic interconnectedness of such a world would be apparent wherever one looked.

At one point my attention was drawn to my hands. The skin looked translucent, and the serpentine pattern was there too. I felt like a wild animal that was about to undergo metamorphosis. A theory in evolutionary biology called *punctuated equilibria* came to mind.

The idea is that evolution proceeds in short, sharp bursts (although still over relatively long periods of time) rather than at a steady pace. I had the notion that life might suddenly change at lightning speed according to contextual forces of which we are ignorant, that sudden dramatic cellular rearrangements might occur, akin, perhaps, to the arresting physiological transformation sequence shown in the movie *An American Werewolf in London,* but obviously not wolf-based but something much stranger. In essence, I could imagine a moment in time when life on earth might suddenly shift into some new configuration. I could even imagine that it was about to happen to me there and then—yet I was not afraid. The sacred pattern adorning everything seemed to exude a kind of psychedelic assurance that there was nothing to fear, that change, growth, and evolution were good, that all life was part of one fabulous creatively purposeful process.

But I digress. My main reason for relating this particular night's experiences is that I was able to study the sacred pattern in great depth. I can state with conviction that it is an actual existing pattern and not a hallucination. With "hallucinations" one thinks of seeing elves, or spaceships, or walls covered in morphing mythological creatures and such. The sacred pattern is nothing like this. As far as I can judge, it is not even related to so-called sacred geometry (popular among the New Age community) because straight lines, circles, and symmetry are not involved. And the bottom line, as I have mentioned elsewhere, is that one can move around the sacred pattern and look at it from different angles. It is simply there, a curiously alluring pattern that does not resemble any known object and that is somehow etched onto, and into, all and any surfaces.

In thinking about why it took me twenty years to get my head around this obscure phenomenon, I think this is to do with repeated journeying and the familiarization with new perceptual territories. What usually happens to mushroom users, even those with a number of sessions under their belt, is that they get overwhelmed with the transcendent nature of the experience, akin to finding oneself in a strange new environment and being bewildered. Certainly at the peak of the psilocybin experience one often has to lie down and surrender oneself to psychedelic bliss. It takes repeated journeying to be able to "stand up," as it were, and study the new landscape in earnest. But it *can* be done. This is what I mean when I talk of being in a state of superconsciousness. Everything becomes crystal clear, and one can feel tremendously empowered. With a certain effort and focus, one can write, send e-mails, play the guitar, go for walks, cycle, and even go up mountains under the influence of psilocybin (although, again, I can in no way condone all these activities and can speak only for myself!). It is precisely in such a keen and enlivened superconscious state that one can study the sacred pattern in detail. First you need to see it, though. Once you have properly noticed it, it can be noticed again.

Having had a few discussions with other psychedelic voyagers about the sacred pattern, I have not actually found anyone else who can describe the exact same kind of phenomenon that I have repeatedly witnessed. I have heard reports of seeing "alien languages" (like an alien alphabet) and that sort of thing, but this does not really tally with what I have perceived and what I have been discussing here. Ordinarily, this might give me pause. Is it just me? Is there something about my nervous system that is unique? I doubt it. As I mentioned above, I reckon the only reason the sacred pattern has not been well delineated is that it is so hard to study properly. This is because it becomes perceivable at the peak of the psilocybin experience, when there is a tendency to be overwhelmed by one's senses.

The aforementioned experiences of August 2012 were extremely clear to me. As I said, I felt focused enough to really study the nature of the sacred pattern, like I was an amateur scientist in the field making observations of a new phenomenon completely unknown to science. In times past, I would have lost focus, overcome with powerful emotions, visions, and all manner of other psychological goings-on, but this time I was able to repeatedly concentrate on the sacred pattern. It is real and robust and seems to be totally compelling once you see it. And it is everywhere, although not normally perceivable—an omnipresent fractal embroidery, a membranous pattern of interrelated information that covers everything.

Having pondered the sacred psilocybin pattern for some time now and suspecting that it is of significance vis-à-vis the fundamental nature of reality, I have come up with a number of interesting hypotheses to account for it. I submit that one of these hypotheses has to be true, or at least one must be closer to the truth than the others. Before I relate these hypotheses, I should make mention of an event that occurred a few days after the auspicious November 5, 2009, psilocybinetic encounter and that I think bears upon the nature of the sacred pattern. I was on my way to see an associate. I was standing on a near-empty bus, and in front of me was a woman with a really young baby. I estimate that this baby could not have been more than three or four months old. Now, I like to stare at young babies and toddlers. The reason for this is that they have what an old friend of mine used to call "the Buddha nature." Which is to say that babies are not "messed up" like many adults are, and if you catch their line of sight, they can have a curious kind of uplifting, and even healing, effect. Indeed, I have always thought that young babies should be carried around hospital wards. Because I reckon that by staring directly into the eyes of a very young child some kind of healing phenomenon occurs. First off, you become more conscious of yourself and can see more clearly the state of your inner world. Second, you make some kind of intimate contact with the pure, unmuddied inner world of the child. There is definitely a flow of information of some kind, which is, I feel, mutually beneficial, as long as the inner world of the adult in the equation is not too compromised.

So it is that I love to catch the gaze of young infants and to really see them (and thus see myself as well). On this bus then, I began to try to lock on to the gaze of the very young baby. It was amazing to study this baby because its eyes were wide open and massive. Its big jeweled eyes were looking all over the place as it tried to make sense of the strange and unfamiliar world around it. I stared hard as I attempted to lock in on its gaze. But at first its line of sight would simply pass across me and would not connect. Being a determined man I kept fixing my eyes on its eyes. Eventually contact was made, and our lines of sight suddenly locked on to each another. The intensity of what happened next was unique. Our gazes firmly locked, this baby's eyes somehow managed to open even more widely, and it was, to put it mildly, wholly agog and amazed. As was I. Moreover, the mutual wide-eyed stare went on for perhaps twenty seconds without a single blink. So intense was the sensation of a meeting of worlds, mine and the still-forming, alienesque psyche of the baby, that I was immediately reminded of the sacred pattern I had seen on the Guru's floor a few days earlier. There was something about the two encounters that was deeply related. In particular it was to do with the alluring felt presence of *sentience*.

Eventually our psyches "decoupled," and I almost staggered off the bus, astonished by the intensity of the experience I had just had. As I say, I felt strongly that the true nature of the sacred pattern had something to do with what had just gone on betwixt me and the newly forming human being. Which brings me neatly around to the first hypothesis: *the sacred pattern is part of an Other, a sentience that somehow saturates the world or is somehow a hidden aspect of the world.* This implies that when you take psilocybin you can potentially access this sentience and perceive its presence. If the sacred pattern is not separate from the real world (i.e., it is simply the real world seen in a new way), then what we call the world around us is, in fact, a *being* of some kind (or "beingness"), but so enormous and so unlike anything else that we cannot recognize it as such. This suggests that it is deliberately hidden, or at least that it remains hidden from our default frames of perception.

The notion of a vast hidden being puts me in mind of something esteemed sci-fi author Philip K. Dick explored in his 1981 book *VALIS* (VALIS is an acronym for "vast active living intelligence system"—a notion that accords well with this first hypothesis about the sacred pattern). Dick wrote about something he called the zebra principle. The idea is that the sophisticated mimicry we find, say, in the insect world (where an insect might look exactly like a leaf) might also exist on a higher level, or on a higher scale. Which is to say that some kind of higher intelligence may be present in the world but be hidden to us through a cunning sort of mimicry. In *VALIS,* Dick writes:

> What if a high form of sentient mimicry existed—such a high form that no human (or few humans) had detected it? What if it could only be detected if it wanted to be detected? Which is to say, not truly detected at all, since under these circumstances it had advanced out of its camouflaged state to disclose itself. "Disclose" might in this case equal "theophany." The astonished human being would say, I saw God; whereas in fact he saw only a highly evolved ultra-terrestrial life form, a UTL, or an extra-terrestrial life form (an ETL).

At this point, let me reiterate the nature of the sacred pattern. I have seen it enough times and studied it closely enough to state with certainty that it is not a hallucination—at least not in the sense of being an object that is not there, like a dancing pixie or a pink spotted elephant or whatever. It is, rather, an actual existing pattern, the medium of which is the regular environment. In addition to my previously mentioned notion of a crocheted fractal membrane, another simple way to think about this is to imagine sprinkling white sand grains onto black paper. The grains would doubtless take up a random arrangement. Now imagine that you suddenly saw a pattern in the grains that enabled you to see *all of them at once,* as part of a single pattern (albeit not representative of any known object). Further imagine that the pattern in the grains could also be seen to be connected to the pattern in the grain of the paper as well. This is what psilocybin perception can be like. Hitherto disparate information in one's environment becomes connected into one single pattern that, ultimately, connects everything. It is like the old adage that everything is interconnected—only in this case the mushroom shows you this fact for real. The interconnectedness of all things goes from being a "nice idea" to a direct holistic perception of the most intensely stimulating kind.

Another useful analogy is that of a familiar landscape. If you are up a mountain or in a helicopter or in an airplane and you gaze at a vast landscape below that you have never seen before, you will not tend to see it all at once, or "all of a piece," because you do not recognize it and are not yet familiar with such a scene. You will see details like rivers and towns and forests and such, but, being unfamiliar with them, you will not see the whole landscape as one integrated pattern. But if, through repeated sightings, you become familiar with the landscape, then it becomes more like a recognizable picture, in that you can see it all at once, as one significant iconic pattern (like a face). I am sure this is how experienced migrating birds see landscapes. They perceive one large, meaningful, picturelike pattern. In fact, this same principle of pattern recognition is apparent when we study the starry heavens. Once you have recognized a constellation, you will always see it. Previously unconnected and disparate, individual stars can, through familiarity, be viewed as connected in coherent iconic patterns.

The other thing to reiterate about the sacred pattern is its compelling quality. Indeed, when locked onto, the pattern seems to expand and exude power. The more you see it, the more filled with transcendental energy you become. How is this possible? If the entire field of reality has a significant coherency and being to it (weakly analogous to the significant coherency and being of an organism), why would perceiving this coherency fill one with blissful awe? It seems bizarre. Unless, of course, the very act of seeing it implies that this larger coherency is somehow simultaneously seeing you, or at least, as Philip K. Dick might say, it is revealing itself to you and thereby inspiring you in some way. Maybe it is interpersonal sensing—akin to what went on with the baby I mentioned—that creates a powerful emotional effect, like a resonance in consciousness.

Whatever the case, this initial hypothesis about the sacred pattern asserts that there is a living coherency and "beingness" to the world around us and that this coherency—the interconnectedness of all things—actually forms a pattern that can become perceivable under the influence of psilocybin. The pattern pervades everything and is particularly evident on surfaces. Moreover, when the pattern is perceived, it seems to have some sort of positive emotion-boosting effect that can reach mystical levels of intensity.

That reality as a single coherent living totality has a lot going for it. After all, science teaches us that the universe can be traced back to a singularity (and a "big bang" event)—which means the universe began from a single unified state. Fourteen or so billion years later it may appear that the universe consists of separate things and has totally lost all trace of its original singular nature—yet this may be an illusion.

I often like to imagine the big bang in terms of a slow-motion explosion. If we imagine a melon exploding in ultraslow motion after the impact of a bullet (most of us will have seen slow-motion movie clips like this) or from an internally planted explosive, then all of the moving fragments of the detonated melon, although seemingly disparate, are actually still connected to one another. How so? Well, if one were to analyze the velocities and trajectories of the fragments very carefully, it would become apparent that there was a *correlation* between them, that all the parts are connected through their combined pattern of movement, which stems from a shared origin. In other words, all the moving fragments, although seemingly disconnected and following their own separate paths, are in actual fact related to one another and part of a single expanding pattern. That is why if one were to take individual measurements of velocity and direction of the exploding melon parts, it would become apparent that all the pieces are connected through the same causal force. A good scientist would be able to deduce from his or her measurements and observations that there was some common feature of all the fragments, that they could be traced back to a common origin and a common factor that imparted energy to them and caused them to explode.

Let me shift perspective slightly to explore this notion of interconnectedness in another way, because it bears heavily upon the nature of patterns. Imagine one of those rooms where security guards watch live video monitors. Let us say there are eight screens and that each screen shows a certain area of a shopping mall. Now imagine that each screen is fed with live video data from a camera and that each camera has a different angle, but they are all focused on one exact spot. In other words, all eight video cameras point to one specific spot—but they all have a different perspective because they are in different positions. Now imagine what the eight video feeds look like. They all look different. They all show the same group of shoppers milling around, but the angles are different. At first blush, if you were to walk into this security room and you saw the eight screens for the first time, you might think all the video feeds were entirely separate and not related to one another. However, after a while you'd notice correlations. Maybe someone in a red suit appears briefly—and you see this person, from a different angle, on all eight monitors. Soon enough it would become clear that all these disparate monitors are being fed by correlated information. You would have spotted a pattern that connects. This is worth bearing in mind for a bit later when we look more closely at what a pattern actually is.

Returning to why I introduced these analogies, it was because of the idea that the universe is a single coherent totality. Well, to be sure this must by definition be true as the etymological root of the word *universe* literally means "all things turned into one." So the idea is that even though the universe appears to be made of a myriad different parts, there is nonetheless a *coherency,* or *single pattern,* to all and sundry. No one thing is truly separate but is, through a network of interrelations, connected to everything else. In fact, there is even a phenomenon in physics known as quantum entanglement that concerns nonlocal connections. Although the physics of nonlocality is beyond my ken, the idea seems to be that fundamental parts of the universe are entangled, or connected, and remain so even if they end up light years apart. This seems to support the idea that everything is deeply unified and that a single pattern, or a single coherency, unites all and everything. It is this underlying pattern connecting all things that may be perceivable with psilocybinetic vision. Although this pattern is always there, it remains hidden to us because of the limits and restrictions of our normal perception.

Let me add one more thought experiment to drive home the notion of coherency—because, whatever the nature of the sacred pattern, I am convinced coherency of some kind is involved. Indeed, I would even go so far as to say that coherency lies at the heart of any kind of mystical experience—in that such experiences involve more coherent forms of consciousness in which information within the brain suddenly assumes a more coherent and integrated state. I would further surmise that any "theory of everything" would have to involve the notion of coherency in some way. In any case, I have mentioned "coherency" a few times and linked it with patterns. This is not surprising as coherency is bound up with interconnectedness. If something has coherency, then its various component parts are joined together in some way.

Imagine, then, a boulder rolling down a mountainside. Rolling as one single object, the boulder clearly evinces coherency. It may be made of zillions of individual atoms but, en masse, the boulder moves as one single unified solid object. The boulder has coherency. Now contemplate the mountain that the boulder is rolling down. We know that mountains move—very slowly, of course—but the evidence is overwhelming that mountains rise (and fall). Charles Darwin was rightly amazed when, during his famous voyages and travels, he found the remains of seashells on top of large mountains in South America. The shells got there because once upon a time the mountain was below sea level and was gradually raised by tectonic plate activity. Thus, the mountain beneath our rolling boulder also evinces coherency in that it too can move as one single, solid mass.

As mentioned, our mountain was formed according to the movement of tectonic plates. These tectonic plates are gargantuan sections of the earth's crust that are continually moving and grinding against one another. Thus, the tectonic plates beneath a mountain have the property of coherency as well, because they likewise move as one single object. It is remarkable to consider this the next time you are witness to a large geographical panorama. All that you see is gradually moving as one whole piece. Even though you can kick the earth into bits at your feet, on a larger scale the whole ground you are standing on is one vast solidly coherent mass.

Continuing to expand our scale of focus, all tectonic plates are themselves part of the whole earth—and the whole earth similarly has coherency as it rotates as one spherical object. And, of course, the whole coherent earth orbits the sun.

These embedded coherencies do not end at the earth. The earth is a part of the solar system, and the solar system likewise has its own specific movement. Unbelievably, the entire solar system moves around the center of the Milky Way galaxy at a speed of more than two hundred kilometers per second! More astonishing still is the fact that it moves as one object and therefore, despite its vast size, has coherency just like our rolling boulder, which is so small in comparison as to be almost nonexistent. And we are still not done. The entire Milky Way galaxy also evinces coherency as it too moves as one unit—in this case at a whopping speed of six hundred kilometers per second relative to the cosmic microwave background radiation! Again, the really astonishing fact is not simply the staggering pace involved but that something as huge as a galaxy with billions of suns can move as one coherent unit.

So what does all this ambitiously grand musing mean? In simple terms, it means that a calm spring day, free of even the slightest of breezes, hides the exceedingly mind-boggling fact that within the larger contextual fabric of nature we are verily zipping, rotating, and orbiting every which way, zipping so fast in fact that if we were to fully grasp the enormity of the speeds and coherencies involved we would likely swoon and keel over. In more important terms, it means that the universe is one whole. Having coherency throughout, the universe must be one coherent object with each one of us (including our conscious experience) woven into it. Reason invariably leads us to this conclusion. But rather than this coherency of everything being nothing more than an intriguing (and reasonable) fact, I am proposing that such coherency is the source of the sacred pattern, that the sacred pattern is, as it were, the actual sign and signature of this coherency. *In other words, through the illuminating power of psilocybin, one can become consciously privy to the interconnected coherency of the world and everything in it.* Moreover, this coherency has lifelike, beinglike characteristics. The "beingness" of the whole can connect with our own being on a local scale through the psilocybinetic perception of the whole's signature pattern. That, then, is the gist of the first hypothesis.

The second hypothesis to account for the sacred pattern is far less quixotic and will doubtless appeal to those readers of a more reductionistic persuasion. This theory holds that what I was seeing in the aforementioned instances was nothing more than the effect of spontaneous pattern recognition, albeit spurious. Which is to say that the human brain is so geared toward pattern recognition that it may, under the influence of psilocybin, synthesize patterns where none exist. This means that one may perceive a pattern when in fact there is none, or at least not a proper pattern with significance.

If you look long enough at a complex surface and you relax your focus, then it is not too difficult to make out faces and other common objects. I am sure that we have all done this—especially in the days when we were simple daydreaming children. Yet these kinds of faces are whimsy and not real. Certainly faces are not deliberately carved into clouds for our viewing pleasure. Nor are the shadowy folds of a curtain deliberately shaped by someone or something into the likeness of an animal of some kind. Our imaginative pattern-seeking minds conjure up these faces and likenesses because it is the business of minds to engage in the pursuit of meaning and significance. So although it may be enjoyable to see faces in clouds or in dimly illuminated curtains, such patterns have no real significance or import. In a similar fashion, the sacred psilocybinetic pattern may be no more than a phenomenon forced into existence because of psilocybin's ability to boost the mind's capacity to construct patterns.

The mind's tendency to synthesize patterns out of often fuzzy visual cues is known as *pareidolia* and is likely to be a hardwired mechanism within the brain. However, as far as I know, pareidolia involves the illusory seeing of *familiar* objects—like faces and such. What is interesting about the sacred pattern is that it does not really look like anything familiar. It is, in fact, wholly novel. So we should bear that in mind when thinking about the brain's innate tendency to see patterns in the environment (such as faces and animals). While there may be good evolutionary reasons for us to see faces where none exist (better to be safe than sorry when erroneously seeing a lion in the bushes when there is in fact no lion there), seeing *abstract* patterns seems to have no obvious evolutionary advantages. Which is to say that the sacred pattern cannot really be categorized as pareidolia. In a way, perceiving the psilocybinetic sacred pattern is almost a curious antithesis of pareidolia, for one detects a pattern, but without recognition of what it is!

In speaking of the common illusory perception of faces that occurs with pareidolia, what is fascinating is that I have thought about that when directly observing the sacred pattern. I would put that down to the training, albeit limited, that I had in the scientific method when I pursued my psychology degree. Good scientists can maintain skepticism in the face of extraordinary claims and sensational suggestions. So should they find themselves experiencing directly the very stuff of extraordinary claims, they can attempt to observe the occurrence as impartially as possible. This may sound rather "stiff," but I would argue that it is necessary to act in this way in the pursuit of the truth—especially if the truth proclaimed is extraordinarily contentious. Thus, although one might be awestruck in the bemushroomed state, it is possible to study the sacred pattern in the same way a scientist might study, say, an enchanting magnetic field or a new species of organism. The thing is, the pattern is just there—in the same way that a magnetic field is just there. It won't go away. Once you have spied it and it has registered, *you cannot not see it*. It is not like a typical visual illusion in which you see some flickering or some motion (such as the various optical illusions that do the rounds of Facebook). Indeed, it is a pattern that appears more real than the writing on this page. More profoundly, viewing it is accompanied by a remarkably uplifting emotion. In combination, these two factors make the pattern absolutely compelling and difficult to dismiss as a mere meaningless artifact of the psilocybin experience. Moreover, the felt presence of some kind of higher intelligence is impossible to shake off when you are in the throes of perceiving the sacred pattern. This is why I am devoting so much time in delineating it. I therefore think it is unlikely that the sacred pattern is a mere illusion with no import. Whatever "thing" it is that the sacred pattern highlights, this "thing" is of great significance and not simply an optical-cum-conceptual illusion.

My third hypothesis concerns the innermost depths of the human psyche. Is it possible that the sacred pattern is somehow "all in the head"? I do not mean synthetic pattern recognition wherein the human mind is constructing a spurious pattern, but more like one is seeing the very foundations of consciousness. In other words, maybe there exists, at the very core of the human psyche, some kind of "pattern of divinity" that is roused by psilocybin? A divinity that can become projected outwardly under certain psychological conditions? That would mean that psilocybin stimulates the "divine spark" within, so to speak, and that this divine element, projected outwardly, mingles into one's perceptions of real-world objects. Thus, maybe when you are bemushroomed and you perchance behold the sacred pattern you are not seeing something divine in the "world out there," but something divine deep within the inner world. In fact, this supports the terminology associated with psilocybin by many researchers these days—namely, that the mushroom is entheogenic, which means "generates the divine within."

This is an intriguing, albeit highly mystical, idea with many ramifications if we go along with it. It suggests that when we look out on the world, we are, in some way, actually viewing the inside of our own minds, or, to be more accurate, we are witness to a projection of our own minds, for the world we perceive certainly seems extended out there in front of us. But what does it really mean to suggest that the world is a projection of the mind? How can the "world out there" not genuinely be "out there"? After all, we can all agree that we see pretty much the same world. No one disputes that we live on the earth and that the sun shines from the sky, or that the oceans are subject to tides, or that Everest is a large snow-capped mountain. Surely these objective facts of nature cannot be projections of the human mind? Surely they cannot be inventions? Or can they? Could reality be a shared projection of some kind rather than something existing independent of us?

I am reminded here of an in-joke within psychedelic circles that says that everyday reality, or normal reality, is little more than a commonly shared serotonergic hallucination (serotonin being one of the brain's chief neurotransmitters). The point of this wry remark is that if we all had psilocybin coursing through our brains (instead of serotonin), then we might all become subject to a commonly shared psilocybinetic hallucination. Although I have already pointed out that hallucinations per se are not really a part of the psilocybin experience, it is still the case that psilocybin alters one's perception of reality—and in this sense one can speak of a psilocybinetic reality as opposed to a normal, or serotonergic, reality.

In other words, could the reality we experience be an elaborate projection of the brain/mind system, underscored by serotonin, and common to everyone because we all have similar brains? And could the psilocybin experience represent a newly projected reality? Further, could the sacred pattern be an indication of what lies at the very bedrock of such a projection system?

Such an assertion seems to raise more questions than it answers. I have never been fond of ideas that suggest that we project reality or that we create reality. Well, to be sure, there is certainly a lot of evidence to suggest that our minds leave an *interpretive mark* on what we call the "world out there." One of the most striking examples of this is revealed by the McGurk illusion. The McGurk illusion is extraordinary, as it works even when you know full well what is going on (examples of it can be found on YouTube). Indeed, it is impossible to stop this illusion from having an effect (such is not true of many visual illusions, which can at least be mitigated once you are wise to them). The McGurk illusion consists of a speaker making some sounds. You see his face and mouth clearly as he repeatedly voices a syllable—"bah." But if you close your eyes or look away from his face and mouth, the sound heard is "dah"!

This remarkable illusion shows that we use visual cues to interpret reality. In the case of a mouth saying the syllable "bah," this is a very pronounced visual cue. When we sound "bah," we purse our lips in a highly specific way. We may not consciously know this, but subconsciously we know it. And if we say the sound "dah," our mouth movements are totally different. So if an audio track with the sound "dah" is carefully dubbed over the "bah" mouth movements, we will still hear "bah" because the visual cues take precedence. Of course, this does not mean our minds are silly or foolish because this kind of scenario would never likely happen in the real world. Besides, the lips *really are* enacting a "bah" sound regardless of what the audio is doing. In this case, seeing really is believing! The McGurk illusion reveals how important visual cues are in our perception of the world. We don't just perceive reality "on a plate"; rather, our minds use various cues to actively interpret the world and make sense of it.

Similar illusions involving colors demonstrate how contextual cues can determine our perceptions of the world. Two pictures can be shown, and specific areas in each of these pictures appear to consist of quite different colors. But if the colored areas are viewed in isolation without any surrounding context, then they are seen to be exactly the same hue. Once again it is clear that contextual cues can determine how we perceive something (one of the best of these context-based visual illusions is known as the checker shadow illusion, in which two nearby checkerboard squares look to be totally different colors but, upon isolated inspection, are in fact the exact same color).

To sum up: in the McGurk illusion a given objective audio reality can, through its processing journey through the mind, be modified into an interpretive subjective reality based on certain visual information that accompanied the audio information. In the case of same-color illusions, objectively existing colors can transform into apparently different shades through a similar process of perceptual interpretation. In each case we clearly do not view the world "as it is," but rather we utilize all manner of contextual cues and thence *form an interpretation of the world around us that makes the most holistic sense.* And we should note that classic illusions are important not because they highlight how poor our brains are but because they highlight how our perceptions constitute the most sensible "fit."

This is actually a very important point because, at first blush, we might be tempted to make much of this ability of the mind to be readily fooled. We might cite such examples, fold our arms, and say: "See, what we call reality is totally subjective. Our minds are making things up as they go along." But this misses the point. And the point is that our minds are striving to make the best sense of all the information we take in. That is actually a very clever capacity when you think about it, especially given that this sense-making process happens unconsciously and really quickly. All that our consciousness gets exposed to is the end result, or most sensible integration, of the array of ambient information that our senses accumulate. So we should not conclude that we are unable to divine objective reality. While it may be true that the mind interprets reality, it is also likely that the gist of objective reality gets through to our consciousness. In fact, the more evolved the brain/mind system (as in *Homo sapiens*), the more likely is objective reality to be perceived. After all, evolution will not long favor a brain/ mind system that perceives in an overtly erroneous way. To live and to be, to survive in the world, requires that we be able to make sense of the world. While our sense-making abilities might not be 100 percent accurate, they have to be pretty accurate. That small range of error might make us perceive lions in the bushes when there are no lions in the bushes, and it might make us see faces in clouds and on rocks, but these will be minor side effects of an otherwise accurate system of pattern recognition.

Let us now return to the notion that the sacred pattern is the result of some deeper projection of reality. While the aforementioned visual illusions elegantly demonstrate how interpretations of reality are what reach our conscious awareness and that such interpretations may be in error, they are, as I intimated, nonetheless built on an original source of information—and this original information must be "out there." In other words, reality cannot be wholly a projection of the mind. Reality may be colored by the mind, it may even be clouded by the mind, but that does not mean it originates in the mind (or at least not in *our* minds). Thus, the most reasonable conclusion to be reached here, as far as I can see, is that there is an objective "world out there" (the sort of world, or reality, that persists even if you die or don't believe in it—this being, in fact, Philip K. Dick's definition of reality) and that information about it arrives at our conscious awareness after having been filtered and sorted by the smart information-processing mechanisms of the brain/mind system. So when you look around you, you are assuredly not creating what you see, but rather you are witness to your mind's best integration of all the information at its disposal.

Intuitively this seems correct—especially if you consider what it is like to look at a really complex scene. Imagine sticking your head out of a tent and seeing a vast mountain range with a flock of birds outlined against a deep blue sky dotted with little fluffy clouds. Moving your head around, it is apparent that you are exposing yourself to a huge ocean of ultra-high-resolution information. If you walk around in such a scene and rapidly take in the panorama and even the details at your feet, the sheer amount of three-dimensional patterned information is staggering. The idea that the human mind effortlessly synthesizes such a complex high-resolution scene is a tad absurd (yet you do hear it said that the brain generates consciousness). It makes much more sense to suppose that the patterned information originates independently outside of us, that this "world out there," or "world in itself," does all the hard patterning work, as it were, and that *our brains essentially reflect a perspective slice of that existing field of information* (like a hologram containing minor reflections of itself). The same could be said of a blind man walking into an unfamiliar room. He may bump into various unknown objects. Obviously he does not randomly create those objects. Rather, they exist independently of him, and their properties can gradually be discerned through sensual interaction, such as tactile handling. This gels with the notion that nature is like some big book that the human mind can learn to read in more and more detail. *The book and its layers of meaning exist regardless of whether we, as individuals, care to read it or not.*

The sacred pattern is therefore unlikely to be something arising solely from the mind alone—inasmuch as nothing can arise solely from the mind alone, but must stem from some larger objective source. In fact, given the "out there" quality of the sacred pattern that I remarked upon several times, it does seem more likely that the pattern is part of the objective world and not simply something cooked up by the mind and projected outwardly. As I remarked, optical and audio illusions are not made out of thin air; rather, they involve alternative perceptions of something. So again, there has to be this "something out there" that we are witness to. Only then can this "something out there" be interpreted by the mind in a new way according to various contextual cues. The sacred pattern must therefore exist "out there." Somehow.

What to make of all this admittedly curious musing? How to decide between the three discussed hypotheses? The first hypothesis is that the sacred pattern indicates that the universe is an interconnected and coherent lifelike totality and that this coherency, or grand "being-ness," can actually be beheld, almost like perceiving the interconnecting strands of fabric in a mysteriously sentient carpet. The second hypothesis is that the sacred pattern is a spurious artifact, nothing real or substantial, little more than a pattern resolved by an overly enhanced pattern-recognition mechanism within the brain/mind. The third hypothesis is that the sacred pattern is an outwardly projected reflection of some divine inner spark.

A good basic question to ask at this point is: What is a pattern exactly? Indeed, what is it that lies at the heart of any given pattern we care to think of? If we humans have evolved to be experts in pattern recognition, if we can even synthesize patterns where none exist, and if psilocybin can allow one to perceive previously occluded patterns, then what do all and any such patterns have in common? What is it that makes a pattern a pattern? Further, what, if anything, is a false pattern? And what defines a very significant or very meaningful pattern?

Let me take three good examples of patterns and see what they all have in common. Like consciousness, patterns are such a common unquestioned aspect of human experience that we never really think about them too deeply. Let us consider fractals, snowflakes, and music—these will suffice as examples of patterns. Everyone would agree that these phenomena involve patterns, and very attractive ones at that. Fractals are particularly interesting. Although a fractal pattern such as the famous Mandelbrot set is infinitely deep and although it can be seen to be all of one piece, there is no exact symmetry to it, and it never repeats exactly the same anywhere (as far as we know). Yet it looks like a single interconnected coherent pattern. Reason tells us that it looks to be all of a piece because actually it *is* all of a piece—in that large groupings of pixels flow together, as opposed to being random. Indeed, what makes the Mandelbrot set such a striking pattern is precisely the nonrandom way in which it flows. When exploring the Mandelbrot set fractal through magnification, it seems as though it is woven from interconnected tendrils—in the same way that a carpet may have complex shapes on it yet be interwoven. With the Mandelbrot set, its interwoven nature is due to each pixel being related to each adjoining pixel in a mathematically significant way. Each pixel is derived from the same equation—each represents a number that falls within certain specific parameters. This automatically means that the numbers are all of a kind, all part of one set, all part of one pattern whose constituent parts "flow" into one another according to their degree of similarity.

As well as interwoven tendrils, the Mandelbrot set also has reoccurring numerical patterns. Eight and sixteen, for instance, crop up a lot (similar to the manner in which Arabic artwork often evinces eight-sided shapes). Thus, within the large overall pattern of fractal sets you will find "island" patterns that have an "eightness" about them, in that there will be eight converging tendrils present. Out around these eight tendrils you will often find a larger ring of sixteen tendrils, then thirty-two tendrils, and so on. These island patterns do display a form of symmetry—yet on close inspection they are not perfectly symmetrical; there are always subtle twisting differences. It is precisely these subtle asymmetries that make fractal patterns so complex and absorbing. The point, though, is that a fractal landscape like the Mandelbrot set is clearly *one* pattern that is derived from *one specific set of related numbers*. A fractal is an interconnected pattern, a single comprehensible mathematical object. Indeed, according to mathematics, any sequence of numbers that may be modeled by a mathematical function is considered to be a pattern. As all such numbers derive from the same function, they are related to one another. In this sense then, a pattern can be defined in terms of *nonrandom interconnectedness*. The more related the parts of the pattern are, the closer together their position will be and the more obvious the pattern will be (as opposed to forms with no patterning or very little patterning).

Now the snowflake. Although I have never personally gone around putting snowflakes under a microscope, snowflakes are apparently all different, their specific pattern determined by the unique ambient conditions in which they form. They all show symmetry of some kind, or at least *sameness*. Indeed, if you have some graph paper at hand, it is easy to apply some basic rules of symmetry and thence create a large geometrical pattern that looks like a snowflake. Unlike fractals, though, snowflakes have a much more obvious symmetry. Indeed, as with interconnectedness, symmetry appears to be a classic feature of patterns—but as we saw with fractals, absolute symmetry is not required for a pattern to exist (the same applies to psilocybinetic patterns, which have no obvious symmetry).

Our third example is music. With music, temporal patterns are evident. Which is to say that patterns of vibration are manifest over time. Before we consider patterns that are made up of individual musical notes, take something really basic, like drumming. What marks out a drumbeat from random thumping? What distinguishes a drumbeat, or even a heartbeat, from the sound made by a garden gate repeatedly banging shut due to a strong wind? The answer is a nonrandom pattern. Indeed, a good drummer can keep accurate time and maintain a mathematically accurate pattern. The less randomly spaced the drum beats and percussive sounds, the better the drummer. Maintaining the same interval between each beat, or precisely halving the time interval, or doing quarter beats or triplets and so on make for good, accurate drumming and percussion. This means that the patterns inherent in drumming have a numerical foundation.

Musical notes played on a guitar or on a piano similarly show mathematical relationships, this time involving vibrations, in which each note, like G or A, has a specific vibration and specific numerical relations with other notes. If you pluck a guitar string, it might sound as G. If you then fret the string exactly halfway along its length, it will again sound as G but will be one octave higher. And if you keep plucking the note G, then suddenly introduce a different accompanying note, the original note G will thence sound slightly different in the context of the accompanying note. All notes sound according to their numerical vibrational relationship to other notes. Thus, as with drumming, music is essentially mathematical. It is the precise nonrandom patterns between mathematical values—played out over time—that lie at the heart of music. And if you take a song, or tune, the sections will generally be related to one another, whereby there is some kind of theme (a specific kind of pattern) or a chorus (a specific kind of pattern) or a repeated verse (again, a specific kind of pattern). In short, with music, the components have a close relationship with one another. This is most obvious if we consider the notion of harmony. If everyone in a group hums any kind of note they like, the result will be a random cacophonous racket. But if voices begin to converge on one note, or mathematically related notes, harmony will take hold. What happened is a concordance of different elements as they become more closely related.

Let's consider the patterns found in fractals, snowflakes, and music; what, then, do they all have in common? I would argue that it involves interrelatedness, some kind of sameness (as in symmetry or near symmetry), along with nonrandom relational properties (i.e., a concordance of parts). More simply, I would boil it down to interconnectedness and coherency. In other words, reason suggests that all and any patterns consist of interconnected parts such that a coherency of some kind is in operation. This might be a static coherency—as in the case of a fractal or a hexagon—or it may be a moving coherency—as in the case of synchronized swimmers or a piece of music.

If we now return from this long detour back to the sacred pattern discernible through psilocybin, this is, in all probability, some new pattern of interconnectedness that we do not yet have the language to describe. In a way, I imagine the situation is akin to when Antonie van Leeuwenhoek first looked down a microscope in the seventeenth century and saw tiny squiggly things. This was a new aspect of reality coming into focus within the collective human mind, new patterns of significance that would forever change our ideas about life. Needless to say, I am in no way suggesting that the sacred psilocybinetic pattern is in the same league, only that it might be of significance and import. In fact, even if the sacred pattern was eventually confirmed to be nothing more than some artifact of the human mind, I think it would still aid in our understanding of reality. It would just mean that the human mind would be the focus of interest and not the "world out there."

Having said that, my conclusion—at least as it stands at the time of writing—is that the sacred psilocybin pattern involves the "world out there" being perceived "all at once," or at least more "all at once" than is usually the case. This idea can be succinctly stated by asserting that psilocybin expands the "fovea of the mind." Now according to science there is no fovea of the mind—this is something I have made up to get my point across. What we do know for sure is that the eye, the normal eye, that is, has a fovea. This fovea is that part of the back of the eye that is most sensitive. As you scan these words, for instance, the light information will be falling on the fovea areas of both your eyes. In other words, when you fix your sight on something and scrutinize it—like these words, for instance—the fovea of the eye is being used. Everything around the periphery of the fovea will not be in focus and cannot be seen as clearly.

The notion of a "fovea of the mind" goes something like this. We have five primary senses—hearing, touch, smell, sight, and taste. Our sense organs are constantly sending signals about the world around us to the brain. Indeed, our bodies are brimming with neurons, which are cells that convey information. To be sure, we each have some 100 billion or so neurons. Which means that at any one moment a tremendous amount of information is being relayed through the human organism. All this incredible wealth of information, this vast stream of incoming signals, is sent to the brain, where, through some kind of sophisticated parallel processing, a single conscious experience results. Imagine you are out walking down a busy street. Think of all the sounds and smells and innervating visual data. Somehow your brain can deal with this influx and can turn an informational onslaught into a single coherent perception of standing on Fifth Avenue or Oxford Street. That is what the brain—in particular, the human cortex—does. It can make sense of streams of information from various sense modalities.

Now to talk about a "fovea of the mind" is simply to say that part of the cortex acts like a fovea, in that at any one time your attention is focused on something or another. Not simply visual information, as in the case of the fovea of the eye, but information from multiple sources. If you are watching a movie, for instance, your attention will be focused on both the visual and audio information emanating from the TV or cinema screen. And you may even be combining that information with certain memories in order to makes sense of the plot. If someone next to you suddenly asks you a question, then your focus of attention will shift and a new set of external visual and audio information will be given priority. It is this ability to shift attention and to focus on specific sources of information (internal or external) that suggests, to me at least, that the mind possesses a kind of fovea, or even that the mind *is* a kind of "higher level fovea."

In other words, at any one moment there is a part of the mind that is the most sensitive and where one's attention is focused. This fovea of the mind is in action now as you read these words and contemplate what they mean and will also be in action whenever your attention is focused on something and not simply wandering aimlessly. Whether, like the eye, there is an actual area of the cortex that is "most sensitive" and where all incoming information gets processed I know not. My point is simply that there may exist such a region and that such a region might account for the phenomenon of attention. Moreover, I am further suggesting that substances like psilocybin cause an expansion of this fovea of the mind. *This means that our attention is able to focus on more at once.* If we again bear in mind that "consciousness" means "knowing together," then the notion that higher consciousness involves knowing more at once is both tenable and logically realizable. And the way that one might come to know more at once is if the fovea of the mind is expanded. Once expanded, our attention could embrace larger fields of information. If so, it means that psilocybin allows one to experience a larger chunk of reality all at once. It may be that with such an expanded perception the sacred pattern, hitherto occluded, becomes suddenly visible.

While it sounds strange to say that there is an informational landscape "out there" (particularly perceptible on surfaces) that is invisible to normal perception but that can suddenly become visible under the influence of psilocybin, this is a conclusion that I feel somewhat compelled to embrace. As mentioned earlier, it is like the effect of a microscope. When people first looked down a microscope and saw strange moving shapes and patterns, they might have wondered whether they were subject to some cunning illusion, to some weird artifact of the microscope apparatus, or even to an artifact connected with the internal structure of the eye (think of "floaters," for instance, little bits of dead tissue floating around inside the eyeball that can sometimes be seen in bright sunlight). Yet repeated viewings and cross-referencing with one another enabled groups of pioneering scientists to establish that there were indeed untold living organisms in a single drop of pond water and that it was not some perceptual illusion. What had once seemed fantastical and even doubtful soon became an accepted aspect of the world. This is what will hopefully transpire from my musings about the sacred psilocybinetic pattern. It remains for others to confirm or deny my findings. Either I am delineating some new holistic aspect of reality indicative of fractal interconnectedness or it is simply an illusion peculiar to my particular brand of nervous system. Time alone will tell. My job in this chapter was to point to this phenomenon and inspire others to explore it. Indeed, as is often the case, certain things only become apparent if they are talked about in detail and shared. This is really a continuation of precedents set by researchers such as Aldous Huxley, Gordon Wasson, and Terence McKenna, who pointed out the significance of the psychedelic experience. Without their cogent and lucid philosophical and metaphysical forays, the psychedelic experience may have lain on the subcultural periphery. By drawing attention to it, by aiding other explorers to cross-reference experiences,

Huxley, Wasson, and McKenna enabled psychedelic phenomenology and psychedelic philosophy to flourish. In the same vein, I will be very interested to learn of the findings of others who have observed the sacred pattern. As they used to say in *The X-Files*—the truth is out there!

6
Idris Nemeton

Let me describe to you a perfectly wonderful moment in time. I am lying flat out, almost spread-eagled, on a soft carpet of living vegetation deep in the heart of *dragon country*. It is nighttime. The ground is not merely soft, but luxury soft, and it is exuding a sweet, fresh, oxygen-rich aroma. It's pretty chilly—it's late autumn, after all—and I can see the misty streams of my breath in the light of my trekking headlamp. Yet this chill in the night air, this nippy tang, serves only to boost the perfection of the moment as it makes me all the more alert and vivified. Indeed, all of my senses are acutely keyed up. This is chiefly due to the exotic molecules coursing their way through my cortex—molecules obtained not from fungi on this occasion but from certain exotic tropical plants. Similar to psilocybin, these rare molecules are boosting and innervating my mind into a state of blissful crystalline clarity.

I am hypervigilant, hyperconscious, hyperhappy as I lie on the soft, earthy organic carpet amid dragon country. Oh, how I wish I could adequately convey my love of that carpet! It is a living, metabolizing carpet spun of moss and numerous other plant forms and expertly tied together with ivy. To be sure, the ivy is everywhere, its tenacious, cord-like tendrils and leaves spreading throughout the large forest in which I am a joyful supine guest. The ivy runs along the ground, snaking in all directions and has effortlessly climbed up oak, beech, and conifer tree alike.

The section of ivy-laced, DNA-writ carpet I am lying on is totally flat and seemingly made to measure. A special place about thirty feet or so from the campfire. A place to lie back and gaze up at the stars twinkling through oak branches and oak leaves. Everything is wondrous here in the mystical land of dragons. I am experiencing an absolutely perfect moment. I even feel compelled to exclaim this fact aloud to my companion, who is over by the fire. I have assuredly partaken of such glorious moments before—but how easily one forgets! Somehow, and by some means, the universe has conspired (once again!) to orchestrate an exhilarating taste of paradise. I appear to be a hominid vehicle for this gift. Myriad biological and psychological events have coalesced into a singularly lucid transcendental experience. I realize with conviction that reality is far more mysterious and far more fantastical than fiction. I—and everyone else—is in good hands even though we may not yet realize it. . . .

Incredible as it may seem, a few hours before this idyllic moment, I was nervous and uneasy. In fact, this unease had been with me for weeks. Why? In order to explain that, I need to explain why exactly my companion and I were camped in a remote forest and why curiously powerful psychedelic molecules, albeit nonfungal, were coursing through our veins. And not any old forest either. This one was deep in the heart of Snowdonia, a mystical region of Wales full of majestic mountains, roaring waterfalls, and rolling green valleys and where, you will recall, I previously had many mushroom adventures. And it really is dragon country—for the national emblem of Wales is the dragon. Wales is also rife with Arthurian legends and connections to Avalon—the mythical isle associated with stories about Arthur. So the secluded wilds of Snowdonia are certainly different from the concrete confines of London. But we were not camped in this mystical region solely for the history, geology, or ambient ecology. Ours was a bigger game—or at least we were inadvertently embroiled in a bigger game. Players, perhaps, characters even, in a biospherical adventure story. How come? Because my companion had conjured up two stiff doses of ayahuasca, a powerful and highly esteemed psychedelic brew obtained in the Peruvian Amazon.

This companion of mine—henceforth known as the Artist—had recently visited the Peruvian Amazon on two occasions. Each time he had gone to a special retreat, where he had taken ayahuasca on a nightly basis for a week or more (it is an interesting fact that, unlike most other psychedelic compounds, one can take ayahuasca repeatedly without developing a tolerance to it, which would render it weaker each successive time). That, in fact, is the purpose of such retreats. They are the principal component of the ayahuasca tourism I mentioned in an earlier chapter, a burgeoning phenomenon at the current time (if you can afford it, that is—these retreats do not come cheap). Wealthy tourists from all over the planet now flock to the Amazon and partake in ayahuasca ceremonies usually presided over by native shamans. Ayahuasca is talked of as a potent spiritual medicine. People can work through psychological issues and can feel reborn and spiritually revivified.

As the author of *The Psilocybin Solution*—a book revolving around the science and psychology of psychedelic mushrooms—I had been long aware of ayahuasca and its revered effects at the time of our sojourn. After all, both the mushroom and ayahuasca are psychedelic sacraments, bedfellows in the ongoing interest in expanded states of consciousness. Yet, having never visited Peru or the Amazon, I had never actually encountered the famous brew. I had seen pictures of it and watched many documentaries that featured ayahuasca, and I also knew that underground ayahuasca sessions were sometimes held in Europe and even in London. Yet ayahuasca was somehow beyond the scope of my radar. Deep down I hoped one day to venture to the Amazon and partake of it, but due to persistent limited finances, such a venture seemed years away.

So imagine my surprise when I got word from the Artist that he had allegedly managed to secure two doses of ayahuasca from the latest Peruvian retreat he had attended. Apparently he had even observed the shamans at the retreat make it. Given that he had taken ayahuasca over a dozen times and was even then working on a graphic novel about his experiences, he was obviously an experienced ayahuasca user. As for me, well, I was but a simple mushroom man. I may have taken psilocybin more than 130 times over a period of twenty-five years or so, but ayahuasca always sounded different. It has a unique and formidable mythos attached to it.

As it happened, the Artist and I had already planned to do a four-day autumnal trek out in Snowdonia, where we hoped we might locate some indigenous psilocybin mushrooms—but now here he was informing me that we would be able to take ayahuasca out in the Welsh wilderness. This seemed decidedly ominous to me. My life, at that point, was not plain sailing. A number of relationship issues were infusing my inner world with bitterness and unease. Moreover, I had not, at that point in time, taken psilocybin for nine months or so, and I felt distant from the realms of numinous experience that psilocybin and other psychedelics can potentiate. In short, I felt nervous about taking ayahuasca. How different would it be compared with psilocybin mushrooms? What if vicious monsters emerged from those bitter parts of my psyche? Or what if some spiritual force or entity smashed me and plunged me into a morass of demonic visions?

To make things even more unnerving, the Artist suggested that we should embark on the four-day Snowdonia trek at a specific time at the end of October 2011 that coincided with one version of the end-date scenario connected to the Mayan calendar. Apparently a few rogue New Age prophets were stating that the traditional end date of the Mayan calendar—December 21, 2012—was erroneously arrived at and, in fact, the actual end date was October 28, 2011. Regardless if this was woolly eschatological hearsay, it still served to increase my state of agitation. What in good Goddess's name would happen to us if we consumed ayahuasca on the putative last day of the final Mayan time cycle? I was worried enough about what I might experience— now I was beginning to wonder if I would verily survive the ayahuasca experience! The prospects of consuming Pachamama's most well-known spiritual medicine seemed intensely daunting, to say the least. My usual store of level-headed reason seemed to be fast evaporating, and I was almost working myself into a neurotic frenzy.

The week before we left for Snowdonia, I tried to prepare myself inwardly. Consuming organic psychedelics is never a frivolous venture. It takes real courage to ingest a psychedelic plant or fungus— particularly if you are well familiar with them. You are forced to confront your neuroses and hang-ups, your unfinished business, your problematic relationships, the frailness of your ego, and all manner of psychological flotsam and jetsam. That which is buried in your subconscious and unconscious becomes suddenly and dramatically exposed. Those issues that need dealing with become apparent. You see yourself for what you are, without the trappings of who you *think* you are. Your worldly goods mean diddly-squat. As does your social position. Strip all that external stuff away and what is left? What is your essence and truly yours? Bereft of your perceived social standing and your usual beloved image of yourself, what remains? This, at least, is the kind of thing that the psilocybin mushroom exposes. Of course, it is not all negative and unpleasant. Once you are "tuned in," so to speak, and have worked through any outstanding psychological issues, then consciousness expands and blooms like a gorgeous exotic flower, allowing one access to what can only be described as a superconscious mystical experience—as I hope I have conveyed in earlier chapters. But the longer you are away from this kind of thing, the harder it can be to find such a place again. And there are no guarantees. In any case, the thought of taking ayahuasca was causing me apprehension.

Given my unease, I went to visit the Guru a few days before the Artist and I left. The Guru sensed my tense mood. He was particularly alarmed at the notion of vomiting—which often accompanies ayahuasca consumption. As it was something he felt he himself would not like to go through, he felt concern for my welfare. I told him that I was not looking forward to that aspect of ayahuasca. Apparently the vomiting episodes can give one the feeling of relief, of being purged of something bad. But I was chiefly worried that I would throw up "snakes of bitterness" or something horrible like that. Fragments of alarming ayahuasca stories were buzzing around my mind, and I was piecing them into negative scenarios that would befall me.

The advice of the Guru was exactly what I would expect of him. He told me to pay attention, to watch, and to go with whatever happened. Just accept whatever transpired and learn from it. See it. Observe it. Be with it. Do not fight it. Fighting the experience, or trying to block unpleasant revelations, is to erect a door. And if you erect a door, then you will hear a relentless and growing pounding on that door. So don't turn away from anything. Flow with the experience. Watch the processes transpiring within your psyche as clearly as you would watch a bird flying across the sky.

The Guru also advised that the Artist and I do some major walking on the day of the ayahuasca session so that we would be physically tired in the evening (the evening being the time we would be drinking the ayahuasca). The Guru reckoned that physical exhaustion would be better for the mind when it undergoes psychedelic transformation. To be sure, the Guru and I had observed this firsthand during our many psilocybinetic treks. Once the body is physically tired from a long day of mountain climbing and walking, it slips into relaxed mode, and the mind can feel similarly relaxed. The Guru then wished me luck, and I left his flat. I still felt nervous. But all the time I was watching my inner world. I was not giving in to apprehension; rather, I was able to consistently observe it with clarity and impartiality. That took the sting off it.

October 27 arrived, and the Artist drove us to Snowdonia. I had not seen the ayahuasca, but I knew that it was on his person somewhere. I set his satellite navigation system to the vicinity of Cadair Idris, the second-highest mountain in Wales. I aimed to get us to a nifty campsite I had established four or five years before. During the car journey, I got to "bitch" about certain people that I was having bitter feelings about. I said to the Artist that it was not enjoyable to observe bitter thoughts and feelings, and that I was often amazed at how negative I had been finding myself. These negative feelings simply would not go away. All one can do when subject to such constant negative emotions about other people in one's life is to impartially observe them. The more one observes them, the less free they run amok in the psyche. They don't always go away, but they do diminish in intensity. Still, as we bombed along the motorway, it was clear that my psyche was far from being in a calm and collected state. But it was good to expose all this to the Artist. Sharing one's emotional unease and relationship problems with friends seems to lessen one's suffering—as if some burden has been shared and energy of some kind has been allowed to vent.

We arrived at our destination in the late afternoon. We parked the car, donned our hefty rucksacks, and within minutes we entered a new world—namely a big beech forest and a path through it that ran alongside a sizable river that had, over the millennia, carved quite a gorge out of the underlying rock. As soon as we entered this forest, a sweet and heavenly aroma filled our senses. It had rained for days prior to our arrival, a late autumn storm, and the forest was damp and absolutely smothered in a dense layer of beech leaves. This organic mix of leaves and damp soil crammed with symbiotic fungi and symbiotic bacteria was giving off a heady scent the intensity of which I had never before encountered (this kind of aroma is due to a substance known as geosmin). We stopped still and became transfixed, snorting lungful after lungful of the divinely sweet air. Such a simple thing—an organic woodland smell. Yet so profoundly intoxicating!

The problem with city life is that one loses touch with this kind of thing. Smells of woodland and forest that our ancestors would have been privy to for thousands of generations have all but vanished from the urban concretized way of life, to be replaced with toxic car exhaust fumes and the stench of old trash. But we are still wired to appreciate forest odors just as we are wired to appreciate other natural stimuli, like the sound of streams, birdsong, and wind rustling through leaves. Biologist E. O. Wilson has called this loving resonance with nature *biophilia*—meaning that we have an innate hardwired affinity for natural things such as forest aromas and the like. Certainly the Artist and I had our biophilia aroused as soon as we entered that forest. In fact, as I have previously mentioned, my long-term mushroom use had caused within me conditions I call chronic biophilia and chronic gaiaphilia—so it was not surprising that the forest odors were innervating me in such stark fashion.

The route up to the intended campsite ran for some way along the roaring river. The path was so laden with leaves that the term *leaf alley* came to mind. In some places the recently fallen brown leaves must have been six inches thick. More biophilia was evoked on account of the sound made as our feet pushed through piles of dry leaves. I am always amazed by the sheer volume of leaves shed by large deciduous trees each autumn. Each fallen leaf is a discarded solar panel that will be broken down by fungi and bacteria and thence recycled into the forest ecosystem, highlighting nature's engineering acumen on several levels. Not only are leaves redolent in naturally intelligent design, such organic solar panels can be easily disassembled and their components recycled and used elsewhere. This is the kind of thing that human sustainability engineers can only dream of emulating. Life has learned, to an astonishingly high degree of proficiency, the art of sustainable living whereby output from one form of life becomes input for another. And here we were happily scrunching our way through piles of evidence of this!

We eventually crossed the river. Then up over a stile. The path—decidedly old and disused—then pretty much frittered out. But there were some very overgrown steps that led the way. We were at the hallowed entrance of the place I would later christen Idris Nemeton. So on up the ancient steps, and then up a steep rocky incline down which flowed a stream. As it had been four or five years since I was last here, I soon lost the way. Up and up we climbed as I looked forlornly for a landmark amid the trees that would jog my memory as to the exact location of the secret campsite. We were now in very wild and very overgrown territory indeed. Our route was barred by massive ferns and an inordinate amount of sprawling prickly brambles. We started to get well and truly scratched and cut as I attempted to locate the camping area that I knew was somewhere in the vicinity. Eventually we headed over toward an old stone wall because I knew that the campsite was somewhere on the other side of it. By the time we reached the wall and I finally recognized some landmarks, my left boot had almost been removed from my foot! Somehow, the thorny brambles had undone my laces and opened up the boot so that it was half off my foot. How strange! Anyhow, we made our way along the high stone wall until we reached one specific spot where it was possible to clamber over by making use of a handy adjacent tree as a kind of stepladder. And so we had arrived at Idris Nemeton proper. It was a really wild and uneven place, brimming with unfettered organic artistry.

We set up our tents on the other side of wall and, because it was getting dark, quickly gathered some deadwood for that night's fire. I confess that this is, as far as I can see, the only morally and ecologically questionable act we engaged in during our stay. As I don't drive a car, and as I use a bicycle a fair bit, I always convince myself that burning deadwood is part of my pollution quota. As to the interference one is causing by denying an ecosystem a portion of recyclable deadwood, I assume that such an impact is negligible. It is not like I indulge in wilderness camping all the time—maybe two brief treks a year.

The evening was pretty uneventful. We did get to test out the Artist's sound system. He had some portable hi-fi gear on his person. A couple of small but powerful speakers meant we could attach our smartphones and play our favorite music all night. I also worked out a route up Cadair Idris, the nearby mountain that we would be ascending the next day immediately prior to taking ayahuasca. And I quizzed the Artist about this Mayan end-date notion because I had noticed that some of his Facebook friends from Peru had been raving on about the specialness of this date. In rather vague terms, he said that it would be a time when "shamans got together" or something along those lines.

That night I had a strange and disturbing dream. I saw an arrow being fired at me from afar. I could not make out who had shot the arrow, but I saw it traveling my way at high speed. It hit me in the left lower jaw area. I felt a sort of numbness and had that kind of embarrassing feeling you get when your face is swollen and throbbing in some way. This arrow stuck firmly in my cheek. Friends seemed unable to remove it. Incredibly, I told someone that it was a kind of acupuncture. After awakening from this dream, I wondered if I had suffered some kind of shamanic attack. I say this because it is well known that some Amazonian shamans indulge in sorcery and will try to harm their perceived enemies with magical poison darts, which they shoot at one another. It seemed inconceivable to me that subconscious fears of some kind had led to this almost cliché-ridden dream. On the other hand, it seemed equally implausible that I was under attack from malevolent forces.

After pondering for some time I suddenly remembered a traumatic incident from my childhood, when I was climbing a pine tree and a branch I was standing on broke. Although I held on to the tree, my left jaw got stabbed by a jagged branch stub (in exactly the same place as in the dream), and my family rushed me to the hospital, where I had stitches put in. To this day I bear a scar from that incident, and I can even picture the offending pine tree in my mind's eye. So was this dream connected with this early painful encounter with nature? Was I being reminded of close encounters with forests and the like? I might have concluded as much, but a week or so later I had another dream in which persons unknown were trying to dart me! I have no idea what it all means. But anytime I dwell upon such malevolent attacks and wonder what one's response should be, all I can come up with that seems fair is to somehow deflect the darts back. That would be a sort of shamanic t'ai chi.

As planned, on the day of the ayahuasca we ascended Cadair Idris. An interesting legend states that anyone who spends the night on top of this mountain will awaken as either a poet or a lunatic. Even this sounded ominous to me as I thought about what lay before us that evening. Although we would not be taking ayahuasca on top of Cadair Idris, we would certainly be in its vicinity. As ever, I was vigilant of my fear and apprehension and endeavored to watch the nervous machinations of my inner world as clearly as possible. As it was, I was actually pretty relaxed, and the trip up and down the mountain was excellent. The day was full of blue sky, and the views were incredible. Many city folk, alas, most of them, never bear witness to the stunning landscapes on offer in areas like Snowdonia and the Lake District. It is very refreshing to look for miles in any direction and see only mountains, green forested valleys, and a seemingly unending coastline.

By the time we arrived back at the campsite, it was dusk. That morning we had gathered a large amount of deadwood and had agreed that keeping the fire going during the ayahuasca session was of the utmost importance. Fire can be a powerful and illuminating ally to the psychedelic voyager out in the wilderness. So as the sun went down and the autumnal darkness swept in, we were all set to do this thing, to complete an ancient psychedelic process of communion—but with what exactly I was still unsure. Again, I was wondering how Amazonian ayahuasca would compare with the European psilocybin mushroom. Would the experience be totally unfamiliar or have similar components? In any case, we were ready. We both had empty stomachs as we had not taken solid food since the early afternoon, when we were descending Cadair Idris. The next thing we would be consuming would be the ayahuasca. There was no going back. Everything had been leading to this moment.

The campfire had reached critical mass and was roaring away. As I lay by the fire, the Artist began to prepare a ceremony. I noted that he was dressed in Peruvian attire. He had a Peruvian wool hat along with a shirt adorned with colorful ayahuasca-inspired imagery. He looked like a Peruvian shaman. We even had our portable sound system playing icaros, these being the songs sung by Peruvian ayahuasca shamans. For all I knew, I had been transported to the heart of the Amazon.

The Artist finally produced the ayahuasca and poured it into a pot so that it could be briefly boiled. This was my idea, because I had read that if you boil something for just one minute it will kill off all and any pathogens. Because the fact was that this ayahuasca was over a month old, had no preservatives in it, and had not been kept chilled. Imagine if you cooked up some vegetable soup, then bottled it and left it in a cupboard. Would you be keen to drink it a month later? If you had to drink it, you would certainly want to heat it before consumption. Hence my insistence that we boil the ayahuasca for one minute. Besides, the alkaloid content would not be significantly affected because it was boiled for hours on end to begin with anyway.

I was curious to see what the ayahuasca looked like. Under the bright light of our trekking headlamps, it had the appearance of melted chocolate. It was gloopy and thick, like viscous brown oil. I then began to wonder about how to drink the stuff. I had read and heard so many bad things about the taste of ayahuasca. Some have described it as tasting like battery acid. I asked the Artist if I should drink it in one go. What would happen if I gagged on it? I started to get somewhat neurotic as I watched the thick brown liquid bubble away.

The Artist then got two small shot glasses and shared out the ayahuasca. He presented me with a glass. I looked down at it. I decided there and then that I would not hold my nose. I remembered how I once hated the taste of psilocybin mushroom tea and used to always hold my nose when gulping it down. Then, on one particular night, I realized the silliness of doing this, drank the stuff properly, and savored (or at least paid attention to) the taste in my mouth so I would know more clearly its nature. To my surprise, the mushroom brew was really not all that bad—it had been my attitude that was the problem, not the actual taste.

So then, steeling myself, I took the shot glass to my lips and boldly drank the warm contents. The weirdest and most confounding thing happened, the kind of thing that is such a surprise that only life itself can deliver such. I actually enjoyed the taste of the ayahuasca! Maybe this was a first for all humankind! It even had a *tang* to it! I exclaimed aloud my amazement. I told the Artist in no uncertain terms that I really liked the taste and that it had an air of prune juice about it. He was as surprised as I was. But I also felt somewhat elated. How remarkable that I should enjoy the taste of something that was legendary for its foulness! In any case, it seemed to bode really well.

As I lay by the fire, the effects came on very slowly. Much more slowly, in fact, than is the case with a mushroom brew. It must have been about an hour before I sensed with certainty that my consciousness was moving into a different realm. At one point I shut my eyes and observed a vision of coiling, spinning, semicircular millipedes, serpentine in appearance and with colorful psychedelic sparks emanating from their glowing surfaces. At that point I realized that I was in the same realm that psilocybin takes me. In other words, I *recognized* the ayahuasca experience as it was almost indistinguishable from the mushroom experience. In fact, I had once smoked DMT and discovered that it too took me to the same inner place as the mushroom. DMT is very similar in structure to psilocybin and is the principal psychedelic component of ayahuasca. When smoked, however, it is extremely short-acting and extremely powerful. Some of the most "far out" psychedelic stories come from the act of smoking DMT. Yet when I had smoked it, I eventually found myself in the same psychological realm that I visit with psilocybin. When this happened, I recall being amazed because I was not expecting it. I really did recognize that visionary realm of the higher self. However, I have never heard of many others remarking upon this similarity, so it might be an idiosyncratic observation.

Anyhow, like the agreeable taste earlier, the fact that ayahuasca seemed to propel me to a recognizable visionary psychological realm was another amazing discovery for me. As I lay there enjoying the psychedelic state, I was in many ways relieved that I was in familiar territory. Thinking about it, it made sense. If all psychedelic agents (or at least tryptamines such as DMT, psilocybin, and LSD) put one into some sort of a direct connection with the unconscious, then it stands to reason that they all possess a similar psychological flavor. Once one becomes accustomed to the tutorial nature of the unconscious and one is well versed in the symbolic language that it uses, then it is almost akin to meeting an old friend or an old teacher, or returning to some tribal homeland or timeless mythical art college.

It was fascinating to look at the fire, then shut my eyes. The after-images were beautiful as they morphed into stunning, contorting landscapes. To be sure, over the last decade or so, I have found many of my closed-eye visions to involve huge landscapes that are bending and folding up in a dramatic way. Although incredible to behold, such visions have never matched the intensity of the visions I had during my formative mushroom fever period of 1992. I think we each must develop a unique relationship with the unconscious (or the mushroom) and that the relationship must necessarily change over time. All I can say for sure is the visionary realm I experience has colors, themes, and dynamics that I recognize, like I am interfacing with some sort of transcendental familial heritage with a distinct style and feel.

With eyes open I saw oak tree branches above me, with a few stars twinkling between the leaves. Then I noticed a peculiar sound that took me by surprise. It was like whispering, but emanating from lots and lots of people. I soon realized that it was the sound that the wind was making as it rustled the oak leaves. The impression of whispering was very strong, but it had never happened with psilocybin before despite identical prevailing conditions.

My impressions were interrupted then by the unholy sound of vomiting. The Artist was on his feet, had moved some distance away from the fire, and was throwing up. I was concerned, but he was apparently used to this kind of physiological evacuation from previous ayahuasca sessions. As for me, my stomach was giving me no problem at all—even though I had been a tad fearful of vomiting prior to consuming that night's strange brew. In addition to enjoying the "new taste sensation," my organism, it seemed, had taken well to ayahuasca.

At some point I got up and started to explore the area—or Idris Nemeton, as I later named that spot (*Idris* from the nearby mountain, the name of a giant as well as a Welsh prince, and *nemeton* being a Celtic word for "sacred grove"). I remember staring intently at the thick green moss covering one of the many rocks strewn on the ground. This particular species of moss was very familiar to me, like an old friend. In fact, it was, for me, one of the chief ingredients of the sacred magic carpet of which all and sundry was woven. As I perceived the moss with the wonder typically evoked by psilocybin but this time by ayahuasca, I asked myself what was different about my perception in that moment. Because everything was really the same as usual, but somehow not the same. This is a fascinating aspect of the psychedelic experience, and I had often wondered about it. There are no hallucinations as such, but rather a radical new way of perceiving the world around one. As I say, the moss looked normal and yet "supernormal" at the same time. What was it that had changed?

It felt like the moss was, in some strange way, "beckoning" me. By this, I mean that the more I looked at it, the more alluring it became (similar to my perceptual interactions with the plants in the Palm House at Kew). The "distance," as it were, between me the observer and the object of my perception seemed greatly decreased, as if there is normally some sort of interference that prevents such direct perception. In other words, I was much, much closer to the world around me than is usually the case. I was, as they say, at one with everything. The moss also had a sort of communicative air about it, similar to the sacred pattern phenomenon.

With a stretch, one can consider these notions in terms of hermeneutics. Hermeneutics is the study of interpretation, mainly of texts (like religious texts), but it can refer to *any kind of communication*. In other words, I reckon that some kind of communication can go on between us and the rest of nature (in this case, plants) and that one can be brought to a state of awareness in which a kind of *new interpretation* occurs. In this light, the psychedelic experience reflects a profound new way of interpreting nature, like the mind has shifted into a new interface with the world at large. New impressions thereby reach the mind and can fuel new interpretations of reality.

Call to mind our ancestors and how they must have wondered about their environment. One can imagine an ancestral hominid staring at a leaf, or a butterfly struggling out of a chrysalis, and having certain ideas occur to him or her. Which is to say that there is a flow of information between the natural environment and the human mind. *Nature is informative.* Whenever our minds quiet down and we look at a living thing, or even something nonliving, such as a vortex in a river, or a snowflake drifting to the ground, or a piece of wood burning, there is an information flow. What I am suggesting is that when one is in the psilocybinetic state (or any similar heightened state of consciousness), this information flow gets raised up a notch or two, and this increased communication of information makes the world seem so richly compelling to the bemushroomed mind. I am not suggesting that the environment "talks" to us in a sort of animistic sense, only that the environment is informative, or at least potentially informative depending on our state of mind. Indeed, I think many discoveries may have been made by our ancestors, maybe even discoveries with historical import, through a sort of passive learning wherein the human mind gains insights through the sustained observation of the larger environment within which the mind is located.

As an example, imagine someone living thousands of years ago, before machines had been invented. Imagine them staring at the edge of a river at small catchment pools in which leaves are floating and being forever drawn around and around in a spiraling vortex. It is not too far-fetched to imagine a keen, observant mind linking this rotary motion to some daily chore that requires rotary motion, maybe the grinding of food or something similar. Through an analogical juxtaposition, the novel idea might occur to marry those two separate scenarios such that the force of water could, if harnessed, do the food grinding. Hence the inspired invention of a watermill, with its clever system of cogs and wheels that can transform water-flow energy into some useful mechanistic motion. The point I am trying to make is that *information is self-organizing*. Nature can be suggestive and can coax ideas and insights in the keenly observant human mind. In fact, when you think of the enterprise of natural philosophy and science (which natural philosophy graduated into), the essential feature of these endeavors has always been connected with learning the ways of nature, with learning how the world works. This means that key sciences such as chemistry and physics require a tutorial input. Chemists and physicists have to learn. What supplies this teaching is, ultimately, nature itself. For even the greatest scientist must learn from nature. None of our learning comes out of thin air or solely out of the mind. There has to be, as it were, some vast ultimate book that we can read and that can educate us. Nature is this book.

Thus, I am of the opinion that there are different layers to nature. This calls to mind a palimpsest. A palimpsest is a manuscript page that has been used more than once, such that it carries the remains of older writings on it that were scraped off and written over. In some cases, there are enough remains of the old writing that it can actually be read in full. Hence what appears to be a single page of text might, upon intense examination, contain older texts. The same must hold true of nature. There must be untold layers of information and meaning inherent in the natural environment—physical information, chemical information, biological information, genetic information, ecological information, and so on. Under the influence of a psychedelic and with eyes open to the natural world, I believe one can access more of these informative layers than is the usual case, particularly once the mind has been stilled.

All this suggests that under the influence of ayahuasca my mind was open to all and any information inherent within that which I was perceiving, and that this flow of otherwise occluded information was what made the perceptual encounters so mysterious and so compelling. Then again, the experience cannot really be worded. It is seemingly ineffable, and one must perforce have the experience to realize its significance. All that I can really state with certainty is that moss, that seemingly simple spongy green organism, *seemed* to communicate something to me, or at least its allure was remarkably deep despite the fact that I did not know why. I also felt that I was somehow a part of what I was seeing—as though I *was* the moss, but seeing myself from another perspective, as it were.

Some ayahuasca aficionados might take me to task here and assert that ayahuasca should be taken only in the presence of a master shaman and that one should not be wandering around investigating flora and fauna while under the influence. I must vehemently disagree. I think there are rules and traditions for good reason, in that they have been learned over millennia in order to foster productive psychedelic journeys. Even the dietary regimens undertaken by those who visit Peru to take ayahuasca are part of that hard-learned lore. But I suspect that these rituals are not essential, but rather a means to get the voyager to focus on the impending journey and approach it with seriousness and sincerity. In other words, traditions, rituals, and rules can be of practical benefit and can embody great wisdom. But I do not believe that they are crucial and set in immutable stone. I think the most essential element of such psychedelic undertakings is *intent*. It is one's intent that makes the difference between profane use and sacred use. This applies equally to the mushroom as it does to ayahuasca. Moreover, what one should be doing in the throes of the experience is not written in stone either. The cosmos does not come with a set of inviolable rules concerning psychedelic pursuits. We are still learning.

The fact that I was moving around and exploring a forest under the influence of ayahuasca is therefore not to be dismissed as Western profanity—because many activities (maybe all and any of them) can be illuminating when one is in the psychedelic state. Indeed, it was at about this time that I gingerly ventured over to the flat bit of mossy ground I mentioned at the start of this chapter. Being farther away from the fire, the area was slightly chilly, and the air was sweet and fresh. It was sheer heaven lying down on that luxury bed of moss, surrounded by oak trees and stars, the light of the campfire flickering in the distance, along with the glowing outline of my good friend the Artist as he tended the fire. As I said, I became joyfully subject to an absolutely perfect moment in time. Whether I was "playing by the shamanic rules" did not matter. Indeed, how can there be inviolable rules of conduct when no one really knows what is going on with psychedelic consciousness? More than that, no one even knows why nature has the potential to craft conscious brains! Everything about life is really a mystery still. The thing to do then is to be attentive and to go with it. If something feels good and natural, then one should, as Timothy Leary once said, trust one's nervous system and go with the flow (despite his notoriety, Leary did come out with some good lines). This includes our perceptual system and the instinctive urge we may have to explore the world around us.

A bit later I was leaning against an old ruined wall not far from the fire, and the ayahuasca seemed to be reaching its peak of effect. The Artist sat opposite me, his head sort of nodding, and I guessed that, like me, he was deep in the psychedelic realm. Things seemed incredibly auspicious. I kept thinking about the fact that ayahuasca comes from the Amazon, the very heart of the biosphere, and yet here it was being imbibed in a Welsh oak forest. I felt like some kind of sacred shamanic current was now flowing from the Amazon to the U.K., from distant Amazonia to local Snowdonia, from a dense tropical jungle to rolling psilocybin country. It was like we were ushering in a new chapter of biospherical alchemy. And the thing we seemed to be channeling was ancient. I could really sense this ancient spirit, or something we have no words for, being channeled by us.

These feelings of awe and profundity were growing by the second. Some fear started to flicker into life within me. I then had a flashback (i.e., a vivid memory) to the intense night I had spent with the Guru on the Snowdonian coast some fourteen years earlier, when I had been almost bowled over by the sacred pattern that had manifested on the rocks. I realized that this current Idris Nemeton campsite was actually only about five miles away from that other place. And I recalled how overwhelmed the Guru and I had become on that occasion. I could feel that the ayahuasca was about to do the same to me here at Idris Nemeton. There was this scary feeling, that I was about to "lose it." But I was able to see this clearly within myself. Fear is a strange beast because if it is observed clearly it loses its strength. In other words, fear is something that can be mitigated to a certain degree as long as one is capable of observing it clearly. In any case, it felt like I had been driven to the very edge of psychedelic turmoil but, through focusing my consciousness, had managed to hold myself together and stand up when ordinarily I may have been knocked to the ground. I put this down to experience, that I was older and wiser than I had been in that other place and time.

With my eyes shut and feeling totally immersed in some higher psychological realm brimming with archaic wisdom, I proceeded to have a very profound spiritual experience that seemed quite unusual for ayahuasca. I saw, or sensed, the presence of a noble Native American chief. The impression was that he was about to address the entire world and had something of the utmost importance to relate. And his message seemed to be delivered in ultraslow motion. "The earth," he intoned, then paused for effect. An age seemed to pass. Finally, he continued: "The earth is our mother." And that was it. So simple yet simultaneously the most deeply meaningful thing I could have been privy to at that time.

I was moved and felt tears welling up in my eyes. Because I knew then that the earth is indeed the mother of us all, for we are all woven from the biosphere, and the biosphere sustains us even though we may be oblivious to it. All other matters seemed to fade into insignificance in comparison to our beleaguered relationship with the biosphere. I saw that it was our understanding of the biosphere that needed readdressing, that life on earth needed to be reappraised and reevaluated. I saw that our relationship with the biosphere was more strained than at any previous time in history. This visionary Native American chief welling up out of my unconscious, or the collective unconscious, seemed to sum it all up in just a few words. Like he had issued a code or signal.

An hour or so later, when I related this vision to the Artist, I felt somewhat defensive. I asserted that although it was a simple message, I could flesh it out with various facts. For instance, what does "mother" mean? And what does it mean that the earth is our mother? What does it mean that the earth nourishes us and provides all manner of ecosystem services? How is one supposed to treat that which sustains us? How does the "mother" concept of the earth contrast with the way modern culture actually treats the biosphere? And so on. In other words, I explained to the Artist that I could expand upon the brief simple message and defend it by using hard science and tough rhetoric. Which is to say that I was confident in my rhetorical abilities such that no one would be able to sneer at the simplicity of the message. However, the Artist suggested that I did not need to do this. He reckoned people would know the truth of it. Well, maybe. In any case, it was a mighty powerful experience.

At about this point, we ventured over to a clearing not far from the fire. It was a cloudless night, and the Milky Way was visible. Planets were also on display—easily noticeable by their brightness and the fact that they did not twinkle. With the ayahuasca I could even perceive that the planets were closer to the earth than all the other points of light. As with psilocybin, ayahuasca allows one to sense scale and a gridlike three-dimensionality to the heavens. That night the starry expanses way above us looked awesome. I believe the Artist shed a tear, so beautiful was that view.

A bit later, as we were coming down, I was musing about the stars and how inspiring it can be to view them on cloudless nights when there is a lack of urban lighting to occlude the view. It occurred to me that, during the autumn and winter months, schools could organize early evening trips at short notice to local vantage points, where stargazing could be facilitated with a few good telescopes and some pairs of binoculars. With schoolchildren contactable by mobile phones and the Internet, it would not be difficult to arrange pickup points and organize outings at short notice when skies are clear. And no matter how deep inside a city a school might be, there will likely be some good vantage points within five miles or so.

The allure of the starry night sky and the gasps of wonder that the sight of thousands of stars can induce is a curious thing. I am sure that I am not alone when I say that I have often felt inspired when viewing the night sky. When I was very young I well remember viewing the stars from out of the back of the car window as my mother drove us along pitch-black country roads at night. I grew up in North Devon, where there is a lot of countryside and less light pollution, and the night sky was often extremely clear. Even though I was young and knew nothing of cosmology, I still enjoyed a sensation of mystery at the sheer scale of the universe. Seeing an immense spread of stars can initiate a brief altered state of consciousness—the epic majesty of the cosmos being apprehended in a flash of exultation. Indeed, that is why I think the idea of organized stargazing trips would be good for children, especially city children, who, by birthright, ought to be able to see the stars.

The odd thing is, when you think about the allure of the starry heavens, there is no obvious economic value in having some sort of unoccluded access to them. A skeptic might proclaim: So what if we can't see the Milky Way? There is no market value in it, is there? Such experiences can't be bought or sold, can they? The economy won't improve simply because we can suddenly behold the glory of the night sky, will it? In other words, a view of the heavenly constellations does not command value because it is not a commodity.

Here we arrive at something very important concerning values. Think about some of the greatest things in life that are essentially free. Not just an unoccluded view of the Milky Way, but things like friendships and love. Walks in the park. Mountains. Sunsets. Sunrises. Fluffy clouds. Sweet fresh air. Feeling alive. Feeling passionate. Blue sky. Butterflies. Birdsong. Flowers. Sex. Hugging. Sharing. Laughing together. Joking together. Storytelling. Learning new facts. Communicating insights. All these are invaluable aspects of human life, of the human journey. Yet they are essentially free. They are not like stocks and shares, or commercial items. Those experiences can be facilitated, but they cannot really be branded or traded. In other words, although we would all agree that they are valuable things, their value is not monetary. This is an important distinction. The sad fact of modern life is that we value monetary things more than we do these other things whose value is not monetary. Thus, even though a good case can be made that seeing the Milky Way is a highly valuable experience that can foster a spiritual and emotional bond with the larger cosmos, nothing much will be done in the current cultural climate to facilitate such because there is no monetary reward in doing so. The same applies to the kind of spiritual experience that psilocybin and ayahuasca can initiate. There is no real market value in this—despite the fact that such experiences might be the most profound that one can have in this life. Something is deeply amiss here with regard to what we value and how we conceive of value.

How to change this unfortunate state of affairs? Well, it seems that we have to take a long hard look at our value system and what we judge to constitute wealth. The notion of wealth is interesting as it is bound up with value. Money, value, and wealth are bedfellows, part of a conceptual complex. As such, this complex can be teased apart and be remade in a new way. The root of the word *wealthy* is connected with "well," as in "well-being." Somehow we have convinced ourselves that well-being involves material possessions. Stuff, in other words. The more stuff we have and the more money we have to buy stuff, the greater our well-being, right? If you are happy with one new smartphone, then acquiring several more might double or even triple our level of well-being, right? Of course, this is nonsense. One may have a hundred top-end mobile phones but have no truly good friends to call. One may have a mansion full of gold bullion but be lonely and miserable (incredibly, I have seen TV commercials advertising gold bullion and the "real wealth in your hands" that it can provide!). One may have the biggest or most expensive car on the block but be an angry bozo who is so empty inside that only copious amounts of cocaine or alcohol can disguise it.

This is not to say that "stuff" has no value. Certain stuff is really useful and can most definitely improve well-being. Like access to free-flowing electricity, free-flowing water, and various medicines, for example. Yet without psychological wealth—namely, the less tangible valuables I mentioned a couple of paragraphs ago—material wealth means very little. So by elevating material wealth above inner psychological wealth we have basically sold out to the dreams being purveyed by all those brands I mentioned at the start of this book. We have become slaves to stuff, forever striving to consume things with no real substance and to amass possessions that do not improve our well-being.

What is truly substantial is not our material possessions but *our relationships to one another and to the larger cosmos.* This was very clear to me on that night of the ayahuasca, as I lay in that mystical oak forest beneath the Milky Way. I realized that in order to realign ourselves with the biosphere and deal with the various ecological and social messes we have created, we need to establish new behaviors that embody new values (such as the stargazing idea). That I was having such thoughts surely testifies that ayahuasca is indeed a strong medicine. Much of the popular mass media might still dismiss psychedelics, but the fact is that the psychedelic experience can afford all manner of healing changes on both a personal and a collective level. I even think this is what most of the pioneering psychedelic explorers were concerned with in the 1960s. There was a feeling in that tumultuous decade that human culture could be shifted on to a new course. It had nothing to do with magic portals or UFOs or hyperdimensional space elves but more to do with making heaven on earth.

Anyhow, back to Idris Nemeton. The following night was just as eventful, for we had located some mushrooms in the vicinity—not a lot, but enough for two average doses. I wondered, though, whether the mushrooms would work in light of the ayahuasca we had consumed the previous night. Usually one will develop a tolerance to a psychedelic drug, but this is not the case with DMT. As I recalled mentioning in *The Psilocybin Solution,* the brain does not develop a tolerance to DMT, meaning that you can take it repeatedly at the same dosage and with the same effect (it is uncertain why this is so, but it might well indicate that endogenous DMT has some sort of regular function in the brain such that tolerance is not allowed to occur). That one does not build up a tolerance to DMT suggested to me that we could take a regular dose of mushrooms and still get substantial effects. This hunch proved to be correct.

Unlike the ayahuasca of the previous evening, the mushrooms came on very fast. There are two things I clearly recall about that night. First, I felt compelled to visit the nearby stream so that I could have a wash. This would mean climbing over the big wall surrounding our camp and then making a short trek to reach the stream. Not too difficult—but when bemushroomed it is not so easy! Especially in the dark of night and with all of one's senses working overtime and with colorful visions appearing every time one so much as blinks. Indeed, these closed-eye psychedelic colors can persist for a few seconds such that one's surroundings appear full of luminescent sparks.

I informed the Artist that I had a compulsion to get to the stream. I could detect that he was somewhat concerned—but I was so confident in my own abilities and soundness of mind that I was able to assure him, in a clear and concise manner, that I would be fine. So off I set. I had soon left the light of the campfire and was clambering over the ancient wall that surrounded our camp. There was the trusty tree on the other side with its handy branches and saddlelike stepping point. Then a brief wade through wiry shrubbery, and on to a makeshift path to the stream. I was hyperalert. As I knelt down by the stream, I could not help but notice all the beech leaves everywhere. Unlike the brown beech leaves we had encountered at a lower elevation in *leaf alley,* these were not long fallen and were still green and yellow. Moreover, they looked like scales. Familiar scales too, homely, like some kind of biospherical tribal symbol spread far and wide. Akin to finely crafted dragon scales, I realized with glee! In my mind, I had all sorts of mythical ideas well up pertaining to dragons and giant serpents. The whole serpentine Gaia thing came alive for me again.

There was a presence there, all around me, made up of the stream, the hillside, and the flora. The entire area was like the living hide of some gargantuan planetary dragon! And then it was like I was in a dream, not my dream but some other being's dream, as if I was being lucidly dreamed of by something bigger than I. It felt distinctly mystical, like I was performing a timeless act, or feat. And yet all I was really doing was having a much-needed wash in the stream!

As I removed my glasses, sweater, and T-shirt, a voice in my head advised me what to do. "Position your headlamp there; place your glasses on that rock; careful how you remove the soap from the bag," and so on. It was like an inner guide helping me to perform my cleaning duties with precision and finesse in spite of my bemushroomed state. And so it was that I had a good wash, then headed back to camp. It was a small satisfying adventure in and of itself.

The other thing I recall from that night was the light splattering of rain. We were lounging by the fire, enjoying music and the flickering, warming firelight when it began to spot with rain. This was like some fascinating new experience. It started with a single prick of cold on the cheek. Although this drop was tiny in scale, I could sense this arrival of water upon my being. Then another tiny prick of cold. After a few more of them, it was as if I was being caressed by a biospherical goddess. The Artist too was enjoying this novel elemental interaction—at least novel in that neither of us had ever experienced fine light rain in such a sensuously enhanced way before. It usually goes unnoticed. We both exclaimed out loud how wonderful the sensation was, how marvelous it was that one could feel each and every minuscule speck of water delivered from unseen clouds far above us. It never turned into a downpour but remained as light specks of cold impinging on one's exposed skin, like a subtle play of sensations orchestrated by Pachamama, a gift so rare in terms of the ingredients required (Welsh ecosystem, human cortex, psilocybin) that the Artist and I were the only recipients. One often hears the phrase "you had to be there"—in this instance it is the definitive descriptor.

The next day we were headed back to civilization. As was the case on numerous occasions before, this return to mainstream culture was somewhat uncomfortable, pretty much a minor shock to the system. How do you return to normalcy, to the mundane affairs associated with modern living, when you have just experienced transcendental realms, where heaven and paradise were glorious states of mind to be enjoyed for hours on end and not abstract places described in old books? How do you explain to family and friends that modes of consciousness exist in which some kind of higher intelligence, or higher wisdom—both within and without—is accessed? How do you persuade people that everything can change for the better if we integrate psychedelic plants and fungi into our culture and make use of their illuminating and informative power? How do you get across such information in a world where fashion, celebrity, and the lust for money and evermore "stuff" rules over people?

The answer is: "with difficulty." The psilocybin experience and ayahuasca experience are so exotic, so strange, so radically different from our normal states of mind that the simplest thing to do if one is hearing about them for the first time is to laugh them off, treat them as "far out" episodes or, worse, temporary forms of psychosis. No wonder then that some deem psychedelic agents to be a threat, both to the user and to society. From this fear comes oppression. Thus, the absurd truth of the matter is that every one of the mind-expanding experiential wonders I have related in this book were catalyzed by substances currently subject to worldwide prohibition. Apart from a few rare places, it is illegal to pick psilocybin mushrooms *anywhere* on the earth. And this is despite the fact that they are a natural part of the ecological fabric of nature. It seems to me no coincidence that our society holds such views at a time when our relationship with the biosphere is at breaking point. Indeed, the idea that people nowadays suffer from "nature deficit disorder" rings disturbingly true. What could be more symptomatic of our broken relationship with nature than our insistence that psychedelic plants and fungi are pernicious and to be avoided like the plague?

Having said that, I often suspect that there is a strange method to such legislative madness. I don't mean that the method lies in our hands, though. I think naturally intelligent self-organizing forces are at play and that, like the script of a good book, timing is everything. In other words, I sometimes entertain the notion that, as Terence McKenna suggested, these plants and fungi have a sort of protection device built around them, to prevent profane mass usage. Indeed, one can think of most currently illegal psychoactive substances as representing catalysts or enzymes—inasmuch as they can saturate human nervous systems and influence the cultural climate. This being so, there is likely a best way, or *optimum method,* of opening the channels of the benign spiritually charged influences that are at hand. In other words, the mushroom's potential needs to be handled with care and to be released with care. Maybe this is what the current legal situation is demanding.

The hope is that in the coming decades the psychedelic story, whose modern Western telling began in earnest in the 1960s, will continue to develop and unfold. All being well, the various proponents for the judicious use of psychedelics such as psilocybin will converge their goals, thereby enabling, finally, psilocybin's integration into Western culture. This could be realistically achieved by opening up "revitalization centers," places where "ordinary healthy people" can visit and where rewarding psilocybin experiences can be facilitated by trained personnel. I imagine large dedicated buildings with tastefully decorated rooms and spacious gardens (access to green space is crucial). Visitors would get as much, or as little, overseeing assistance as they require. I would also like to see the licensed trade of psilocybin-mushroom-growing equipment such that adults would be able to grow personal supplies of the mushroom in their own home (such grow kits would come with information leaflets). Should either of these possibilities come to pass, the fruits would be tremendous. I predict that a new cultural climate would take hold, one that places great value on creating healthy relationships with one another and with the biosphere and one in which ever new connections are forged between humanity and the larger cosmos. From then on, anything will become possible as natural intelligence continues to evolve, bloom, and flourish. Heaven may yet be made on earth.

About the Author

Simon G. Powell, a graduate from University College of London, is the author of *The Psilocybin Solution: The Role of Sacred Mushrooms in the Quest for Meaning* (2011) and *Darwin's Unfinished Business: The Self-Organizing Intelligence of Nature* (with a foreword by Dorion Sagan) (2012). He has written and directed two full-length experimental documentary films—*Manna,* a psilocybin mushroom inspired documentary (2003), and *Metanoia: A New Vision of Nature* (2007)—along with several short films with his original music, including *The Greatest Story Ever Told* and *Good Trip* (all available on YouTube). He is also a frequent radio guest and lecturer on the subject of natural intelligence and the importance of our relationship with the rest of the biosphere. He lives in London.